West's Law School Advisory Board

JESSE H. CHOPER
Professor of Law,
University of California, Berkeley

DAVID P. CURRIE
Professor of Law, University of Chicago

YALE KAMISAR
Professor of Law, University of San Diego
Professor of Law, University of Michigan

MARY KAY KANE
Chancellor, Dean and Distinguished Professor of Law,
University of California,
Hastings College of the Law

LARRY D. KRAMER
Dean and Professor of Law, Stanford Law School

WAYNE R. LaFAVE
Professor of Law, University of Illinois

JONATHAN R. MACEY
Professor of Law, Yale Law School

ARTHUR R. MILLER
Professor of Law, Harvard University

GRANT S. NELSON
Professor of Law,
University of California, Los Angeles

JAMES J. WHITE
Professor of Law, University of Michigan

2005 SUPPLEMENT TO
CORPORATIONS
LAW AND POLICY
MATERIALS AND PROBLEMS
Fifth Edition

By

Jeffrey D. Bauman
Professor of Law
Georgetown University Law Center

Alan R. Palmiter
Professor of Law
Wake Forest University School of Law

Frank Partnoy
Professor of Law
University of San Diego School of Law

AMERICAN CASEBOOK SERIES®

THOMSON
———★———
WEST

Mat #40383177

Thomson/West have created this publication to provide you with accurate and authoritative information concerning the subject matter covered. However, this publication was not necessarily prepared by persons licensed to practice law in a particular jurisdiction. Thomson/West are not engaged in rendering legal or other professional advice, and this publication is not a substitute for the advice of an attorney. If you require legal or other expert advice, you should seek the services of a competent attorney or other professional.

American Casebook Series and West Group are trademarks registered in the U.S. Patent and Trademark Office.

© West, a Thomson business, 1996, 1999–2002, 2004
© 2005 Thomson/West
     610 Opperman Drive
     P.O. Box 64526
     St. Paul, MN 55164–0526
     1–800–328–9352

Printed in the United States of America

ISBN 0–314–16205–4

TEXT IS PRINTED ON 10% POST CONSUMER RECYCLED PAPER

Table of Contents

	Page
TABLE OF CASES	vii
Chapter 1. Introduction	**1**
B. Corporate Governance in the Modern Corporation	1
Chapter 3. An Introduction to the Law of Corporations	**3**
C. Choice of the State of Incorporation: An Introduction	3
2. The History of States' Competition for Corporate Charters	3
Chapter 5. The Corporation and Society	**6**
A. Introduction	6
2. Corporate Maximization Choices	6
Yochi J. Dreazen, Trying to Balance Profit, Christian Giving	6
Sarah Kershaw, Microsoft Comes Under Fire For Reversal on Gay Rights Bill	8
Sarah Kershaw, Microsoft C.E.O. Explains Reversal on Gay Rights Bill	9
Sarah Kershaw, In a Reverse, Microsoft Says It Supports Gay Rights Bill	11
Chapter 7. Forming the Corporation	**13**
Model Rules of Professional Conduct	13
1.6 Confidentiality of Information	13
1.7 Conflict of Interest: Current Clients	16
1.13 Organization of Client	19
Chapter 9. Financial Structure of the Corporation	**24**
A. Corporate Securities	24
4. Options	24
Chapter 13. Governance Role of Shareholders	**30**
C. Shareholders' Power to Initiate Action	30
2. What Actions Can Shareholders Initiate?	30
c. Removal and Replacement of Directors	30
Note: Board Removal of Directors	30
3. Board Responses to Shareholder Initiatives	31
Note: Effect of Shareholder-Approved Shark Repellents	31
Chapter 14. The Role of Shareholder in the Governance of the Public Corporation	**33**
B. Shareholder Proposals	33
2. The Rule in Operation	33
b. Substantive Grounds for Omission	33

	Page
Sarah Ivry, A Social Concern Turns Economic for Best Buy	33
Note: Shareholder Activism in 2005	34

Chapter 16. Outside Directors' Role in the Public Corporation — 38

D. Do Independent Directors Matter? — 38
   2. How "Independent" Is Defined? — 38
   4. Concerns Precipitated by the "Fall of Enron" — 39
      b. When Should Courts Defer to "Independent" Directors' Judgments? — 39
         In re eBay, Inc. Shareholders Litigation — 39

Chapter 17. The Duty of Care of Corporate Directors — 45

B. Duty of Oversight — 45
   2. Monitoring Legal Compliance — 45
      Note: Update of Internal Controls Under Sarbanes-Oxley — 45
      Note: Europe's Response to Accounting Scandals—Eighth Company Law Directive — 47
   3. Director's Criminal Liability — 48
C. Business Judgment Rule — 49
   1. Scope of the Business Judgment Rule — 49
D. Duty to Become Informed — 49
   1. The *Trans Union* Case — 49
      Note: An "Options" Perspective on Trans Union — 49
      Frank Partnoy, Adding Derivatives to the Corporate Law Mix — 49
   3A. Deference to Management — 53

Chapter 18. Duty of Loyalty — 58

A. Introduction: Conflicts of Interest — 58
B. An Overview of the Issues — 62
C. Evolving Standards of Review — 63
   1. The Common Law Standard: 1880–1960 — 63
   2. Contemporary Statutory Approaches — 64
      a. The Traditional Analysis — 65
         Remillard Brick Co. v. Remillard–Dandini Co. — 65
      b. MBCA Subchapter F — 71
      c. Company Codes: The European Approach — 74
         Communication From the Commission to the Council and the European Parliament — 74
         Modernising Company Law and EnhancingCorporate Governance in the European Union—A Plan to Move Forward (2003) — 74
D. Entire Fairness: Fair Dealing and Fair Price — 76
   1. Fair Dealing (Procedural Fairness) — 77
      a. Director Approval — 77
         Who Is an Interested or Independent Director? — 77
         In re the Walt Disney Company Derivative Litigation — 80
         In re Oracle Corp. Derivative Litigation — 85
         How Far Does Oracle Reach? — 101
         The Attorney as Director — 104
         Can Directors Be Truly Independent? — 106
      b. Shareholder Approval — 107

SUMMARY OF CONTENTS

	Page
Lewis v. Vogelstein	108
Harbor Finance Partners v. Huizenga	112
c. Disclosure	116
2. Fair Price (Substantive Fairness)	118
E. Corporate Opportunity	120
1. Traditional Corporate Opportunity Doctrine	122
Farber v. Servan Land Company, Inc.	122
2. What Is a Corporate Opportunity?	127
a. Interest or Expectancy	127
b. Line of Business	128
c. Fairness	130
3. When Can a Manager Take a Corporate Opportunity?	131
a. Financial or Economic Capacity	131
b. Corporate Rejection of an Opportunity	133
i. Fairness and the Role of Disclosure	133
ii. The Delaware Statutory Approach	136
4. Remedies for Usurping a Corporate Opportunity	137

Chapter 18A. Executive Compensation — **139**

A. The Compensation Puzzle — 141
  1. Forms of Executive Compensation — 141
  2. Process for Setting Executive Compensation — 145
  3. Debate over Executive Compensation — 149
B. State Law — 151
  1. Traditional Approach — 153
  2. Evolving Delaware Approach — 155
    Lewis v. Vogelstein — 156
    In Re the Walt Disney Company Derivative Litigation ("Disney II") — 163
    The Good Faith Thaumatrope: A Model of Rhetoric in Corporate Law Jurisprudence — 166
C. Federal Law — 167
  1. Disclosure — 167
  2. Deductibility of Executive Compensation — 168
  3. Sarbanes–Oxley Act — 168

Chapter 19. Duty of Controlling Shareholders — **171**

B. Cash Out Mergers — 171
  In Re Emerging Communications, Inc. Shareholders Litigation — 171

Chapter 20. Shareholder Litigation — **186**

B. Direct and Derivative Actions — 186
  Tooley v. Donaldson, Lufkin, & Jenrette, Inc. — 188
C. Who Qualifies as a Plaintiff? — 191
  2. Standing — 191
    d. Encumbered Shares — 191

Chapter 21. Regulation of Securities Trading — **193**

C. Insider Trading: Rule 10b–5 — 193

		Page
4.	Tipping Liability (Or When 15% Is Not Enough)	193
	Note: Martha Stewart	193
5.	Misappropriation Liability	197

Chapter 22. Protecting and Selling Control — 201

C. Case Law Developments — 201
   1. The Delaware Courts' Approach — 201
      b. The Contemporary Framework — 201
         Note: Do Takeover Defenses Help Directors Negotiate Better Deals? — 201
      c. Post–Unitrin Developments — 202
         Note: Have Delaware Courts Re-Written the Takeover Rules for Delaware Corporations? — 202
         Note: Joint Ventures and the Sale of Control — 204
         Steven Fraidin & Radu Lelutiu, Strategic Alliances and Corporate Control — 204

Table of Cases

The principal cases are in bold type. Cases cited or discussed in the text are roman type. References are to pages. Cases cited in principal cases and within other quoted materials are not included.

A. C. Petters Co., Inc. v. St. Cloud Enterprises, Inc., 301 Minn. 261, 222 N.W.2d 83 (Minn.1974), 132
Aronson v. Lewis, 473 A.2d 805 (Del. Supr.1984), 105

Beam ex rel. Martha Stewart Living Omnimedia, Inc. v. Stewart, 845 A.2d 1040 (Del.Supr.2004), 101
Blasius Industries, Inc. v. Atlas Corp., 564 A.2d 651 (Del.Ch.1988), 31, 32, 203
Brehm v. Eisner, 746 A.2d 244 (Del. Supr.2000), 53, 54, 162
Broz v. Cellular Information Systems, Inc., 673 A.2d 148 (Del.Supr.1996), 134
Brundage v. New Jersey Zinc Co., 48 N.J. 450, 226 A.2d 585 (N.J.1967), 107

Chestman, United States v., 947 F.2d 551 (2nd Cir.1991), 198
Cinerama, Inc. v. Technicolor, Inc., 663 A.2d 1134 (Del.Ch.1994), 70
Citron v. E.I. Du Pont de Nemours & Co., 584 A.2d 490 (Del.Ch.1990), 71
Cohen v. Beneficial Indus. Loan Corp., 337 U.S. 541, 69 S.Ct. 1221, 93 L.Ed. 1528 (1949), 186
Cooke v. Oolie, 1997 WL 367034 (Del.Ch. 1997), 70

David J. Greene & Co. v. Dunhill Intern., Inc., 249 A.2d 427 (Del.Ch.1968), 107
Dirks v. S.E.C., 463 U.S. 646, 103 S.Ct. 3255, 77 L.Ed.2d 911 (1983), 199
Durfee v. Durfee & Canning, 323 Mass. 187, 80 N.E.2d 522 (Mass.1948), 130

eBay, Inc. Shareholders Litigation, In re, 2004 WL 253521 (Del.Ch.2004), **39**
Eliasberg v. Standard Oil Co., 23 N.J.Super. 431, 92 A.2d 862 (N.J.Super.Ch.1952), 107
Emerging Communications, Inc. Shareholders Litigation, In re, 2004 WL 1305745 (Del.Ch.2004), **171,** 183, 184

Farber v. Servan Land Co., Inc., 662 F.2d 371 (5th Cir.1981), **122,** 138
Fisher v. State Mut. Ins. Co., 290 F.3d 1256 (11th Cir.2002), 74
Fliegler v. Lawrence, 361 A.2d 218 (Del. Supr.1976), 69

Gauger v. Hintz, 262 Wis. 333, 55 N.W.2d 426 (Wis.1952), 132
Gaynor v. Buckley, 203 F.Supp. 620 (D.Or. 1962), 133
Globe Woolen Co. v. Utica Gas & Electric Co., 224 N.Y. 483, 121 N.E. 378 (N.Y. 1918), 116
Gottlieb v. Heyden Chemical Corp., 33 Del. Ch. 177, 91 A.2d 57 (Del.Supr.1952), 107
Gries Sports Enterprises, Inc. v. Cleveland Browns Football Co., Inc., 26 Ohio St.3d 15, 496 N.E.2d 959 (Ohio 1986), 104
Guth v. Loft, Inc., 23 Del.Ch. 255, 5 A.2d 503 (Del.Supr.1939), 120, 128

Harbor Finance Partners v. Huizenga, 751 A.2d 879 (Del.Ch.1999), **112**
Hayes Oyster Co., State ex rel. v. Keypoint Oyster Co., 64 Wash.2d 375, 391 P.2d 979 (Wash.1964), 118
Heller v. Boylan, 29 N.Y.S.2d 653 (N.Y.Sup. 1941), 154, 160

In re (see name of party)
International Radio Telegraph Co. v. Atlantic Communication Co., 290 F. 698 (2nd Cir.1923), 119
Irving Trust Co. v. Deutsch, 73 F.2d 121 (2nd Cir.1934), 132

Johnston v. Greene, 35 Del.Ch. 479, 121 A.2d 919 (Del.Supr.1956), 129, 133

Kahn v. Lynch Communication Systems, Inc., 669 A.2d 79 (Del.Supr.1995), 71

TABLE OF CASES

Kahn v. Lynch Communication Systems, Inc., 638 A.2d 1110 (Del.Supr.1994), 70, 120

Kerrigan v. Unity Sav. Ass'n, 58 Ill.2d 20, 317 N.E.2d 39 (Ill.1974), 133

Keypoint Oyster Co., State ex rel. Hayes Oyster Co. v., 64 Wash.2d 375, 391 P.2d 979 (Wash.1964), 118

Klinicki v. Lundgren, 298 Or. 662, 695 P.2d 906 (Or.1985), 134

Lagarde v. Anniston Lime & Stone Co., 126 Ala. 496, 28 So. 199 (Ala.1900), 127

Lewis v. Vogelstein, 699 A.2d 327 (Del. Ch.1997), **108, 156**

Litwin v. Allen, 25 N.Y.S.2d 667 (N.Y.Sup. 1940), 128

Lovenheim v. Iroquois Brands, Ltd., 618 F.Supp. 554 (D.D.C.1985), 33

Marciano v. Nakash, 535 A.2d 400 (Del. Supr.1987), 69, 71, 118

Miller v. Miller, 301 Minn. 207, 222 N.W.2d 71 (Minn.1974), 130, 131

MM Companies, Inc. v. Liquid Audio, Inc., 813 A.2d 1118 (Del.Supr.2003), 203

Murray v. Conseco, Inc., 795 N.E.2d 454 (Ind.2003), 30

Murray v. Conseco, Inc., 766 N.E.2d 38 (Ind.App.2002), 31

Northeast Harbor Golf Club, Inc. v. Harris, 661 A.2d 1146 (Me.1995), 134

Oberly v. Kirby, 592 A.2d 445 (Del. Supr.1991), 70

Oracle Corp. Derivative Litigation, In re, 824 A.2d 917 (Del.Ch.2003), **85,** 101, 103, 104

Orman v. Cullman, 794 A.2d 5 (Del.Ch. 2002), 80

Ostrowski v. Avery, 243 Conn. 355, 703 A.2d 117 (Conn.1997), 135

Pappas v. Moss, 393 F.2d 865 (3rd Cir. 1968), 107

Phoenix Airline Services, Inc. v. Metro Airlines, Inc., 194 Ga.App. 120, 390 S.E.2d 219 (Ga.App.1989), 138

Puma v. Marriott, 283 A.2d 693 (Del.Ch. 1971), 70

Remillard Brick Co. v. Remillard–Dandini Co., 109 Cal.App.2d 405, 241 P.2d 66 (Cal.App. 1 Dist.1952), **65,** 68, 107

Rogers v. Hill, 289 U.S. 582, 53 S.Ct. 731, 77 L.Ed. 1385 (1933), 153, 160

S.E.C. v. Gemstar–TV Guide Intern., Inc., 401 F.3d 1031 (9th Cir.2005), 169

S.E.C. v. Yun, 327 F.3d 1263 (11th Cir. 2003), 197

Shlensky v. South Parkway Bldg. Corp., 19 Ill.2d 268, 166 N.E.2d 793 (Ill.1960), 76, 119

Southeast Consultants, Inc. v. McCrary Engineering Corp., 246 Ga. 503, 273 S.E.2d 112 (Ga.1980), 131

State ex rel. v. _____ (see opposing party and relator)

Steiner v. Meyerson, 1995 WL 441999 (Del. Ch.1995), 155

Tooley v. Donaldson, Lufkin & Jenrette, Inc., 845 A.2d 1031 (Del. Supr.2004), **188,** 191

United States v. _____ (see opposing party)

Walt Disney Co. Derivative Litigation, In re (Disney I), 731 A.2d 342 (Del.Ch. 1998), 54, **80,** 104, 161

Walt Disney Co. Derivative Litigation, In re (Disney II), 825 A.2d 275 (Del. Ch.2003), **163,** 167

Weinberger v. UOP, Inc., 457 A.2d 701 (Del.Supr.1983), 77, 107, 120

Young v. Higbee Co., 324 U.S. 204, 65 S.Ct. 594, 89 L.Ed. 890 (1945), 186

2005 SUPPLEMENT TO
CORPORATIONS
LAW AND POLICY
MATERIALS AND PROBLEMS
Fifth Edition

*

Chapter 1

INTRODUCTION

B. CORPORATE GOVERNANCE IN THE MODERN CORPORATION

Add at page 9 (before "C. Architecture of This Casebook"):

The reinvention of corporate governance in the 1980s described by Professors Holmstrom and Kaplan can also be seen as a shift from a "technocratic" to "proprietary" understanding of the role for corporate management. See Ernie Englander & Allen Kaufman, *Executive Compensation, Political Economy, and Managerial Control: The Transformation of Managerial Incentive Structures and Ideology, 1950–2000*, George Washington University SMPP Working Paper No. 03–01, SSRN Paper No. 408820 (January 2003):

> We characterize the period from the end of World War Two to the early 1980s as technocratic and the period since as proprietary. During the technocratic period, compensation differences between CEOs and senior management were "marginal" in that they reflected their economic contributions to the firm. This facilitated team cohesion among the senior managers, who, like the CEO, had membership "rights" to the board over which they, as a team, controlled. Though constrained by antitrust regulations, managers shared knowhow across industries and built a corporate-wide identity through a system of interlocking directorates. While this network educated its participants in corporate-wide issues, those within it still identified first and foremost with their firm, where they spent most of their career. Finally, managers continued to conceive of their profession as one that served a larger social good. First, they accepted a legal duty of care to further the interests of the corporation as a whole. And secondly, they [adopted] a second fiduciary duty to advance democracy.
>
> In contrast, the coalesced proprietary system has encouraged managers to think of themselves as a special class of shareholders. The extensive use of stock options to supplement their base salary has contributed heavily to this shareholder (as opposed to technocratic) managerial self-definition. This occurred as managers weight-

ed their compensation packages with stock options to take advantage of an explosive equities market and alterations in the tax code. As "insider shareholders" who aimed merely to enhance their personal fortunes, managers turned their internal labor market into a contest for the prized CEO position. The compensation differential between the one who wins and those who lose have become substantial. Indeed, winners receive packages so large that they enter into the truly privileged sector of the very rich—the top 1 percent of the general population.

Consider the dichotomy identified by Englander and Kaufman. What corporate model should we prefer—corporate managers who see themselves as stewards of the public good (as they choose to define it) or as highly-paid servants of capitalism (as expressed through product and stock markets)? Can you imagine any other models?

Chapter 3

AN INTRODUCTION TO THE LAW OF CORPORATIONS

C. CHOICE OF THE STATE OF INCORPORATION: AN INTRODUCTION

2. THE HISTORY OF STATES' COMPETITION FOR CORPORATE CHARTERS

Add at page 61 (before "3. The Preeminence of Delaware"):

The empirical results of Daines' study have been questioned by Professor Guhan Subramanian, who recently examined more recent data on the effect of incorporation in Delaware. Guhan Subramanian, *The Disappearing Delaware Effect*, 20 J. LAW, ECONOMICS & ORGANIZATION 32 (2004):

> Refining and extending the methodology introduced by Daines (2001), I present evidence that small Delaware firms were worth more than small non-Delaware firms during the period 1991–1996 but not afterwards. I also present evidence that larger firms, which comprise 98% of my sample by size, exhibit no Delaware effect for any year during the period 1991–2002. Thus the Delaware effect "disappears" when examined over time and when examined for firms that are economically meaningful. These new contours of the Delaware effect suggest that the benefit associated with Delaware incorporation was an order of magnitude smaller than estimated by Daines (2001) during the early 1990s, and non-existent by the late 1990s. The trajectory of the Delaware effect further suggests that it cannot provide support for the "race to the top" view of regulatory competition, as some commentators have argued, and may in fact provide support for the "race to the bottom" view. Finally, the findings presented here identify two puzzles: first, why did small Delaware firms exhibit a positive Delaware effect during the early 1990s but larger firms did not? And second, why did this effect disappear in the late 1990s? I identify doctrinal changes in Delaware corporate law in the mid–1990s, increased managerial incentives to

sell during this period, and a cohort selection effect during the 1980s as potential explanations.

Whatever the status of Delaware in the "state chartering" debate, Professor Mark Roe has suggested the debate may miss the point. Roe explains that there really is no race, to the top or bottom, for chartering of out-of-state public corporations. Mark Roe, *Delaware's Competition*, 117 HARV. L. REV. 588 (2003). According to Roe, Delaware has won the race "with the overwhelming number of American large corporations chartering there." Instead, Roe asserts that the long-standing "top or bottom" debate is misconceived:

> Delaware's chief competitive pressure comes not from other states but from the federal government. When the issue is big, the federal government takes the issue or threatens to do so, or Delaware players are conscious that if they mis-step, Federal authorities could step in. These possibilities of ouster, threat, and consciousness have conditioned Delaware's behavior. Moreover, even if Delaware were oblivious to the Federal authorities, those authorities can, and do, overturn Delaware law. That which persists is tolerable to the Federal authorities. This reconception a) explains corporate law developments and data that neither theory of state competition can explain well, b) fits several developments in takeover law, going private transactions, and the rhetoric of corporate governance in Delaware, and c) can be detected in corporate law-making in Washington and Wilmington from the very beginning in the early 20th century "origins" of Delaware's dominance right up through last summer's Sarbanes–Oxley corporate governance law and the corporate governance failure in Enron and WorldCom.

> This analysis upsets the long-standing analysis of state corporate law competition as a strong race (whether to the top or to the bottom) because when a corporate issue is important, the federal government takes it over, or threatens to do so, or Delaware fears federal action. As such, we cannot tell whether Delaware, if it indeed raced to the top, did so because of the looming federal "threat". Nor can we tell whether Delaware, if it raced to the bottom, a) did so because national politics meant that, had they taken the locally efficient path, Congress, subject to wider pressures than is Delaware, would have taken the issue away, or b) would have instead raced to the top on other, more important issues that directly affected the mechanisms of a race to the top, had the states fully controlled them. Nor can we tell if that which persists is that which the Federal players approved of, or at least found tolerable. Too many of the truly important decisions, the ones that could affect capital costs—the mechanism driving the race-the-top theory—are taken away from Delaware or are at risk of removal or the Delaware actors know could be taken away if they seriously damaged the national economy or riled powerful interests. That is not to say that what happens at the state level in corporate law is trivial, but that the results are ambiguous in terms of the race debate. If efficiency is

the usual result, then the Federal vertical element could correspond to the strengths of other organizational structures (like separating proposals from ratification in decision-making, of the checks and balances in the M-form corporation). If inefficiency is the usual result, we do not know whether the states, if free to compete without a federal "veto" possibility, would have raced toward efficiency. When we add this "vertical," Federal-state competition atop the horizontal state competition in corporate law, the state race debate—one that has stretched across the 20th century from Brandeis to Cary and beyond—is rendered empirically and theoretically indeterminate.

An example of Roe's thesis may be found in the Delaware judiciary's response to the federal Sarbanes–Oxley Act of 2002 which federalized critical elements of corporate governance, including the composition, functions and responsibilities of the audit committee of the boards of directors of public corporations. See Renee Jones, *Rethinking Corporate Federalism in the Era of Corporate Reform*, 29 J. CORP. L. 625 (2004) (finding that recent Delaware court decisions respond to the preemptive threat by "moving to more restrictive application of the business judgement rule and more vigorous enforcement of officers' and directors' fiduciary duties").

Chapter 5

THE CORPORATION AND SOCIETY

A. INTRODUCTION

Add at page 107 (before "B. Corporate Social Responsibility Trends"):

2. CORPORATE MAXIMIZATION CHOICES

May a corporation choose to maximize values other than shareholder wealth, such as by preferring specified customers or serving some larger social or religious purpose? If a corporation chooses a non-shareholder perspective, is that choice binding? Consider the following story about the dilemma that LifeLine, a phone service company originally established with a specific religious mission, confronts as it struggles between making profits and fulfilling its mission.

Yochi J. Dreazen, TRYING TO BALANCE PROFIT, CHRISTIAN GIVING

THE WALL STREET JOURNAL (Aug. 21, 2003).
2003 WL–WSJ 3977569.

If making money and serving God are at odds, what does one do? Robert Cook, the new chief executive of Christian long-distance provider LifeLine Communications, is wrestling with just that question.

When Mr. Cook, a former Air Force officer and longtime telecommunications executive, took over as CEO of closely held LifeLine late last year, he found a company in turmoil. Launched in 1991, Lifeline had expanded impressively by signing up hundreds of thousands of evangelical Christians attracted by its promise to provide low-cost long-distance phone service while also giving 10% of its revenue to charities and ministries. By 1998, the Oklahoma City company had $124 million a year in revenue, millions of dollars a year in profit, and had given away tens of millions of dollars to various Christian charities.

Then the bottom fell out of the nation's phone market, sending the company's revenue and profit margin plummeting.

In a struggle for the company's survival, Mr. Cook wants to broaden its appeal by playing down its religious nature and offering non-Christians the ability to divert a portion of their bills to the secular charity or university of their choice. He proposes tweaking the company's logo—a stylized cross—to make it look more like a lighthouse. He suggests eliminating the company's long-held slogan, "Serving God. Connecting People, Changing Lives," from some of its advertising and marketing materials. And he hopes to expand the company's advertising from Christian media into secular newspapers, TV and radio stations. "We may have shortchanged ourselves by not reaching out to people who aren't associated with these huge ministries," he says. "We're a Christian organization, but we can support groups that aren't Christian if they're providing important, family-friendly services." But the proposals are angering many of the company's longtime customers and investors, mostly individuals from the evangelical community in and around Oklahoma City. And they particularly rankle LifeLine co-founder Carl Thompson, who now works for a rival company and accuses LifeLine of abandoning its Christian mission.

Founded by Mr. Thompson and Tracy Freeny, LifeLine has relied on a grass-roots marketing campaign built around televised national ministries and independent Christian churches. Working off a particular church's mailing lists, the company uses mail, e-mail and telemarketing to sell its services to members of that congregation, often by highlighting its connection to their church or minister. A flier sent to the parishioners of charismatic black preacher T.D. Jakes, for instance, features photos of the minister and tells recipients that "one decision allows you to stay in touch with family and friends, receive rates as low as 4.9 cents a minute and support T.D. Jakes Ministries." Rev. Jakes's church then gets a percentage of the revenue Lifeline raises from his congregation.

The company makes its money by buying long-distance minutes in bulk from companies such as MCI or Broadwing, often for a penny or less per minute, and then reselling them for roughly five cents a minute, a rate comparable with those offered by larger long-distance providers. LifeLine also keeps its overhead low.

Yet the company's early years were a struggle. It got its first break when it signed on a large national ministry, American Family Association, of Tupelo, Miss. The association gave the young company the names of 1.5 million people that it could solicit and added material about LifeLine to its monthly journal sent to hundreds of thousands of churches and individuals. Other large groups, such as Concerned Women for America, based in Washington, and the Trinity Broadcasting Network, of Santa Ana, Calif., soon signed up as well.

Mr. Freeny, then a life-insurance salesman, and Mr. Thompson, a landscape gardener, both committed Christians, launched the venture as a way to make money while aiding religious causes.

However, turmoil dogged the company's growth: The partners were subject to a two-year investigation by the Securities and Exchange Commission after they illegally sold $25 million in shares to individuals (a move, they said, they didn't know at the time was illegal). The partners also bitterly disagreed about the company's direction and religious mission. Now working for a rival company, Mr. Thompson criticizes LifeLine for trying to broaden its appeal to secular customers and for failing to take as strong a line as he has against abortion, pornography and homosexuality.

Compounding the upheaval: In 1998 LifeLine appointed a professional CEO who infuriated shareholders by eliminating the company's dividend and proposing a reduction in the percentage of revenue LifeLine devoted to charity to 7% from 10%. Shareholders, many of them small investors who relied on the dividend for income, demanded a public meeting and, in surprise move, voted to oust the entire management team and appoint a dissident shareholder, Kenneth Kolek, as CEO. However, Mr. Kolek resigned last fall because he didn't want to move his family from Cedar Rapids, Iowa.

Despite turbulence within LifeLine and the telecom-industry collapse, the company remains profitable. But its revenue has dropped in recent years, making its margins ever thinner, as long-distance rates keep falling. Under Mr. Cook, LifeLine began offering local phone service nationally this summer. The company also has high hopes for its Internet-access offerings, centered on a filtered Internet service that blocks access to sites customers could deem offensive. The service's home page, MyLifeLine.net, is an AOL-lookalike with Christian-themed news and entertainment. The company also is trying to expand into the wireless broadband market.

Yet, sitting in his office, Mr. Freeny wonders if such new products are even necessary. "The Lord has plans for us," he says. "It's all just matter of who's still standing when the game ends."

Remembering *Bellotti* and *Austin* from Chapter 4, consider the pressures facing a corporation in balancing social and economic concerns in the legislative context.

Sarah Kershaw, MICROSOFT COMES UNDER FIRE FOR REVERSAL ON GAY RIGHTS BILL

NEW YORK TIMES.
April 22, 2005.

SEATTLE, April 21 The Microsoft Corporation, at the forefront of corporate gay rights for decades, is coming under fire from gay rights groups, politicians and its own employees for withdrawing its support for a state bill that would have barred discrimination on the basis of sexual orientation. Many of the critics accused the company of bowing to pressure from a prominent evangelical church in Redmond, Wash., located a few blocks from Microsoft's sprawling headquarters.

The bill, or similar versions of it, has been introduced repeatedly over three decades; it failed by one vote Thursday in the State Senate.

Gay rights advocates denounced Microsoft, which had supported the bill for the last two years, for abandoning their cause. Blogs and online chat rooms were buzzing on Thursday with accusations that the company, which has offered benefits to same-sex partners for years, had given in to the Christian right.

"I think people should feel betrayed," said Tina Podlodowski, a former Microsoft senior manager and former Seattle city councilwoman who now runs an advocacy group for AIDS patients. "To me, Microsoft has been one of the big supporters of gay and lesbian civil rights issues, and they did it when it wasn't an issue of political expediency, when it was the right thing to do."

Microsoft officials denied any connection between their decision not to endorse the bill and the church's opposition, although they acknowledged meeting twice with the church minister, Ken Hutcherson.

Dr. Hutcherson, pastor of the Antioch Bible Church, who has organized several rallies opposing same-sex marriage here and in Washington, D.C., said he threatened in those meetings to organize a national boycott of Microsoft products.

After that, "they backed off," the pastor said Thursday in a telephone interview. "I told them I was going to give them something to be afraid of Christians about," he said.

Microsoft officials said that the recent meetings with the minister did not persuade them to back away from supporting the bill, because they had already decided to take a "neutral" position on it. They said they had examined their legislative priorities and decided that because they already offer extensive benefits to gay employees and that King County, where Microsoft is based, already has an anti-discrimination law broader than what the state bill proposed, they should focus on other legislative matters.

"Our government affairs team made a decision before this legislative session that we would focus our energy on a limited number of issues that are directly related to our business," said Mark Murray, a company spokesman. "That decision was not influenced by external factors. It was driven by our desire to focus on a smaller number of issues in this short legislative session. We obviously have not done a very good job of communicating about this issue."

"We're disappointed that people are misinterpreting those meetings," he said.

Sarah Kershaw, MICROSOFT C.E.O. EXPLAINS REVERSAL ON GAY RIGHTS BILL

NEW YORK TIMES.
April 24, 2005.

SEATTLE, April 23 The chief executive of Microsoft, Steven A. Ballmer, sent what company officials described as an unusual e-mail message on Friday evening to roughly 35,000 employees in the United States, defending Microsoft's widely criticized decision not to support an antidiscrimination bill for gay people in Washington State this year.

The e-mail message came as company officials, inundated by internal messages from angry employees, withering attacks on the Web and biting criticism from gay rights groups, sought to quell rancor following the disclosure this week that the company, which had supported the bill in past years, did not do so this year. Critics argue that the decision resulted from pressure from a prominent local evangelical Christian church.

In his message, posted on several Web logs on Saturday and confirmed by company officials, Mr. Ballmer wrote that he had done "a lot of soul searching over the past 24 hours." He said that he and Bill Gates, the founder of Microsoft, both personally supported the bill but that the company had decided not to take an official stance on the legislation this year. He said they were pondering the role major corporations should play in larger social debates.

"We are thinking hard about what is the right balance to strike—when should a public company take a position on a broader social issue, and when should it not?" he wrote. "What message does the company taking a position send to its employees who have strongly held beliefs on the opposite side of the issue?"

Critics, including some Microsoft employees and a state legislator, who said they had conversations with company officials about their decision, said a high-level Microsoft executive had indicated that the company withdrew its support because of pressure from a local minister, Ken Hutcherson. Dr. Hutcherson opposed the bill and said he had threatened a national boycott of Microsoft.

Company officials have denied any connection between the threatened boycott and their decision not to support the bill.

Microsoft, which is based in Redmond, Wash., east of Seattle, has long been known for being at corporate America's forefront on gay rights, extending employee benefits to same-sex couples. In his e-mail message, Mr. Ballmer said, "As long as I am C.E.O., Microsoft is going to be a company that is hard-core about diversity, a company that is absolutely rigorous about having a nondiscriminatory environment, and a company that treats every employee fairly."

Mr. Ballmer described the antidiscrimination measure as posing a "very difficult issue for many people, with strong emotions on all sides." He wrote, "both Bill and I actually both personally support this legislation," adding, "but that is my personal view, and I also know that many employees and shareholders would not agree with me."

Sarah Kershaw, IN A REVERSE, MICROSOFT SAYS IT SUPPORTS GAY RIGHTS BILL

NEW YORK TIMES.
May 7, 2005.

Microsoft, faced with unrelenting criticism from employees and gay rights groups over its decision to abandon support of a gay rights bill in Washington state, reversed course again yesterday and announced that it was now in support of the bill.

Steve Ballmer, the company's chief executive, announced the reversal in an e-mail message sent to 35,000 employees in the United States. "After looking at the question from all sides, I've concluded that diversity in the workplace is such an important issue for our business that it should be included in our legislative agenda," Mr. Ballmer said.

He added: "I respect that there will be different viewpoints. But as C.E.O., I am doing what I believe is right for our company as a whole."

Long known for its internal policies protecting gay employees from discrimination and offering them benefits, Microsoft sparked an uproar when officials decided to take a "neutral" stance on the antidiscrimination bill this year, after having supported it the two previous years.

Critics, including employees who said they were told that Microsoft would back the bill, said the decision to withdraw support had been made under pressure from a local evangelical preacher who threatened to boycott the company if it supported the legislation this year. Company officials have disputed the accusation.

The bill, which would have extended protections against discrimination in employment, housing and other areas to gay men and lesbians, failed by one vote on April 21. But it is automatically up for a new vote next year because bills introduced in the Washington Legislature are active for two years even if they are voted down the first time.

After the defeat, Mr. Ballmer sent an e-mail message to company employees, defending the decision to withdraw support. In that note, Mr. Ballmer said that he and Microsoft's founder, Bill Gates, personally supported the measure but felt the company needed to focus its legislative efforts on measures that had a more direct connection to their business.

In yesterday's message Mr. Ballmer suggested that employees' responses had helped persuade Microsoft officials to renew their backing of the measure. More than 1,500 employees signed an internal petition demanding that the company support the bill, and scores wrote in protest to Mr. Ballmer and Mr. Gates.

A Microsoft executive, speaking on condition of anonymity, said that senior company officials met after Microsoft's widely publicized turnaround on the bill prompted an uproar, and that they had decided to change the company's stance because of pressure from employees.

"This issue got attention at the highest levels of the company in a way it didn't before," said the executive, who did not attend the meeting but was briefed on it. "It was a rocky path, but we got to the right place."

Some lawmakers had said that Microsoft, based in Redmond, Wash., could have lent crucial backing to the legislation through influence on lawmakers representing Redmond and the suburbs outside Seattle.

In explaining why the company had not supported the bill this year, Mr. Ballmer and other Microsoft officials had said over the last two weeks that they were re-examining their legislative priorities and debating when and whether to become involved in public policy debates.

Gay rights groups said they were contacted by Microsoft officials before Mr. Ballmer's statement was publicly released. They applauded the decision.

"We're very happy," said Joe Solmonese, president of the Human Rights Campaign, a national gay advocacy group.

Mr. Solmonese met recently with several Microsoft employees after he learned of the earlier decision not to back the bill, which was first disclosed by The Stranger, an alternative weekly newspaper in Seattle.

The Microsoft officials, Mr. Solmonese said, "took it very seriously."

"They said that there had been a huge outpouring of concern via e-mail, both internally and externally," he said.

Ed Murray, an openly gay state legislator from Seattle and a sponsor of the bill, said of the company's reversal: "I think it's important. It sent a message that this issue is not simply a so-called social issue or cultural war issue, but it's an issue that is good for business, and it's an issue that business considers important."

But the company's decision disappointed others, including Microsoft employees who belong to the Antioch Bible Church in Redmond. The church is led by the Rev. Ken Hutcherson, who met with Microsoft officials twice about the bill and claimed to have persuaded them to change their position on it.

"I feel that it's been kind of a stressful day," said a Microsoft employee who is a member of the church and who spoke on condition of anonymity. "I feel that it was wrong for the company to say that they will be supporting issues such as this. Businesses should not actually be publicly taking a stance on that, regardless of their internal policies."

The employee, who has worked at Microsoft for four years, said the company should "stay out of it" when it comes to the debate over gay rights.

Dr. Hutcherson, whose church offices are near Microsoft's headquarters, said earlier that he believed his boycott threat had persuaded Microsoft not to support the bill. He did not respond to messages left yesterday on his cellphone and at his office.

Chapter 7

FORMING THE CORPORATION

Substitute the following for American Bar Association Model Rules of Professional Conduct Rules 1.6, 1.7 and 1.13 at pages 171–176:

Rule 1.6 Confidentiality of Information

(a) A lawyer shall not reveal information relating to the representation of a client unless the client gives informed consent, the disclosure is impliedly authorized in order to carry out the representation or the disclosure is permitted by paragraph (b).

(b) A lawyer may reveal information relating to the representation of a client to the extent the lawyer reasonably believes necessary:

(1) to prevent reasonably certain death or substantial bodily harm;

(2) to prevent the client from committing a crime or fraud that is reasonably certain to result in substantial injury to the financial interests or property of another and in furtherance of which the client has used or is using the lawyer's services;

(3) to prevent, mitigate or rectify substantial injury to the financial interests or property of another that is reasonably certain to result or has resulted from the client's commission of a crime or fraud in furtherance of which the client has used the lawyer's services;

(4) to secure legal advice about the lawyer's compliance with these Rules;

(5) to establish a claim or defense on behalf of the lawyer in a controversy between the lawyer and the client, to establish a defense to a criminal charge or civil claim against the lawyer based upon conduct in which the client was involved, or to respond to allegations in any proceeding concerning the lawyer's representation of the client; or

(6) to comply with other law or a court order.

COMMENT

[2] A fundamental principle in the client-lawyer relationship is that, the absence of the client's informed consent, the lawyer must not reveal information relating to the representation. * * * This contributes to the trust that is the hallmark of the client-lawyer relationship. The client is thereby encouraged to seek legal assistance and to communicate fully and frankly with the lawyer even as to embarrassing or legally damaging subject matter. The lawyer needs this information to represent the client effectively and, if necessary, to advise the client to refrain from wrongful conduct. Almost without exception, clients come to lawyers in order to determine their rights and what is, in the complex of laws and regulations, deemed to be legal and correct. Based upon experience, lawyers know that almost all clients follow the advice given, and the law is upheld.

[3] The principle of client-lawyer confidentiality is given effect by related bodies of law: the attorney-client privilege, the work product doctrine and the rule of confidentiality established in professional ethics. The attorney-client privilege and work product doctrine apply in judicial and other proceedings in which a lawyer may be called as a witness or otherwise required to produce evidence concerning a client. The rule of client-lawyer confidentiality applies in situations other than those where evidence is sought from the lawyer through compulsion of law. The confidentiality rule, for example, applies not only to matters communicated in confidence by the client but also to all information relating to the representation, whatever its source. A lawyer may not disclose such information except as authorized or required by the Rules of Professional Conduct or other law. See also Scope.

Disclosure Adverse to Client

[6] Although the public interest is usually best served by a strict rule requiring lawyers to preserve the confidentiality of information relating to the representation of their clients, the confidentiality rule is subject to limited exceptions. Paragraph (b)(1) recognizes the overriding value of life and physical integrity and permits disclosure reasonably necessary to prevent reasonably certain death or substantial bodily harm. Such harm is reasonably certain to occur if it will be suffered imminently or if there is a present and substantial threat that a person will suffer such harm at a later date if the lawyer fails to take action necessary to eliminate the threat. Thus, a lawyer who knows that a client has accidentally discharged toxic waste into a town?s water supply may reveal this information to the authorities if there is a present and substantial risk that a person who drinks the water will contract a life-threatening or debilitating disease and the lawyer's disclosure is necessary to eliminate the threat or reduce the number of victims.

[7] Paragraph (b)(2) is a limited exception to the rule of confidentiality that permits the lawyer to reveal information to the extent necessary to enable affected persons or appropriate authorities to prevent the

client from committing a crime or fraud, as defined in Rule 1.0(d), that is reasonably certain to result in substantial injury to the financial or property interests of another and in furtherance of which the client has used or is using the lawyer's services. Such a serious abuse of the client-lawyer relationship by the client forfeits the protection of this Rule. The client can, of course, prevent such disclosure by refraining from the wrongful conduct. Although paragraph (b)(2) does not require the lawyer to reveal the client's misconduct, the lawyer may not counsel or assist the client in conduct the lawyer knows is criminal or fraudulent. See Rule 1.2(d). See also Rule 1.16 with respect to the lawyer's obligation or right to withdraw from the representation of the client in such circumstances, and Rule 1.13(c), which permits the lawyer, where the client is an organization, to reveal information relating to the representation in limited circumstances.

[8] Paragraph (b)(3) addresses the situation in which the lawyer does not learn of the client's crime or fraud until after it has been consummated. Although the client no longer has the option of preventing disclosure by refraining from the wrongful conduct, there will be situations in which the loss suffered by the affected person can be prevented, rectified or mitigated. In such situations, the lawyer may disclose information relating to the representation to the extent necessary to enable the affected persons to prevent or mitigate reasonably certain losses or to attempt to recoup their losses. Paragraph (b)(3) does not apply when a person who has committed a crime or fraud thereafter employs a lawyer for representation concerning that offense.

[12] Other law may require that a lawyer disclose information about a client. Whether such a law supersedes Rule 1.6 is a question of law beyond the scope of these Rules. When disclosure of information relating to the representation appears to be required by other law, the lawyer must discuss the matter with the client to the extent required by Rule 1.4. If, however, the other law supersedes this Rule and requires disclosure, paragraph (b)(6) permits the lawyer to make such disclosures as are necessary to comply with the law.

[13] A lawyer may be ordered to reveal information relating to the representation of a client by a court or by another tribunal or governmental entity claiming authority pursuant to other law to compel the disclosure. Absent informed consent of the client to do otherwise, the lawyer should assert on behalf of the client all nonfrivolous claims that the order is not authorized by other law or that the information sought is protected against disclosure by the attorney-client privilege or other applicable law. In the event of an adverse ruling, the lawyer must consult with the client about the possibility of appeal to the extent required by Rule 1.4. Unless review is sought, however, paragraph (b)(6) permits the lawyer to comply with the court's order.

[14] Paragraph (b) permits disclosure only to the extent the lawyer reasonably believes the disclosure is necessary to accomplish one of the purposes specified. Where practicable, the lawyer should first seek to

persuade the client to take suitable action to obviate the need for disclosure. In any case, a disclosure adverse to the client's interest should be no greater than the lawyer reasonably believes necessary to accomplish the purpose. If the disclosure will be made in connection with a judicial proceeding, the disclosure should be made in a manner that limits access to the information to the tribunal or other persons having a need to know it and appropriate protective orders or other arrangements should be sought by the lawyer to the fullest extent practicable.

Former Client

[18] The duty of confidentiality continues after the client-lawyer relationship has terminated. See Rule 1.9(c)(2). See Rule 1.9(c)(1) for the prohibition against using such information to the disadvantage of the former client.

Rule 1.7 Conflict of Interest: Current Clients

(a) Except as provided in paragraph (b), a lawyer shall not represent a client if the representation involves a concurrent conflict of interest. A concurrent conflict of interest exists if:

(1) the representation of one client will be directly adverse to another client; or

(2) there is a significant risk that the representation of one or more clients will be materially limited by the lawyer's responsibilities to another client, a former client or a third person or by a personal interest of the lawyer.

(b) Notwithstanding the existence of a concurrent conflict of interest under paragraph (a), a lawyer may represent a client if:

(1) the lawyer reasonably believes that the lawyer will be able to provide competent and diligent representation to each affected client;

(2) the representation is not prohibited by law;

(3) the representation does not involve the assertion of a claim by one client against another client represented by the lawyer in the same litigation or other proceeding before a tribunal; and

(4) each affected client gives informed consent, confirmed in writing.

COMMENT

General Principles

[2] Resolution of a conflict of interest problem under this Rule requires the lawyer to: 1) clearly identify the client or clients; 2) determine whether a conflict of interest exists; 3) decide whether the representation may be undertaken despite the existence of a conflict, i.e., whether the conflict is consentable; and 4) if so, consult with the clients

affected under paragraph (a) and obtain their informed consent, confirmed in writing. The clients affected under paragraph (a) include both of the clients referred to in paragraph (a)(*l*) and the one or more clients whose representation might be materially limited under paragraph (a)(2).

[3] A conflict of interest may exist before representation is undertaken, in which event the representation must be declined, unless the lawyer obtains the informed consent of each client under the conditions of paragraph (b).* * *

[4] If a conflict arises after representation has been undertaken, the lawyer ordinarily must withdraw from the representation, unless the lawyer has obtained the informed consent of the client under the conditions of paragraph (b). See Rule 1.16. Where more than one client is involved, whether the lawyer may continue to represent any of the clients is determined both by the lawyer's ability to comply with duties owed to the former client and by the lawyer's ability to represent adequately the remaining client or clients, given the lawyer's duties to the former client. See Rule 1.9. * * *

Identifying Conflicts of Interest: Material Limitation

[8] Even where there is no direct adverseness, a conflict of interest exists if there is a significant risk that a lawyer's ability to consider, recommend or carry out an appropriate course of action for the client will be materially limited as a result of the lawyer's other responsibilities or interests. For example, a lawyer asked to represent several individuals seeking to form a joint venture is likely to be materially limited in the lawyer's ability to recommend or advocate all possible positions that each might take because of the lawyer's duty of loyalty to the others. The conflict in effect forecloses alternatives that would otherwise be available to the client. The mere possibility of subsequent harm does not itself require disclosure and consent. The critical questions are the likelihood that a difference in interests will eventuate and, if it does, whether it will materially interfere with the lawyer's independent professional judgment in considering alternatives or foreclose courses of action that reasonably should be pursued on behalf of the client.

Informed Consent

[18] Informed consent requires that each affected client be aware of the relevant circumstances and of the material and reasonably foreseeable ways that the conflict could have adverse effects on the interests of that client. The information required depends on the nature of the conflict and the nature of the risks involved. When representation of multiple clients in a single matter is undertaken, the information must include the implications of the common representation, including possible effects on loyalty, confidentiality and the attorney-client privilege and the advantages and risks involved. * * *

Consent Confirmed in Writing

[20] Paragraph (b) requires the lawyer to obtain the informed consent of the client, confirmed in writing. * * * The requirement of a writing does not supplant the need in most cases for the lawyer to talk with the client, to explain the risks and advantages, if any, of representation burdened with a conflict of interest, as well as reasonably available alternatives, and to afford the client a reasonable opportunity to consider the risks and alternatives and to raise questions and concerns. * * *

Consent to Future Conflict

[22] Whether a lawyer may properly request a client to waive conflicts that might arise in the future is subject to the test of paragraph (b). The effectiveness of such waivers is generally determined by the extent to which the client reasonably understands the material risks that the waiver entails. The more comprehensive the explanation of the types of future representations that might arise and the actual and reasonably foreseeable adverse consequences of those representations, the greater the likelihood that the client will have the requisite understanding.* ** If the consent is general and open-ended, then the consent ordinarily will be ineffective, because it is not reasonably likely that the client will have understood the material risks involved.

Nonlitigation Conflicts

[28] Whether a conflict is consentable depends on the circumstances. For example, a lawyer may not represent multiple parties to a negotiation whose interests are fundamentally antagonistic to each other, but common representation is permissible where the clients are generally aligned in interest even though there is some difference in interest among them. Thus, a lawyer may seek to establish or adjust a relationship between clients on an amicable and mutually advantageous basis; for example, in helping to organize a business in which two or more clients are entrepreneurs, working out the financial reorganization of an enterprise in which two or more clients have an interest or arranging a property distribution in settlement of an estate. The lawyer seeks to resolve potentially adverse interests by developing the parties' mutual interests. Otherwise, each party might have to obtain separate representation, with the possibility of incurring additional cost, complication or even litigation. Given these and other relevant factors, the clients may prefer that the lawyer act for all of them.

Special Considerations in Common Representation

[29] In considering whether to represent multiple clients in the same matter, a lawyer should be mindful that if the common representation fails because the potentially adverse interests cannot be reconciled, the result can be additional cost, embarrassment and recrimination. Ordinarily, the lawyer will be forced to withdraw from representing all of the clients if the common representation fails. In some situations, the

risk of failure is so great that multiple representation is plainly impossible. * * * Moreover, because the lawyer is required to be impartial between commonly represented clients, representation of multiple clients is improper when it is unlikely that impartiality can be maintained. * * *

[30] A particularly important factor in determining the appropriateness of common representation is the effect on client-lawyer confidentiality and the attorney-client privilege. With regard to the attorney-client privilege, the prevailing rule is that, as between commonly represented clients, the privilege does not attach. Hence, it must be assumed that if litigation eventuates between the clients, the privilege will not protect any such communications, and the clients should be so advised.

[31] As to the duty of confidentiality, continued common representation will almost certainly be inadequate if one client asks the lawyer not to disclose to the other client information relevant to the common representation. This is so because the lawyer has an equal duty of loyalty to each client, and each client has the right to be informed of anything bearing on the representation that might affect that client's interests and the right to expect that the lawyer will use that information to that client's benefit. The lawyer should, at the outset of the common representation and as part of the process of obtaining each client's informed consent, advise each client that information will be shared and that the lawyer will have to withdraw if one client decides that some matter material to the representation should be kept from the other. * * *

[32] When seeking to establish or adjust a relationship between clients, the lawyer should make clear that the lawyer's role is not that of partisanship normally expected in other circumstances and, thus, that the clients may be required to assume greater responsibility for decisions than when each client is separately represented. Any limitations on the scope of the representation made necessary as a result of the common representation should be fully explained to the clients at the outset of the representation.

Rule 1.13 Organization as Client

(a) A lawyer employed or retained by an organization represents the organization acting through its duly authorized constituents.

(b) If a lawyer for an organization knows that an officer, employee or other person associated with the organization is engaged in action, intends to act or refuses to act in a matter related to the representation that is a violation of a legal obligation to the organization, or a violation of law that reasonably might be imputed to the organization, and that is likely to result in substantial injury to the organization, then the lawyer shall proceed as is reasonably necessary m the best interest of the organization. Unless the lawyer reasonably believes that it is not necessary in the best interest of the organization to do so, the lawyer shall refer the matter to higher authority in the organization, including, if warranted by the circumstances, to the highest authority that can act on behalf of the organization as determined by applicable law.

(c) Except as provided in paragraph (d), if

(1) despite the lawyer's efforts in accordance with paragraph (b) the highest authority that can act on behalf of the organization insists upon or fails to address in a timely and appropriate manner an action or a refusal to act, that is clearly a violation of law, and

(2) the lawyer reasonably believes that the violation is reasonably certain to result in substantial injury to the organization,

then the lawyer may reveal information relating to the representation whether or not Rule 1.6 permits such disclosure, but only if and to the extent the lawyer reasonably believes necessary to prevent substantial injury to the organization.

(d) Paragraph (c) shall not apply with respect to information relating to a lawyer's representation of an organization to investigate an alleged violation of law, or to defend the organization or an officer, employee or other constituent associated with the organization against a claim arising out of an alleged violation of law.

(e) A lawyer who reasonably believes that he or she has been discharged because of the lawyer's actions taken pursuant to paragraphs (b) or (c), or who withdraws under circumstances that require or permit the lawyer to take action under either of those paragraphs, shall proceed as the lawyer reasonably believes necessary to assure that the organization's highest authority is informed of the lawyer's discharge or withdrawal.

(f) In dealing with an organization's directors, officers, employees, members, shareholders or other constituents, a lawyer shall explain the identity of the client when the lawyer knows or reasonably should know that the organization's interests are adverse to those of the constituents with whom the lawyer is dealing.

(g) A lawyer representing an organization may also represent any of its directors, officers, employees, members, shareholders or other constituents, subject to the provisions of Rule 1.7. If the organization's consent to the dual representation is required by Rule 1.7, the consent shall be given by an appropriate official of the organization other than the individual who is to be represented, or by the shareholders.

COMMENT

The Entity as the Client

[1] An organizational client is a legal entity, but it cannot act except through its officers, directors, employees, shareholders and other constituents. Officers, directors, employees and shareholders are the constituents of the corporate organizational client. The duties defined in this Comment apply equally to unincorporated associations. "Other constituents" as used in this Comment means the positions equivalent to

officers, directors, employees and shareholders held by persons acting for organizational clients that are not corporations.

[2] When one of the constituents of an organizational client communicates with the organization's lawyer in that person's organizational capacity, the communication is protected by Rule 1.6. Thus, by way of example, if an organizational client requests its lawyer to investigate allegations of wrongdoing, interviews made in the course of that investigation between the lawyer and the client's employees or other constituents are covered by Rule 1.6. This does not mean, however, that constituents of an organizational client are the clients of the lawyer. The lawyer may not disclose to such constituents information relating to the representation except for disclosures explicitly or impliedly authorized by the organizational client in order to carry out the representation or as otherwise permitted by Rule 1.6.

[3] When constituents of the organization make decisions for it, the decisions ordinarily must be accepted by the lawyer even if their utility or prudence is doubtful. Decisions concerning policy and operations, including ones entailing serious risk, are not as such in the lawyer's province. Paragraph (b) makes clear, however, that when the lawyer knows that the organization is likely to be substantially injured by action of an officer or other constituent that violates a legal obligation to the organization or is in violation of law that might be imputed to the organization, the lawyer must proceed as is reasonably necessary in the best interest of the organization. As defined in Rule 1.0(1), knowledge can be inferred from circumstances, and a lawyer cannot ignore the obvious.

[4] In determining how to proceed under paragraph (b), the lawyer should give due consideration to the seriousness of the violation and its consequences, the responsibility in the organization and the apparent motivation of the person involved, the policies of the organization concerning such matters, and any other relevant considerations. Ordinarily, referral to a higher authority would be necessary. In some circumstances, however, it may be appropriate for the lawyer to ask the constituent to reconsider the matter; for example, if the circumstances involve a constituent's innocent misunderstanding of law and subsequent acceptance of the lawyer's advice, the lawyer may reasonably conclude that the best interest of the organization does not require that the matter be referred to higher authority. If a constituent persists in conduct contrary to the lawyer's advice, it will be necessary for the lawyer to take steps to have the matter reviewed by a higher authority in the organization. If the matter is of sufficient seriousness and importance or urgency to the organization, referral to higher authority in the organization may be necessary even if the lawyer has not communicated with the constituent. Any measures taken should, to the extent practicable, minimize the risk of revealing information relating to the representation to persons outside the organization. Even in circumstances where a lawyer is not obligated by Rule 1.13 to proceed, a lawyer may bring to the attention of an organizational client, including its highest authority,

matters that the lawyer reasonably believes to be of sufficient importance to warrant doing so in the best interest of the organization.

[5] Paragraph (b) also makes clear that when it is reasonably necessary to enable the organization to address the matter in a timely and appropriate manner, the lawyer must refer the matter to higher authority, including, if warranted by the circumstances, the highest authority that can act on behalf of the organization under applicable law. The organization's highest authority to whom a matter may be referred ordinarily will be the board of directors or similar governing body. However, applicable law may prescribe that under certain conditions the highest authority reposes elsewhere, for example, in the independent directors of a corporation.

Relation to Other Rules

[6] The authority and responsibility provided in this Rule are concurrent with the authority and responsibility provided in other Rules. In particular, this Rule does not limit or expand the lawyer's responsibility under Rules 1.8, 1.16, 3.3 or 4.1. Paragraph (c) of this Rule supplements Rule 1.6(b) by providing an additional basis upon which the lawyer may reveal information relating to the representation, but does not modify, restrict, or limit the provisions of Rule 1.6(b)(1)—(6). Under paragraph (c) the lawyer may reveal such information only when the organization's highest authority insists upon or fails to address threatened or ongoing action that is clearly a violation of law, and then only to the extent the lawyer reasonably believes necessary to prevent reasonably certain substantial injury to the organization. It is not necessary that the lawyer's services be used in furtherance of the violation, but it is required that the matter be related to the lawyer's representation of the organization. If the lawyer's services are being used by an organization to further a crime or fraud by the organization, Rules 1.6(b)(2) and 1.6(b)(3) may permit the lawyer to disclose confidential information. In such circumstances Rule 1.2(d) may also be applicable, in which event, withdrawal from the representation under Rule 1.16(a)(1) may be required.

[7] Paragraph (d) makes clear that the authority of a lawyer to disclose information relating to a representation in circumstances described in paragraph (c) does not apply with respect to information relating to a lawyer's engagement by an organization to investigate an alleged violation of law or to defend the organization or an officer, employee or other person associated with the organization against a claim arising out of an alleged violation of law. This is necessary in order to enable organizational clients to enjoy the full benefits of legal counsel in conducting an investigation or defending against a claim.

[8] A lawyer who reasonably believes that he or she has been discharged because of the lawyer's actions taken pursuant to paragraph (b) or (c), or who withdraws in circumstances that require or permit the lawyer to take action under either of these paragraphs, must proceed as

the lawyer reasonably believes necessary to assure that the organization's highest authority is informed of the lawyer's discharge or withdrawal.

Clarifying the Lawyer's Role

[10] There are times when the organization's interest may be or become adverse to those of one or more of its constituents. In such circumstances the lawyer should advise any constituent, whose interest the lawyer finds adverse to that of the organization of the conflict or potential conflict of interest, that the lawyer cannot represent such constituent, and that such person may wish to obtain independent representation. Care must be taken to assure that the individual understands that, when there is such adversity of interest, the lawyer for the organization cannot provide legal representation for that constituent individual, and that discussions between the lawyer for the organization and the individual may not be privileged.

[11] Whether such a warning should be given by the lawyer for the organization to any constituent individual may turn on the facts of each case.

Derivative Actions

[13] Under generally prevailing law, the shareholders or members of a corporation may bring suit to compel the directors to perform their legal obligations in the supervision of the organization. Members of unincorporated associations have essentially the same right. Such an action may be brought nominally by the organization, but usually is, in fact, a legal controversy over management of the organization.

[14] The question can arise whether counsel for the organization may defend such an action. The proposition that the organization is the lawyer's client does not alone resolve the issue. Most derivative actions are a normal incident of an organization's affairs, to be defended by the organization's lawyer like any other suit. However, if the claim involves serious charges of wrongdoing by those in control of the organization, a conflict may arise between the lawyer's duty to the organization and the lawyer's relationship with the board. In those circumstances, Rule 1.7 governs who should represent the directors and the organization.

Chapter 9

FINANCIAL STRUCTURE OF THE CORPORATION

A. CORPORATE SECURITIES

Add at page 245 (at bottom of page):

4. OPTIONS

Another important piece of the financial accounting and valuation puzzle is a financial instrument known as an option. Students who were apprehensive about basic accounting and financial concepts when reading the beginning portion of this chapter might shudder at the thought that now they must understand options, too. But don't worry too much—the basics of options are no more complex than the concepts already covered in this chapter. In any event, lawyers have no choice but to understand options. Corporate lawyers in particular frequently deal with options, in part because most publicly traded companies and many private companies award stock options to managers and employees. Business litigators also encounter options in various contexts.

The definition of an option is simple: it is the right to buy or sell something in the future. Options are everywhere. A tenant with the right to renew a lease at a particular monthly rate owns an option. A car rental company that permits a client to purchase the car's tank of gasoline in advance is selling an option. Any company that gives its employees the right to buy stock at a set time and price also has sold options.

Options generally are known as contingent claims, because they are assets whose value and future payoff depend on the outcome of some uncertain contingent event, such as fluctuations in rental markets, gasoline use on a trip, or changes in the price of stock. Remember: a party who owns an option has a contractual *right* (to buy or sell), but not any contractual *obligation*. A tenant with a right to renew is not obligated to renew the lease; a car renter who prepurchases a tank of gas is not obligated to use all of it; and an employee with stock options is not obligated to buy company stock. Simply stated, option holders have rights, not obligations.

The most familiar type of option is the stock option. Companies frequently grant stock options to their employees, particularly senior managers, as compensation. Again, stock options give the holder the right–but not the obligation–to buy shares of a company. The company whose shares are subject to purchase or sale typically is the employer. For example, in 1995, when Disney hired Michael Ovitz, the Hollywood talent broker, Disney agreed to pay Ovitz a base salary of $1 million, a discretionary bonus, and stock options that effectively entitled Ovitz to purchase five million shares of Disney stock. The right to buy five million shares of Disney stock is a valuable right, which becomes more valuable if the stock price increases.

Options have a special terminology:

1. The right to buy shares is known as a *call option*, whereas the right to sell is known as a *put option*.
2. The price specified in an option contract is known as the *strike price* or *exercise price*.
3. The date specified in an option contract is known as the *maturity date* or *expiration date*.

Options are more than merely types of corporate securities. They also are conceptual tools that help illuminate the roles of various participants in a corporation. For example, in the Precision Tools problem at the beginning of this chapter, the relative positions of Michael, Jessica, and Bernie, on one hand, and Columbia National Bank, on the other hand, can be described using options.

To simplify the example, for purposes of this discussion assume that Precision Tools Corporation has $2 million of assets, and that Jessica is the only shareholder of PTC (for purposes of this example, Michael and Bernie are no longer involved). Further assume Jessica has invested $1.5 million to buy all of PTC's shares, and that PTC has then borrowed $500,000 from Columbia National Bank. In other words, the total capital of PTC, equity plus debt, is $2 million, which is also the value of the firm's assets overall. These details are summarized in the balance sheet for PTC below:

PTC Assets	$2,000,000	PTC Debt (Bank)	$ 500,000
		PTC Equity (Jessica)	$1,500,000
Total Assets	$2,000,000	Total Debt + Equity	$2,000,000

Now consider the following question: who owns the corporation's $2 million of assets? Technically, of course, the corporation itself owns the assets. But looking more deeply at the concept of ownership, instinctively we assume that whoever owns the equity should be considered as if they owned the underlying assets, and the law generally does so. However, as the assets of a corporation begin to decline in value and the corporation comes closer to insolvency, lawyers and judges sometimes begin to think of the debtholders as if they were the owners of the assets. And if the corporation ultimately does become insolvent, it is the debtholders rather than the stockholders (the owners of the equity) who control the assets.

Applying that framework to PTC, there are only two possibilities. Conceptually, either the assets are owned by Jessica, who owns all the equity in PTC, or they are owned by the bank which owns all of PTC's debt. Let us consider what that might mean in each case.

If Jessica is considered to own all $2 million of PTC's assets, what is the Bank left with? Effectively, the Bank has the obligation to take on the assets if the value of the assets falls to below $500,000, the point at which Jessica's equity investment of $1.5 million would be wiped out. Put another way, Jessica has the right to force the Bank to buy PTC's assets for $500,000, even if they are worth less than that, so that the most Jessica can lose is $1.5 million, the value of her initial investment.

This is just another way of saying that Jessica, as a shareholder, has limited liability. She does not bear the risk of loss if the assets decline in value by more than $1.5 million. Instead, she has the right to rid herself of exposure to the assets of PTC if those assets decline in value by more than $1.5 million. Once the assets are worth only $500,000 or less, the Bank effectively has the obligation to buy them from Jessica.

If Jessica has the right to sell the assets to the Bank, and the Bank has the obligation to buy the assets from Jessica, then Jessica has bought a *put option*. Conversely, the Bank has sold a put option. Recall that a put option is the right to sell assets for a specified price during a specified period of time. In this case, the exercise price of the put option is $500,000, the amount of the Bank's debt. The exercise date is the maturity date of the Bank's debt. In other words, Jessica can be thought of as owning, not $1.5 million of shares, but rather $2 million of PTC's assets along with a put option entitling her to sell those assets back to PTC for $500,000.

In the event Jessica exercises her put option, the Bank, as the debtholder of PTC, becomes obligated to take on the economic risk of the assets–this is another way of saying, as lawyers and judges sometimes do, that as the corporation comes closer to insolvency the debtholder sometimes is treated as the owner of the assets. Once the assets have declined in value so much that the equity is worthless, the corporation is on the cusp of insolvency. Beyond that point, if the value of the corporation's assets decline any more, the debtholder–not the equity–will suffer the losses.

From the perspective of the equity owner, the put option acts as an insurance policy. In other words, the put option protects Jessica against losing more than $1.5 million. If the corporation's assets decline by more than that amount, the Bank loses money. In exchange for this downside protection, Jessica agrees to permit PTC to pay the Bank an insurance "premium," in the form of interest payments during the term of the debt. This premium can be thought of as the cost of the put option, which is passed on from Jessica through PTC and then, over time, to the Bank. Again, in options terminology, Jessica has sold a put option to the Bank.

Alternatively, one can view the corporation through an entirely separate lens by picturing the Bank, not Jessica, as the owner of PTC's assets. If the Bank owns all $2 million of PTC's assets, what is Jessica left with? Effectively, Jessica still has the potential for gain associated with PTC's assets. After all, she, rather than the Bank, owns the equity and therefore has a claim to the residual profits of the corporation. In other words, if the assets are worth more than $500,000, that benefit goes to Jessica, not the bank. This is true regardless of the label one applies to Jessica's holdings.

It might sound strange at first, but one way of describing Jessica's holdings is that she effectively has the acquired the right to buy PTC's assets from the Bank if those assets are worth more than $500,000. Put another way, Jessica has the right to enjoy the benefits of PTC's assets above and beyond $500,000 in value. In this second way of thinking about the corporation, the Bank might "own" the assets, but its economic benefit from the assets would be capped at the $500,000 face amount of its debt, plus interest.

In this instance, Jessica can be thought of as buying a *call option* with an exercise price of $500,000, the amount of the Bank's debt. The exercise date of the call option also corresponds to the maturity of the Bank's debt. Effectively, Jessica pays $1.5 million to PTC in exchange for the right to enjoy any upside associated with PTC's assets being worth more than $500,000. Because PTC's assets are worth $2 million at the time it raises capital from Jessica and the Bank, this call option is very valuable, and can be described as *deep in-the-money*. From a conceptual perspective, the Bank pays a net amount of $500,000 (the cost of $2 million for PTC's assets minus the proceeds of $1.5 million from Jessica's call option), in exchange for the right to interest payments during the term of the debt plus repayment of $500,000 at maturity.

Like any call option, Jessica's position increases in value as the underlying assets increase in value. And like any call option, Jessica has limited downside. If the value of PTC's assets declines below the exercise price of the option, $500,000, Jessica can simply walk away from her investment. This is another way of saying she has limited liability. Because she effectively has purchased a call option, she has the right, but not the obligation, to the upside associated with PTC's assets. If those assets are worth less than $500,000, Jessica simply declines to exercise her call option, which becomes worthless (along with her initial investment). The Bank, which has the obligation to take on the risk associated with PTC's assets as they decline in value, suffers the losses.

Finally, thinking about Jessica and the Bank from the perspective of options theory helps illuminate the principal of leverage, discussed in the next section. A person who owns assets and buys a put option is limiting her downside, just as a person who borrows money to invest in a business is limiting her downside. Likewise, a person who buys a call option is magnifying her exposure to the underlying assets: she has the potential to increase the profit associated with an investment, with limited downside risk.

Options offer new ways of thinking about the economic positions of equity and debt. But they also present challenging questions. What if, in the example above, PTC had sold $1,500,000 of call options to Jessica and $500,000 of equity to the Bank? PTC still would have raised the same amount of equity and capital, and Jessica and the Bank still would have the same priority in PTC's capital structure. Compare the revised balance sheet of PTC to the balance sheet above. (Typically, options are not listed on the balance sheet; instead, they are described in the footnotes to financial statements. We will return to this issue in Chapter 18. For now, we have included options as part of the balance sheet below for illustrative purposes, so you can compare this version of PTC's capital structure to the previous balance sheet set forth above.)

PTC Assets	$2,000,000	PTC Debt	$ 0
		PTC Equity (Bank)	$ 500,000
		PTC Options (Jessica)	$1,500,000
Total Assets	$2,000,000	Total Debt + Equity + Options	$2,000,000

How has the capital structure of PTC changed? How do these changes affect the relative positions of the parties? Should you think about the corporation any differently now that the labels associated with each of the participants has changed, in other words, now that Jessica is "options" instead of "equity," and Bank is "equity" instead of "debt"? As you read the next section, consider how changes in the relative composition of options, equity, preferred stock, and debt might affect how corporate law allocates rights to the various participants in the corporation.

Add at page 269 (before "b. Legal Capital Under the Revised Model Act")

Effective July 1, 2004, Delaware amended its corporate statute to liberalize significantly its legal capital rules on the issuance of stock. Borrowing language from the MBCA, DGCL § 152 now permits a Delaware corporation to issue stock for any consideration deemed adequate by the board:

> The consideration, as determined pursuant to subsections (a) and (b) of § 153 of this title, for subscriptions to, or the purchase of, the capital stock to be issued by a corporation shall be paid in such form and in such manner as the board of directors shall determine. The board of directors may authorize capital stock to be issued for consideration consisting of cash, any tangible or intangible property

or any benefit to the corporation, or any combination thereof. In the absence of actual fraud in the transaction, the judgment of the directors as to the value of such consideration shall be conclusive. The capital stock so issued shall be deemed to be fully paid and nonassessable stock upon receipt by the corporation of such consideration....

Chapter 13

GOVERNANCE ROLE OF SHAREHOLDERS

C. SHAREHOLDERS' POWER TO INITIATE ACTION

2. WHAT ACTIONS CAN SHAREHOLDERS INITIATE?

c. *Removal and Replacement of Directors*

Add at page 437 (before "3. Board Responses to Shareholder Initiatives"):

Note: Board Removal of Directors

Generally, removal of directors is a matter entrusted to shareholders, not the board. MBCA § 8.08 (permitting shareholders to remove directors with or without cause, unless articles specify removal only for cause). In egregious cases, the board acting for the corporation (or a shareholder in a derivative suit) can seek judicial removal of a director who engaged in fraudulent conduct, grossly abused his position, or intentionally inflicted harm on the corporation. MBCA § 8.09 (requiring also a finding that removal would be in corporation's best interests).

An unusual provision of Indiana's corporate statute permits removal of a director by the board with or without cause. What rights to incumbency does a director have? In *Murray v. Conseco, Inc.,* 795 N.E.2d 454 (Ind. 2003), a director removed by the board brought an action for declaratory judgment challenging his removal. Although the removal apparently stemmed from a disagreement between the director and the board about pursuing litigation over corporate setbacks, the board treated the removal as one "without cause." On an appeal from a summary judgment for the corporation, Indiana's supreme court pointed out that Indiana allows the board to remove directors without cause.

Indiana's BCL is largely drawn from the Model Business Corporation Act (MBCA), but includes a number of unusual provisions. Unlike the MBCA, the Indiana version has a provision expressly addressing the authority of the board of directors to remove a director without cause. The BCL not only addresses this subject, but expressly authorizes removal by directors for every Indiana corporation unless the articles of incorporation provide otherwise. The same section of the BCL includes provisions retained from the MBCA addressing removal of directors elected by a "voting group," removal of directors elected by cumulative voting, and procedures for convening a shareholder meeting to remove a director. Indiana Code section 23–1–33–8.

795 N.E.2d at 457. The court held that the provisions prohibiting a board from removing a director elected by a separate "voting group" does not apply to a director elected by all voting shares. Furthermore, the director presented no evidence that his removal was a breach of contract, was in bad faith, or was without reasonable investigation.

One effect of giving the board the power to remove directors without cause, as pointed out in the opinion below [*Murray v. Conseco*, 766 N.E.2d 38 (Ind. App. 2002)], is to make takeovers more difficult in a public corporation with a staggered board. Consider an Indiana corporation with a staggered board whose articles permit shareholders to remove directors only for cause, but leave in place the board's power to remove directors without cause. With a staggered board, this could be a real show-stopper. After the election of a new class of directors, the holdover directors could remove and replace the newly-elected directors, but the shareholders (or new controlling shareholder) would be powerless to remove the holdovers. Arguably, this is precisely what the takeover-wary Indiana legislature had in mind. See Paul F. Banta, *Note, The New Indiana Business Corporation Law: "Reckless" Statute or New Standard?*, 1987 COLUM. BUS. L.REV. 233, 234–35 (1987). As the Indiana appeals court pointed out, other states (including Delaware) have shunned this approach:

> To allow the Board to remove one of its own members at any time without cause would seem to be completely violative of shareholder rights. It would be absurd to require an annual meeting of shareholders to elect directors and then allow the remaining members of a staggered Board to remove the newly elected directors without cause and replace them, in total frustration of the stockholders' voting rights. Dillon v. Berg, 326 F.Supp. 1214, 1225 (D. Del.1971), aff'd, 453 F.2d 876 (3rd Cir.1971).

766 N.E.2d 38, 44 n.4 (Ind.App.2002). Is there anything to keep the holdover directors of an Indiana corporation from acting in this manner?

---

3. BOARD RESPONSES TO SHAREHOLDER INITIATIVES

Add at page 443 (before "Quickturn Design Systems"):

Note: Effect of Shareholder–Approved Shark Repellents

In *Blasius* the staggered board was added to the articles and approved by the Atlas shareholders. The articles gave the Atlas board, without further intervention by the shareholders, the power to create a 15–member board, which would be immune from a board-packing ploy. The board, however, exercised this power only after Blasius began his insurgency.

Should a court in a voting contest take into account that the purpose of the shareholder-approved articles was to make the company more resistant to an unsolicited takeover? That is, had the shareholders not delegated to the board some of their governance authority? Arguing that just as Odysseus had ordered his men to tie him to the mast (to keep him from heeding the sirens' call) and to plug their ears with wax (to keep them from heeding his change of heart), Professors Kahan and Rock argue that the *Blasius* court should have respected the shareholders' binding delegation to the board of control over the electoral cycle for directors. See Marcel Kahan & Edward B. Rock, *Corporate Constitutionalism: Antitakeover Charter Provisions as Pre-Commitment*, 152 U. PA. L. REV. 473 (2003) (arguing that Delaware courts should defer to shareholder-approved entrenchment structures, even when board implementation is tardy, as happened when the board in *Blasius* increased the size of the staggered board as anticipated in the shareholder-approved charter provisions). For a more complete summary of their article, see this Supplement, Chapter 22.

Chapter 14

THE ROLE OF SHAREHOLDER IN THE GOVERNANCE OF THE PUBLIC CORPORATION

B. SHAREHOLDER PROPOSALS

2. THE RULE IN OPERATION

b. *Substantive Grounds for Omission*

Add at page 502 (after *Lovenheim v. Iroquois Brands, Ltd*) :

Sarah Ivry, A Social Concern Turns Economic for Best Buy

NEW YORK TIMES.
May 23, 2005.

Youngsters who want to buy adult video games may have run up against a higher authority. Last week, Best Buy agreed to strengthen and publicize its efforts to keep minors from buying violent or sexually explicit video games after the company was pressured by the Christian Brothers Investment Services, which manages assets for Roman Catholic organizations.

The store's policy threatens disciplinary action against clerks who fail to check the ages of shoppers who look as if they may be under 21. It also permits the use of mystery shoppers—spies, in other words—to check whether clerks are observing the rules.

Best Buy agreed to post its policy on its Web site and on store signs after being threatened with a shareholder resolution asking for a report on how Best Buy complied with efforts to restrict the sale of explicit material. Also last week, the Illinois Senate approved the levying of fines against store owners who sell explicit games to minors.

Sue Busch, Best Buy's directory of public relations, rejected the suggestion that the disclosure action was simply to appease a bloc of investors. "We wanted to make sure we were as open as possible so people could see how seriously we take their concerns," she said.

Cathy Rowan, who co-filed the proposed shareholder resolution on behalf of Trinity Health, a Catholic health care provider, said that she was particularly concerned over the games Halo, Manhunt, Hitman and Grand Theft Auto. Grand Theft Auto where players are rewarded if they kill cops or rape prostitutes, she said. "Kids are going to play video games but are they being sold games that are really age inappropriate?"

Nell Minow, the editor of the Corporate Library, an independent research firm, said . "There's not a bright line distinction between what used to be social policy issues and straight shareholder-value concerns."

Substitute the following for the first full paragraph on page 508:

Note: Shareholder Activism in 2005

Investor Responsibility Research Center, Corporate Governance Bulletin

January–March 2005, 1–8

In 2005, shareholder activists are squarely focused on gaining more influence over executive pay and on ensuring that directors will be more accountable to the shareholders they are obligated to represent. Once again, union pension funds are leading the charge by filing resolutions on both of these fronts, but individual activists also are raising their voices by submitting a considerable number of these types of proposals as well as more standard governance proposals that historically have enjoyed strong shareholder support. Overall at this point, IRRC is tracking 264 proposals on executive pay, and 159 related to director elections.

The total number of shareholder proposals dealing with corporate governance issues submitted through March 14 stands at 700.

Making pay performance-based

The most popular of those proposals that take the direct approach to curbing executive pay, with 39 submitted so far, asks companies to award performance-based stock options. These proposals usually are targeted both at companies that recently have moved from options to time-based restricted stock and at companies that continue to rely heavily on options. To date, 11 have been withdrawn, mostly, say proponents, as a result of "positive communications" with the companies.

* * *

A related proposal that is also very popular this year, with 22 submitted so far, asks companies to award performance or time-based restricted shares. Specifically, the proposal urges companies to adopt a performance-and time-based restricted shares grant program that includes: 1) operational performance-vesting measures with "justifiable operational performance criteria combined with challenging performance benchmarks for each criteria utilized" (with performance criteria and associated performance benchmarks clearly disclosed to shareholders); and 2) time-based vesting of at least three years that would need to be met in addition to the performance criteria. The majority of these proposals also were filed by the building trades funds.

The funds may submit both the restricted stock and the performance-based stock option proposals at the same companies this year. In 2004, the proposals seeking performance-and time-based vesting stock received average support of about 15 percent of the votes cast, while performance-based option proposals garnered more than 40 percent on average.

* * *

More say on golden parachutes. Shareholders also continue to take issue with excessive golden parachutes, so far submitting 36 proposals asking boards to seek shareholder approval for future severance agreements with senior executives that provide benefits in an amount exceeding 2.99 times the sum of the executive's base salary plus bonus. Although a few of these severance proposals were filed by the building trades, a substantial number were submitted to companies by either Amalgamated Bank's LongView Funds or by individual activists such as John Chevedden.

LongView's more forceful approach to the issue at CSX has recently paid off. The activist fund submitted a binding proposal that would amend the company's bylaws to include a provision saying that the board will seek shareholder approval of future severance agreements that provide benefits exceeding 2.99 times the sum of the an executive's base salary plus bonus. Last year, a similar proposal submitted to CSX by LongView received the support of 72 percent of the votes cast. The company announced on January 24 that beginning immediately it will seek shareholder approval for new severance packages for senior executives that exceed 2.99 times annual compensation of base salary plus bonus. That prompted LongView to withdraw its proposal requesting the company implement the policy. Since 2003, Corning, NSTAR, AK Steel, Sprint, Norfolk Southern and Union Pacific have agreed to adopt LongView's proposal.

In 2004, about 26 proposals asking for a vote on certain golden parachute agreements garnered an average of 52 percent of the votes cast.

* * *

Requiring a majority to elect directors

In fact, shareholders have become so focused on gaining more influence over board composition that the most frequently filed proposal this season, submitted to 81 companies so far, asks that boards "initiate the appropriate process to amend the company's governance documents to provide that director nominees shall be elected by the affirmative vote of the majority of votes cast at an annual meeting of shareholders."

Delaware state law allows for the election of directors by a plurality, and under these rules, says the proposal, "a director nominee in a director election can be elected or re-elected with as little as a single affirmative vote, even while a substantial majority of the votes cast are 'withheld' from that director nominee." * * *

Proposal proponents got a shot in the arm on February 14 when the SEC required Citigroup to include the non-binding proposal in its proxy. Despite the decision, the Carpenters' fund decided to settle with a number of companies so long as they agreed to study the majority vote issue with building trades funds.

Under terms of the settlement, companies must agree to participate in a "Majority Vote Work Group" comprised of corporate representatives and pension fund representatives that "will examine all aspects of the director majority vote standard issue." The goal of the group will be to "promote informed shareholder and corporate consideration of the director majority vote standard issue." The group will meet three times between June and November "to study legal and practical issues associated with the adoption of a director election majority vote standard." After the third meeting, the group will present its findings on the majority vote issue, identify areas of agreement and disagreement among the participants, and outline possible continued joint collaboration on the issue. * * *

Proxy access proposal ruled out at Disney

The number of proposals calling for a majority vote to elect directors may continue to grow following recent SEC rulings allowing Walt Disney, Halliburton, Qwest Communications and Verizon Communications to omit from their proxy statement a more direct proxy access proposal submitted by Calpers, the American Federation of State, County and Municipal Employees' (AFSCME) pension plan, the New York State Common Retirement Fund and others. The Disney resolution asked that it become subject to the shareholder right of access provision included in the SEC's proposed proxy access Rule 14a–11, which would allow shareholder groups that have held more than 5 percent of Disney's outstanding common shares for more than two years to nominate up to a specified number of candidates who are independent from both the nominating shareholder and from Disney for election to the board. * * *

The December 28 decision by the SEC's Division of Corporation Finance on the Disney proposal simply says, "The division has reconsidered its position, and there appears to be some basis for your view that Disney may exclude the proposal under rule 14a–8(i)(8)." Rule 14a–8(i)(8) allows proposals relating to the election of directors to be omitted from proxy statements.

All of the institutional investors that submitted the proposal to Disney sent a letter to SEC Chairman William Donaldson on December 29 requesting that the full commission reconsider the staff's recent decision. "In the event that the commission declines to review staff's position, we request that the commission direct staff to explain its position so that shareholders and public companies have clear guidance on the viability of open access shareholder proposals and properly draft any such proposals," says the letter. The pension giants also argued in their correspondence that, "the commission's interpretation of rule 14a–8(i)(8) was modified by the proposed rule and authorizes the proposal filed at the company." The letter also said that shareholders will file additional shareholder proposals on the issue of proxy access, and, therefore, "the commission should review staff's position and provide clear guidance on open access proposals so that shareholders and public companies can avoid costly and lengthy appeals to the staff and commission regarding additional open access proposals."

The request had little effect on regulators, who five weeks later again sided with companies seeking to omit proxy access proposals. Halliburton, Qwest and Verizon were granted no-action relief in a February 7 letter from Corporation Finance division director Alan Beller, who approved the exclusion because it relied on an SEC proposal that, he said, had languished. "We are disappointed that the Commission changed the ground rules in the eleventh hour," said Gerald McEntee, chairman of the AFSCME Employees Pension Plan, which joined New York and Connecticut retirement plans in submitting the proposal to Halliburton. "It is disingenuous for the SEC to first establish an interim process to allow shareholders to offer advisory proxy access proposals and then take away that right because they have taken too long to make their own decision. We hope this is not a trend on the heels of the Commission's flip-flop on Disney." AFSCME vowed to pursue the issue until a broader proxy access rule is established.

In keeping with that pledge, the fund filed suit on February 25 against the American International Group in U.S. District Court over the issue of proxy access. The suit sought to require the Delaware-incorporated firm to include a binding proxy access shareholder proposal in its proxy materials and to bring the matter to a vote of shareholders at the company's annual meeting in May.* If passed, the proposal would amend the company's bylaws to allow shareholders future access to AIG's proxy materials to nominate individuals to the company's board of directors. The new bylaws would require AIG to include the names and other information on candidates nominated by shareholders who own 3 percent or more of the company's stock for at least one year, the fund said.

Independence at board helm

Another proposal that seeks more shareholder influence over board composition asks companies to appoint an independent chair. So far proponents have submitted 38 of these. A handful have so far been omitted because, the SEC said, they deal with matters beyond the company's power to effectuate.

* * *

The push to appoint independent board leadership is gaining serious momentum. Based on a review of 1,275 companies' disclosures, IRRC found that independent directors served as the chair at 11 percent of the companies, and the percentage of companies with lead directors, the vast majority of whom are independent, more than doubled between 2003 and 2004. In fact, just two years ago only 3 percent of companies named a lead or presiding director as compared to 17 percent in 2003 and 42 percent in 2004. At its annual fall conference last month, the Council of Institutional Investors adopted a policy stating that, "The board should be chaired by an independent director...[except] in very limited circumstances." In addition, a blue ribbon commission convened by the National Association of Corporate Directors just released a report recommending that all boards have an independent leader of the board, which they can do either by appointing a non-executive chairman who is leader of the whole board or by naming a lead director who is leader of the board's independent directors.

* On March 22, 2005 the District Court refused to compel the inclusion of the proposal. The court found that the proposal could be excluded under Rule 14a–8(i)(8) because it related to the election of directors and that state law did not require its inclusion. [Ed.]

Chapter 16

OUTSIDE DIRECTORS' ROLE IN THE PUBLIC CORPORATION

D. DO INDEPENDENT DIRECTORS MATTER?

2. HOW "INDEPENDENT" IS DEFINED?

Add at page 586 (substitute for second, third and fourth paragraphs of section):

Effective November 4, 2003, the SEC approved new rules proposed by the NYSE and NASD governing outside directors of public corporations. See NASD and NYSE Rulemaking: Relating to Corporate Governance, SEC Release No. 34–48745 (Nov. 4, 2003). These rules require that listed companies have a majority of independent board members, have independent committees, and publish certain guidelines.

Independent board members. Each listed company must have a majority of independent directors. The board must affirmatively determine that each independent director has no "material relationship" with the company (either directly or as a partner, shareholder, or officer of an organization that has a relationship with the company), and it must disclose the basis for its determination in its annual proxy statement. Non-management directors must hold regularly scheduled meetings without management.

To be independent, a director generally must not have had a substantial financial relationship with the company during the previous three years. Specifically, a person cannot become independent until three years after she is no longer an employee of the company (or her immediate family member is an executive officer), receives more than $100,000 in direct compensation from the company, is affiliated with an auditor or the company, or is affiliated with a company that makes substantial payments to or receives substantial payments from, the company (e.g., $1 million or 2% of gross revenues).

Independent committees. Companies must have a nominating/corporate governance committee and a compensation committee composed entirely of independent directors. Companies must have a minimum three-person audit committee composed entirely of independent directors. Each member of the audit committee must be "financially literate, as such qualification is interpreted by the board in its business judgment, or must become financially literate within a reasonable period of time after his or her appointment to the audit committee." At least one member of the audit committee must have accounting or related financial management expertise. Audit committee members cannot serve on the audit committee of more than three public companies unless the company permits, and the board approves, such simultaneous service.

Published guidelines. Companies must adopt and disclose corporate governance guidelines, which cover: director qualification standards; director responsibilities; director access to management and, as necessary and appropriate, independent advisors; director compensation; director orientation and continuing education; management succession; and annual performance evaluation of the board.

Companies also must adopt and disclose a code of business conduct and ethics for directors, officers and employees, and promptly disclose any waivers of the code for directors or executive officers. Topics include: conflicts of interest; corporate opportunities; confidentiality of information; fair dealing; protection and proper use of company assets; compliance with laws, rules, and regulations (including insider trading laws); and encouraging the reporting of any illegal or unethical behavior. Companies must post these guidelines on their websites, along with the charters of important committees.

4. CONCERNS PRECIPITATED BY THE "FALL OF ENRON"

b. When Should Courts Defer to "Independent" Directors' Judgments?

Add at page 606 (at end):

IN RE eBAY, INC. SHAREHOLDERS LITIGATION
2004 WL 253521 (Del. Ch. 2004).

CHANDLER, CHANCELLOR.

Shareholders of eBay, Inc. filed these consolidated derivative actions against certain eBay directors and officers for usurping corporate opportunities. Plaintiffs allege that eBay's investment banking advisor, Goldman Sachs Group, engaged in "spinning," a practice that involves allocating shares of lucrative initial public offerings of stock to favored clients. In effect, the plaintiff shareholders allege that Goldman Sachs bribed certain eBay insiders, using the currency of highly profitable investment opportunities-opportunities that should have been offered to, or provided for the benefit of, eBay rather than the favored insiders. Plaintiffs accuse Goldman Sachs of aiding and abetting the corporate insiders' breach of their fiduciary duty of loyalty to eBay.

I. BACKGROUND FACTS

In 1995, defendants Pierre M. Omidyar and Jeffrey Skoll founded nominal defendant eBay, a Delaware corporation, as a sole proprietorship. eBay is a pioneer in online trading platforms, providing a virtual auction community for buyers and sellers to list items for sale and to bid on items of interest. In 1998, eBay retained Goldman Sachs and other investment banks to underwrite an initial public offering of common stock.

Goldman Sachs was the lead underwriter. The stock was priced at $18 per share. Goldman Sachs purchased about 1.2 million shares. Shares of eBay stock became immensely valuable during 1998 and 1999, rising to $175 per share in early April 1999. Around that time, eBay made a secondary offering, issuing 6.5 million shares of common stock at $170 per share for a total of $1.1 billion. Goldman Sachs again served as lead underwriter. Goldman Sachs was asked in 2001 to serve as eBay's financial advisor in connection with an acquisition by eBay of PayPal, Inc. For these services, eBay has paid Goldman Sachs over $8 million.

During this same time period, Goldman Sachs "rewarded" the individual defendants by allocating to them thousands of IPO shares, managed by Goldman Sachs, at the initial offering price. Because the IPO market during this particular period of time was extremely active, prices of initial stock offerings often doubled or tripled in a single day. Investors who were well connected, either to Goldman Sachs or to similarly situated investment banks serving as IPO underwriters, were able to flip these investments into instant profit by selling the equities in a few days or even in a few hours after they were initially purchased.

The essential allegation of the complaint is that Goldman Sachs provided these IPO share allocations to the individual defendants to show appreciation for eBay's business and to enhance Goldman Sachs' chances of obtaining future eBay business. In addition to co-founding eBay, defendant Omidyar has been eBay's CEO, CFO and President. He is eBay's largest stockholder, owning more than 23% of the company's equity. Goldman Sachs allocated Omidyar shares in at least forty IPOs at the initial offering price. Omidyar resold these securities in the public market for millions of dollars in profit.

Defendant Whitman owns 3.3% of eBay stock and has been President, CEO and a director since early 1998. Whitman also has been a director of Goldman Sachs since 2001. Goldman Sachs allocated Whitman shares in over a 100 IPOs at the initial offering price. Whitman sold these equities in the open market and reaped millions of dollars in profit.

Defendant Skoll, in addition to co-founding eBay, has served in various positions at the company, including Vice–President of Strategic Planning and Analysis and President. He served as an eBay director from December 1996 to March 1998. Skoll is eBay's second largest stockholder, owning about 13% of the company. Goldman Sachs has allocated Skoll shares in at least 75 IPOs at the initial offering price, which Skoll promptly resold on the open market, allowing him to realize millions of dollars in profit. Finally, defendant Robert C. Kagle has served as an eBay director since June 1997. Goldman Sachs allocated Kagle shares in at least 25 IPOs at the initial offering price. Kagle promptly resold these equities, and recorded millions of dollars in profit.

II. ANALYSIS

A. *Demand Futility*

Plaintiffs bring these actions on behalf of nominal defendant eBay, seeking an accounting from the individual director defendants of their profits from the IPO transactions as well as compensatory damages from Goldman Sachs for its participation (aiding and abetting) in the eBay insiders' breach of fiduciary duty. Court of Chancery Rule 23.1 requires that a shareholder make a demand that the corporation's board pursue potential litigation before initiating such litigation on the corporation's behalf. When a plaintiff fails to make a demand on the board of directors, the plaintiff must plead with factual particularity why the demand is excused.

eBay's board of directors consists of seven members. Three are the individual defendants—Whitman, Omidyar and Kagle; defendant Skoll is not presently a director. All four of these individual defendants received IPO allocations from Goldman Sachs. As a result, the three current directors of eBay who received IPO allocations (Omidyar, Whitman and Kagle) are clearly interested in the transactions at the core of this controversy.

Although the other four directors of eBay (Cook, Lepore, Schultz and Bourguignon) did not participate in the "spinning," plaintiffs allege that they are not independent of the interested directors and, thus, demand is excused as futile. Since three of the seven present eBay directors are interested in the transactions that give rise to this litigation, plaintiffs need only demonstrate a reason to doubt the independence of one of the remaining four directors. Plaintiffs allege that directors Cook, Lepore, Schultz and Bourguignon all have "close business and personal ties with the individual defendants" and are incapable of exercising independent judgment to determine whether eBay should bring a breach of fiduciary duty action against the individual defendants. Plaintiffs allege, for example, that Schultz is a member of Maveron LLC, an investment advisory company in which Whitman has made significant personal investments. More significantly, plaintiffs allege that Cook, Lepore, Schultz and Bourguignon have received huge financial benefits as a result of their positions as eBay directors and, furthermore, that they owe their positions on the board to Omidyar, Whitman, Kagle and Skoll. eBay pays no cash compensation to its directors, but it does award substantial stock options. For example, in 1998, when Cook joined eBay's board, it awarded him 900,000 options at an exercise price of $1.555. One fourth of these options (225,000) vested immediately, and an additional 2% vests each subsequent month so long as Cook remains a director. In 1998, after Cook had joined the board, eBay adopted a director's stock option plan pursuant to which each non-employee director was to be awarded 30,000 options each year (except for 1999, when no additional options were awarded). As of early 2002, Cook beneficially owned 903,750 currently exercisable options, and an additional 200,000 shares of eBay stock. The complaint notes that the exercise price on 900,000 of the options originally awarded to Cook is $1.555 per share. At the time the complaint was filed in this case, eBay stock was valued at $62.13 per share. At an exercise price of $1.555, Cook's original option grant is thus worth millions of dollars. In addition, the stock options awarded in 2000, 2001 and 2002, which are not yet fully Vested, and will never vest unless Cook retains his position as a director, are worth potentially millions of dollars.

The complaint further alleges that director Schultz, Lepore and Bourguignon are similarly situated. That is, the stock options granted to these directors, which are both vested and unvested, are so valuable that they create a financial incentive for these directors to retain their positions as directors and make them beholden to the defendant directors. As a result, plaintiffs contend that it is more than reasonable to assume that an individual who has already received, and who expects to receive still more, options of such significant value could not objectively decide whether to commence legal proceedings against fellow directors who are directly responsible for the outside directors' continuing positions on the board.

I need not address each of the four outside directors, as I agree with plaintiffs that the particularized allegations of the complaint are sufficient to raise a reasonable doubt as to Cook's independence from the eBay insider directors who accepted Goldman Sachs' IPO allocations. Defendants resist this conclusion by pointing out that Whitman, Kagle, Omidyar and Skoll, collectively with management, control 40% of eBay's common stock, which they argue is insufficient to allege control or domination. Defendants also contend that the options represent past compensation and would not effectively disable a director from acting fairly and impartially with respect to a demand. These arguments are unpersuasive in these circumstances.

First, defendants must concede that certain stockholders, executive officers and directors control eBay. For example, eBay's form 10–K for the fiscal year ending December 31, 2000 notes that eBay's executive officers and directors Whitman, Omidyar, Kagle and Skoll (and their affiliates) own about one-half of eBay's outstanding common stock. As a result, these eBay officers and directors effectively have the ability to control eBay and to direct its affairs and business, including the election of directors and the approval of significant corporate transactions. Although the percentage of ownership may have decreased slightly from the time eBay filed the 2000 10–K, the decrease is insufficient to detract from the company's acknowledgement that these four individual defendants control the company and the election of directors.

Second, although many of the options awarded to Cook and the other purported outside directors have in fact vested, a significant number of options have not yet vested and will never vest unless the outside directors remain directors of eBay. Given that the value of the options for Cook (and allegedly for the other outside directors) potentially run into the millions of dollars, one cannot conclude realistically that Cook would be able to objectively and impartially consider a demand to bring litigation against those to whom he is beholden for his current position and future position on eBay's board. With the specific allegations of the complaint in mind, I conclude that plaintiffs have adequately demonstrated that demand on eBay's board should be excused as futile.

B. *Corporate Opportunity*

Plaintiffs have stated a claim that defendants usurped a corporate opportunity of eBay. Defendants insist that Goldman Sachs' IPO allocations to eBay's insider directors were "collateral investments opportunities" that arose by virtue of the inside directors status as wealthy individuals. They argue that this is not a corporate opportunity within the corporation's line of business or an opportunity in which the corporation had an interest or expectancy. These arguments are unavailing.

First, no one disputes that eBay financially was able to exploit the opportunities in question. Second, eBay was in the business of investing in securities. The complaint alleges that eBay "consistently invested a portion of its cash on hand in marketable securities." According to eBay's 1999 10–K, for example, eBay had more than $550 million invested in equity and debt securities. eBay invested more than $181 million in "short-term investments" and $373 million in "long-term investments." Thus, investing was "a line of business" of eBay. Third, the facts alleged in the complaint suggest that investing was integral to eBay's cash management strategies and a significant part of its business. Finally, it is no answer to say, as do defendants, that IPOs are risky investments. It is undisputed that eBay was never given an opportunity to turn down the IPO allocations as too risky.

Defendants also argue that to view the IPO allocations in question as corporate opportunities will mean that every advantageous investment opportunity that comes to an officer or director will be considered a corporate opportunity. On the contrary, the allegations in the complaint in this case indicate that unique, below-market price investment opportunities were offered by Goldman Sachs to the insider defendants as financial inducements to maintain and secure corporate business. This was not an instance where a broker offered advice to a director about an investment in a marketable security. The conduct challenged here involved a large investment bank that regularly did business with a company steering highly lucrative IPO allocations to select insider directors and officers at that company, allegedly both to reward them for past business and to induce them to direct future business to that investment bank. This is a far cry from the defendants' characterization of the conduct in question as merely "a broker's investment recommendations" to a wealthy client.

Nor can one seriously argue that this conduct did not place the insider defendants in a position of conflict with their duties to the corporation. One can realistically characterize these IPO allocations as a form of commercial discount or rebate for past or future investment banking services. Viewed pragmatically, it is easy to understand how steering such commercial rebates to certain insider directors places those directors in an obvious conflict between their self-interest and the corporation's interest. It is noteworthy, too, that the Securities and Exchange Commission has taken the position that "spinning" practices violate the obligations of broker-dealers under the "Free-riding and Withholding Interpretation" rules. As the SEC has explained, "the purpose of the interpretation is to protect the integrity of the public offering system by ensuring that members make a bona fide public distribution of 'hot issue' securities and do not withhold such securities for their own benefit or use the securities to reward other persons who are in a position to direct future business to the member."

Finally, even if one assumes that IPO allocations like those in question here do not constitute a corporate opportunity, a cognizable claim is nevertheless stated on the common law ground that an agent is under a duty to account for profits obtained personally in connection with transactions related to his or her company. The complaint gives rise to a reasonable inference that the insider directors accepted a commission or gratuity that rightfully belonged to eBay but that was improperly diverted to them. Even if this conduct does not run afoul of the corporate opportunity doctrine, it may still constitute a breach of the fiduciary duty of loyalty. Thus, even if one does not consider Goldman Sachs' IPO allocations to these corporate insiders—allocations that generated millions of dollars in profit—to be a corporate opportunity, the defendant directors were nevertheless not free to accept this consideration from a company, Goldman Sachs, that was doing significant business with eBay and that arguably intended the consideration as an inducement to maintaining the business relationship in the future.

* * *

For all of the above reasons, I deny the defendants' motions to dismiss the complaint in this consolidated action.

Chapter 17

THE DUTY OF CARE OF CORPORATE DIRECTORS

B. DUTY OF OVERSIGHT

2. MONITORING LEGAL COMPLIANCE

Add at page 635 (before "3. Director's Criminal Liability"):

Note: Update of Internal Controls Under Sarbanes–Oxley

What are the obligations of a lawyer whose corporate client appears to be engaged in a securities fraud? In the post-Enron regulatory climate, the answer is changing. Pressure on lawyers to protect shareholder interests is coming from multiple directions.

As discussed in the Casebook, the Sarbanes–Oxley Act called on the SEC to adopt rules requiring corporate lawyers to report "credible evidence" of securities fraud (such as accounting improprieties) to a firm's top executives or chief counsel. If that doesn't produce results, lawyers must then to go to the board of directors. The SEC's rule compels lawyers who see signs of "material" wrongdoing to bring it up the corporate ladder.

The SEC rule applies to all U.S. attorneys who "appear and practice" before the SEC—that is, who work on securities matters whether for public or private companies. Lawyers outside the U.S. who handle SEC-related work, such as corporate filings, are also subject to the rules. The SEC can't disbar lawyers, but it can prevent them from working for a public company. Lawyers who violate SEC rules are also subject to fines and other civil penalties.

Federal securities duties vs. state legal ethics duties. What if a lawyer brings a violation to the attention of corporate officials, but they fail to respond? Originally, the SEC floated the possibility that lawyers would have to resign in a public fashion once internal "reporting up" did not work. This has raised the question whether such public disclosure of corporate misdeeds would violate state ethics rules requiring lawyers not to disclose client confidences. Some have argued the SEC "noisy withdrawal" proposal would put lawyers in the untenable position of having to choose between violating federal or state law.

Bringing the issue to a head, the Washington State Bar Association's board of governors voted in July 2003 to reaffirm state ethical rules that bar lawyers from revealing confidences without a client's permission. According to this body, Washington State lawyers would be barred, at least under state ethics rules, from revealing confidential information to the SEC or face being sued or barred from practice in the state. See Judith Burns, *Attorneys Face a Paradox in the SEC's Conduct Rules*, WALL ST. J., Aug. 19, 2003, C1.

SEC general counsel Giovanni Prezioso issued a stern warning to the Washington State Bar Association, pointing out that federal regulation would be supreme and that SEC rules for lawyers would be "frustrated" if states could discipline attorneys who comply with them.

In August 2003 the American Bar Association weighed in on the issue by voting to soften its rules on client confidentiality. The ABA's House of Delegates amended the ABA's Model Rule 1.6 (in a vote of 218–201) to permit lawyers to disclose company wrongdoing, and in some cases require them to do so within the company. (The new rule, which supercedes the version at page 171 of the Casebook, is an about-face by the ABA, which two years before had voted against a similar rule change.) Under the new rules, lawyers can disclose their corporate client's confidence if they believe it necessary to prevent fraud or crime that would cause financial harm. Previously, the ABA rule allowed lawyers to do so only to prevent physical injury or death.

The amended ABA rules, however, do not require a "noisy withdrawal," as the SEC has proposed. Some question whether the SEC has authority under Sarbanes–Oxley to require lawyers to break clients' confidences. Others point out that a disclosure requirement might lead corporate executives to not give lawyers access to confidential information, thus disserving investors. Recognizing this problem, some have suggested that the SEC should require companies to report whenever a lawyer resigns in frustration after reporting up the ladder, forcing firms to blow the whistle on themselves.

One important aspect of the ABA rule is that it would apply to all lawyers, including those representing partnerships and closely-held corporations that are not subject to SEC regulation. Although the ABA's deliberations focused on the role of lawyers for public corporations, up-the-ladder reporting would also be expected of lawyers of small businesses. Moreover, the ABA rule would apply to any violations of law, not just securities fraud. Some have argued it would give corporate counsel in a small firm significant leverage to push a personal agenda, armed with the threat of revealing corporate wrongdoing.

Interpretive issues. The SEC's lawyer-disclosure rule raises a number of interpretive questions:

- Is it sufficient if an outside lawyer brings her concerns of corporate wrongdoing to a lawyer in the company's legal department, other than the general counsel. (The SEC's Deputy General Counsel has said the rule requires reporting to the "chief legal officer" or CEO or "qualified legal compliance committee.")

- Is it "credible evidence" if the outside lawyer hears credible hearsay ("he said that he said") of wrongdoing, but not from the original source? (A former SEC general counsel has opined that hearsay is not credible under the SEC rule.)
- How soon must a lawyer who identifies "credible evidence" of wrongdoing begin reporting it up the ladder? How long must the lawyer wait for there to be appropriate responses?

Lawyers' incentives. Ultimately, the question becomes whether outside corporate lawyers, who won their position with the company by proving their allegiance to the managers who hired them, are likely to be watchdogs of manager misbehavior. Some have doubts. See Stephen Bainbridge, *The Tournament at the Intersection of Business and Legal Ethics*, 1 U. St. Thomas L. J. 781 (2004). Professor Bainbridge argues that "Section 307 and the SEC's rules thereunder do too little to address the strong incentives lawyers have to refrain from antagonizing the corporate managers who hire and fire them.... Lawyers who win the tournament develop a set of skills, attitudes, and cognitive biases that systematically skew their analysis of client conduct." He predicts that such lawyers "will turn a blind eye to client misconduct."

Add at page 635 (after "Note: Internal Controls under Sarbanes–Oxley):

Note: Europe's Response to Accounting Scandals— Eighth Company Law Directive

To avert future accounting scandals like Enron and Parmalat (a fraud by an Italian company, built largely on a forged fax showing a fictitious 3.9 billion bank account), the finance ministers of the European Union have endorsed new proposals similar to the auditing provisions of the Sarbanes–Oxley Act. If adopted, the new rules—to be contained in an Eighth Company Law Directive that would call for implementation by each EU member state—would clarify the duties of statutory auditors, introduce a requirement for external quality assurance and public oversight of the auditing practice, and improve co-operation between regulatory authorities in the EU.

The proposed directive first aims at the audit process. It sets out a clear responsibilities when groups of companies are audited by several firms in different locations worldwide. It also seeks to weaken links between company management and audit firms by requiring audit rotation and holding the group auditor fully liable for the audit reports on consolidated accounts. Member States would have the choice of requiring "internal rotation" (a change of key audit partner dealing with an audited company every five years) or "external rotation" (a change of audit firm every seven years). Additionally, if a company dismisses an auditor, it would have to explain the reasons to the relevant authority in the Member State concerned.

The proposed directive also seeks to strengthen public oversight of the audit profession. But, unlike the United States that adopted a national board, the directive would require each Member State to organize a system, independent of the profession, with the ultimate responsibility for overseeing the regulation of auditors. This would include approval of audit firms,

..., internal quality control and auditing, and ... education, quality assurance and investigative and ... To be credible, each Member State would create a ... by knowledgeable, non-practitioners.

... the Sarbanes–Oxley Act, the proposed directive would regulate ... nal corporate governance—a significant step in Europe. Audited companies would have to set up an audit committee, with independent members, which would choose the auditor, oversee the audit process, and communicate directly with the auditor without going through management. Audit firms would be prohibited from providing additional services that would compromise their independence and could in no way be involved in management decisions.

3. DIRECTOR'S CRIMINAL LIABILITY

Add at page 637 (at bottom of page):

In April 2004 the U.S. Sentencing Commission approved and sent to Congress amendments to the Organizational Guidelines, which apply broadly to corporations, partnerships, labor unions, nonprofit entities, and governmental units. 69 Fed. Reg. 28994–01 (2004). The amended Guidelines carry forward the original purpose of encouraging organizations to implement systematic compliance programs. By instituting an effective compliance program, an organization convicted of criminal behavior can obtain mitigation credits and lower the range of potential fines dramatically (sometimes by 95%).

Under the amended Guidelines, organizations must "exercise due diligence to prevent and detect criminal conduct," and must "promote an organizational culture that encourages ethical conduct and a commitment to compliance with law." There are seven minimum requirements a compliance and ethics program *must* meet to earn a sentencing reduction. In a corporation, the board must be knowledgeable about the program; specific high-level executives must be assigned overall responsibility for compliance; and specific individuals (with authority and resources) must have day-to-day operational duties and make regular reports to high-level executives and the board. The program must include auditing and monitoring systems, must be periodically evaluated, and must have mechanisms for anonymous or confidential whistleblowing without fear of retaliation. The program must also provide incentives for compliance and disciplinary measures for failing to detect or prevent criminal conduct. If criminal conduct is detected, the corporation must respond appropriately. Guidelines § 8C2.5(f).

An important, and controversial, change comes in an "application note" accompanying the Guidelines that suggests corporations may have to waive the attorney-client privilege and work-product protections to qualify for mitigation based on cooperation with the government. According to the commentary, waiver may be "necessary in order to provide timely and thorough disclosure of all pertinent information known to the organization." Corporate counsel objected to this interpretation, arguing that waiver will effectively become a necessary part of cooperation if the government can determine whether there has been "thorough cooperation.". Corporate counsel lost the argument.

C. BUSINESS JUDGMENT RULE

1. SCOPE OF THE BUSINESS JUDGMENT RULE

Add at page 642 (before *Note: Corporate Best Interests*):

What is the business judgment rule? Professor Bainbridge identifies two conceptions. One views the business judgment rule as "a standard of liability under which courts undertake some objective review of the merits of board decisions." The other is that the rule is not a standard of review but "a doctrine of abstention, pursuant to which courts simply decline to review board decisions." Stephen Mark Bainbridge, *The Business Judgment Rule as Abstention Doctrine*, UCLA, School of Law, Law and Econ. Research Paper No. 03–18, SSRN Paper No. 429260 (July 29, 2003).

According to Bainbridge, some members of the Delaware supreme court seem to have accepted the "standard of liability" view, making it more likely that claims against the board of directors will survive to summary judgment, thus raising the settlement value of shareholder litigation and producing outcome-determinative effects. Bainbridge criticizes this approach as based on a shareholder primacy-based theory of the corporation. Instead, he argues the board of directors should be viewed as "the nexus of the set of contracts" that makes up the firm. In this model, making directors more accountable infringes on their exercise of authority, and courts should review director decisions only when evidence of self-dealing raises "very serious accountability concerns."

D. DUTY TO BECOME INFORMED

1. THE *TRANS UNION* CASE

Add at page 673 (before *Note: The Board as Individuals or Collective Body*):

Note: An "Options" Perspective on Trans Union

Frank Partnoy, ADDING DERIVATIVES TO THE CORPORATE LAW MIX

34 GA. L. REV. 599 (2000).

* * *

How can option valuation contribute to an understanding of the *Van Gorkom* case? First, it is important to note that Pritzker's option was quite valuable when granted. Its value can be calculated with some precision using the Black–Scholes option pricing model. Only a handful of data points are required, and it is not necessary to understand the intricacies of the model in order to intuit and use its results.

Some of the data required are given in the case; the other data are available elsewhere. The six required variables are: the stock price at the time the option was granted, the exercise price of the option, the time remaining before expiration, the risk-free interest rate, the stock's dividend yield, and the stock's volatility. The value of a call option increases as the stock price increases, the exercise price decreases, the risk-free interest rate increases, the dividend yield decreases, or the volatility increases. First, the stock price at the relevant time is given in the opinion as $37.25. Second, the exercise price of the option also is given, $38. Third, the time remaining before expiration is 134 days, the number of days from September 20, 1980, until February 1, 1981. Fourth, the risk-free interest rate in effect until the date of maturity of the option can be estimated, based on available data for the yields on comparable maturity United States treasury bills, to be 10.17%. Fifth, Trans Union paid an annual dividend of $2.36 per share during 1980; therefore, the dividend yield was approximately 6.3%.

The remaining variable, volatility, is more difficult to estimate. The most accurate method of estimating volatility would be to calculate the volatility implied by the prices of Trans Union options being traded in September 1980; however, there were no such options traded at the time. The next most accurate method is to calculate volatility using historical prices of Trans Union stock. The court provides some data about the stock price history. An accurate estimate, however, requires more frequent and recent data. I estimated volatility based on Trans Union's closing stock price values for the seventy-five business days prior to and including September 20 to be approximately 25.4%. Given these data, the Black–Scholes estimate of the value of Pritzker's option on September 20 is approximately $2.49 million.

Table 1

Stock price	$37.25
Exercise price	$38.00
Days to expiration	134
Risk-free rate	10.17%
Dividend yield	6.3%
Volatility	29.3%
Option value	$2.49 per share

At least three important new insights arise from this information. First, the grant of one million options to Pritzker on September 20, 1980, was extremely valuable ($2.49 million). Moreover, this value does not include several million dollars of value associated with the increase in the price of the stock as a result of the board's approval of the merger agreement. In fact, the price of Trans Union stock rocketed to $51.50 the next day of trading, and the option would have been much more valuable then. [In fact, even without adjusting for any change in the volatility of the stock the value of the option on Monday, September 22, would have been approximately $13.8 million, based on a stock price of $51.50 and a time to expiration of 132 days.] Because this increase was virtually certain to occur once the merger agreement was disclosed, the option arguably was worth much more than the conservative estimate of $2.49 million.

Suppose that instead of granting Pritzker an option, the board had given him a suitcase filled with several million dollars of cash. One can imagine that the board would have considered a grant of such size with greater deliberation. It is possible that the board properly understood the value of the option intuitively, based on the directors' experience with the stock's performance over time. In any event, a simple option valuation would have assisted the board's deliberation. Moreover, if the court had been presented with such a valuation, it likely would have included this value as support for its conclusion that the directors violated their duty of care.

Second, the board's efforts to negotiate the grant of the option down to one million from 1.75 million shares saved Trans Union a considerable sum of money, conservatively estimated at $1.87 million (option on 750,000 shares at $2.49). [A grant of 1.75 million options would have been worth approximately $4.36 million on September 20 based on the pricing methodology described above (approximately $2.49 per share).] Including the informational value of the merger agreement, this savings was over $10 million. Again, the court neither stressed the importance or value of this negotiation, nor is it obvious that the board was aware of its magnitude.

Assuming the board understood the relative values of the options, it may have concluded that a substantial grant was necessary to persuade Pritzker to consider the merger agreement. If so, the board's business judgment would seem to have been better informed than the court's findings indicated. On the other hand, if the move from 1.75 million to one million was simply an arbitrary attempt to "round down" Pritzker's initial offer (which may have been based on the assumption that the board would feel the need to negotiate the offer downward), then the board's grant of even a one million share option would not have been well-considered. In any event, the size of the numbers is staggering, and the court did not address any of these issues.

Third, and perhaps more interesting, Pritzker gave up enormous "time value" (the value associated with the right to wait until the expiration date before exercising the option) when he exercised the option early and purchased one million shares on October 9, 1980. To see the time value Pritzker gave up, consider his alternatives on October 9. Instead of buying one million shares of Trans Union for $38 million, Pritzker could have sold a mirror option (in effect, sold a call) on one million shares to another option purchaser (such as an investment bank) on the same date. He would have received approximately $17.3 million for such a sale. Then, he could have waited until the expiration date of the option to consider how many shares of Trans Union he wanted to own at that point. Even if the shareholders ultimately had rejected the merger agreement, Pritzker could have exercised his option, delivering those shares to the bank to satisfy his short mirror position, or he could have purchased additional shares.

Pritzker was a sophisticated financier; why would he have chosen to give up this time value by exercising early? A simple answer is that Pritzker made a mistake. This answer, however, ignores several critical factors related to the market for Trans Union stock.

A more likely answer is that Pritzker was taking advantage of the fact that Trans Union stock already was trading close to the merger price of $55 per share at the time. As noted above, the value of the option on September 22 was approximately $13.8 million. On October 9, just nineteen days after the option was granted, it was worth approximately $17.3 million. Pritzker probably did not anticipate the option appreciating any more, given that the difference between the $55 per share merger price and the $38 exercise price was $17 million.

However, the above explanation still does not explain why Pritzker would leave the option's time value on the table, even if it was small relative to his overall profit. Another possible explanation for Pritzker's early exercise is that he was concerned about how his ultimate purchase of shares would affect the market price of Trans Union stock. Because Pritzker had the option to purchase treasury stock (held by the company), this purchase would not necessarily affect the public market price.

Before September 1980, the average daily trading volume in Trans Union stock was in the tens of thousands of shares. A purchase of one million shares, even staggered over several days, would have been extraordinary. Again, consider the above figure. On Monday, September 22, 1980, the next business day after the grant of the option, there were 84,400 shares traded. The next day, Tuesday, volume exploded, with 708,200 shares traded. Average volumes remained high during the following weeks, but only in the 100,000 to 200,000 share range. No other single day had volume above 250,000 shares.

Still, even if Pritzker had been concerned about a large purchase moving the market (and potentially making the merger more difficult or expensive), a similar problem would have arisen later if Pritzker had decided he wanted to sell the one million shares (perhaps because the shareholders rejected the merger). There is no reason to think selling one million shares of stock would depress the price any less than purchasing one million shares of stock would increase it. Pritzker may have been concerned only about the latter cost (from purchasing) because he did not assign a high probability to his selling the stock later. He seems to have assumed either that shareholders would approve the merger or some other bidder would offer more than $55 for Trans Union stock. In either case, he would not be selling stock on the open market.

In sum, the options grant in Van Gorkom can be seen as adding three new insights: (1) the board gave Pritzker at least $2.49 million of option value (one million shares at $2.49 apiece) and probably much more, (2) Pritzker requested, and the board rejected, a grant with option value of at least $4.36 million (1.75 million shares at $2.49 apiece) and probably much more, and (3) after the option was granted, Pritzker immediately relinquished its time value by exercising early, presumably in exchange for the substantial benefits associated with a pre-expiration, non-public, off-market purchase of one million shares of stock.

Today, one would expect both the prospective purchaser of a company and its board to attempt to evaluate such an option using the above methodology. In such instances, lawyers advising participants in mergers need to understand the basics of option valuation. Trans Unions directors, and its counsel, might have fared better if they had.

Substitute the following for the discussion of *Brehm v. Eisner* at pages 678–679:

3A. DEFERENCE TO MANAGEMENT

A significant question in cases challenging board decision-making is the extent to which directors can defer to management. Generally, the accepted wisdom (the *Trans Union* case an exception) has been that directors can defer to management unless there is reason to doubt the managers' information, competence or judgment. Recently, the courts in Delaware have signaled that management may not enjoy as much leeway.

In *Brehm v. Eisner*, 746 A.2d 244 (Del. 2000), plaintiffs' alleged that the board of the Walt Disney Company violated its duty of due care by approving a severance payment valued at more than $100 million to Michael Ovitz, an executive who Disney had hired only a year earlier. Responding to a cursory complaint of board inattention and waste, the board moved to dismiss on the ground that it had relied on a well-known compensation expert to review Disney's contract with Ovitz, which included the provision that led to the severance payment. *See* DGCL § 141(e). The court stated that to overcome the presumption of good faith reliance and survive a motion to dismiss,

> the complaint must allege particularized facts (not conclusions) that, if proved, would show, for example, that: (a) the directors did not in fact rely on the expert; (b) their reliance was not in good faith; (c) they did not reasonably believe that the expert's advice was within the expert's professional competence; (d) the expert was not selected with reasonable care by or on behalf of the corporation, and the faulty selection process was attributable to the directors; (e) the subject matter (in this case the cost calculation) that was material and reasonably available was so obvious that the board's failure to consider it was grossly negligent regardless of the expert's advice or lack of advice; or (f) that the decision of the Board was so unconscionable as to constitute waste or fraud.

Id. at 262.

Concluding that the complaint had not adequately alleged waste or lack of due care, the Delaware Supreme Court remanded the case for the plaintiffs to amend their complaint. The court, offering the plaintiff a primer on Delaware fiduciary law, drew a sharp distinction between the standard directors must meet to avoid liability and the higher standards to which directors should aspire, stating:

> This is a case about whether there should be personal liability of the directors of a Delaware corporation to the corporation for lack of due care in the decisionmaking process and for waste of corporate assets. This case is not about the failure of the directors to establish and carry out ideal corporate governance practices.
>
> All good corporate governance practices include compliance with statutory law and case law establishing fiduciary duties. But the law of corporate fiduciary duties and remedies for violation of those duties are distinct from the aspirational goals of ideal corporate governance practices. Aspirational ideals of good corporate governance practices for boards of directors that go beyond the minimal legal requirements of the corporation law are highly desirable, often tend to benefit stockholders, sometimes reduce litigation and can usually help directors avoid liability. But they are not required by the corporation law and do not define standards of liability.

Id. at 255–256.

On remand in *Brehm v. Eisner,* plaintiffs filed an amended complaint (after obtaining information from Disney by exercising their statutory right to inspect the company's "books and records") and spun quite a different story of what the Disney board and its compensation committee had known about the hiring of Michael Ovitz and his compensation agreement. *In re The Walt Disney Company Derivative Litigation,* 825 A.2d 275 (Del.Ch.2003).

Chancellor Chandler described the lackluster attention by the Disney compensation committee that approved Ovtiz's hiring:

> The compensation committee, consisting of defendants Ignacio Lozano, Jr., Sidney Poitier, Russell, and Raymond Watson, met on September 26, 1995, for just under an hour. Three subjects were discussed at the meeting, one of which was Ovitz's employment. According to the minutes, the committee spent the least amount of time during the meeting discussing Ovitz's hiring. In fact, it appears that more time was spent on discussions of paying $250,000 to Russell for his role in securing Ovitz's employment than was actually spent on discussions of Ovitz's employment. * * *
>
> No copy of the September 23, 1995 draft employment agreement was actually given to the committee. Instead, the committee members received, at the meeting itself, a rough summary of the agreement. The summary, however, was incomplete. It stated that Ovitz was to receive options to purchase five million shares of stock, but

did not state the exercise price. The committee also did not receive any of the materials already produced by Disney regarding Ovitz's possible employment. No spreadsheet or similar type of analytical document showing the potential payout to Ovitz throughout the contract, or the possible cost of his severance package upon a non-fault termination, was created or presented. Nor did the committee request or receive any information as to how the draft agreement compared with similar agreements throughout the entertainment industry, or information regarding other similarly situated executives in the same industry.

The committee also lacked the benefit of an expert to guide them through the process. Graef Crystal, an executive compensation expert, had been hired to provide advice to Disney on Eisner's new employment contract. Even though he had earlier told Russell that large signing bonuses, generally speaking, can be hazardous, neither he nor any other expert had been retained to assist Disney regarding Ovitz's hiring. Thus, no presentations, spreadsheets, written analyses, or opinions were given by any expert for the compensation committee to rely upon in reaching its decision. Although Crystal was not retained as a compensation consultant on the Ovitz contract, he later lamented his failure to intervene and produce a spreadsheet showing the potential costs of the employment agreement.

825 A.2d at 280–281. A similar lack of information characterized the full board's approval of the employment agreement. According to the minutes of the board meeting, no expert was present to advise the board; no documents on the Ovitz agreement were presented for board review; no presentation was made by director Russell who had helped obtain Ovitz; no consideration was given to the consequences of termination or the payout scenarios. Nonetheless, the board appointed Ovitz president of Disney and left to Eisner, his close friend of 25 years, to negotiate the final details of the employment agreement. These negotiations, conducted by Eisner and Ovitz and their attorneys, resulted in a final agreement with significantly more favorable terms to Ovitz than had been originally described to the compensation committee. The final agreement was signed without the board or compensation committee ever having reviewed or approved it.

On the question of whether the directors could rely on Graef Crystal, the compensation expert on whose advice the defendants claimed they had relied, Chancellor Chandler pointed out that the amended complaint alleged Crystal was hired to advise on Eisner's employment agreement, not Ovitz's. If so, "Disney's board is not entitled to invoke § 141(e)'s protection based on a board's reliance upon a qualified expert selected with reasonable care." 825 A.2d at 288 n.31.

Chancellor Chandler was scathing in his conclusion that the allegations stated a valid claim of a "breach of the directors' obligation to act honestly and in good faith in the corporation's best interests ... outside the protection of the business judgment rule."

These facts, if true, do more than portray directors who, in a negligent or grossly negligent manner, merely failed to inform themselves or to deliberate adequately about an issue of material importance to their corporation. Instead, the facts alleged in the new complaint suggest that the defendant directors consciously and intentionally disregarded their responsibilities, adopting a "we don't care about the risks" attitude concerning a material corporate decision. Knowing or deliberate indifference by a director to his or her duty to act faithfully and with appropriate care is conduct, in my opinion, that may not have been taken honestly and in good faith to advance the best interests of the company.

825 A.2d at 289 (emphasis in original).

Since the decision, Disney's corporate governance has remained in the news. In the fall of 2003 Roy Disney, nephew of Walt Disney and former vice chair of the board and chair of Disney's feature animation division, resigned after the company's governance committee determined he could no longer serve because he had passed the retirement age of 72. Stanley P. Gold followed Disney's resignation with his own, expressing discontent with the corporate governance committee's decision to remove Disney and instead calling for the removal of Michael Eisner as chair and CEO. Gold alleged in his letter the rules regarding age only applied to nonmanagement directors, and Disney was a management director. Gold called the committee's decision "clearly disingenuous."

In early 2004, perhaps to put a better face on events, Disney's board unanimously adopted new corporate governance guidelines, modified the board's governance and nominating committee charter, adopted a directors' code of conduct and business ethics, and reorganized the membership of board committees. According the company, the changes "strengthened standards relating to the independence of directors" and "meet or exceed newly adopted New York Stock Exchange requirements."

The changes, however, did not end Disney's corporate governance woes. In the annual board election in March 2004, shareholders (including many mutual funds and other institutional investors) cast a strong vote of no-confidence in Disney management. More than 42% of Disney's votes at the meeting (an unprecedented percentage) were withheld from Eisner's re-election to the board. Immediately after the shareholders' meeting, the board met and split the CEO and board chair positions, retaining Eisner as CEO but electing former Senator George Mitchell as chair.

Adding to the drama, Comcast Corp. in February 2004 made a $54 billion all-stock hostile takeover bid for Disney, which the Disney board rejected as inadequate. Although not explicitly framed as a bid to install new management, Comcast heralded its bid as a way "to restore the Disney brand." In April, however, faced with the Disney board's continued refusal to consider selling and the falling price of Comcast stock, Comcast withdrew the offer. With the bid off the table, agitation among Disney shareholders again grew for the board to begin a succession plan for Eisner, and Roy Disney and Stanley Gold reiterated their commitment to help install a board more responsive to shareholder concerns.

Replace Chapter 18 (pages 718–803) with the following and with Chapter 18A:

Chapter 18

DUTY OF LOYALTY

A. INTRODUCTION: CONFLICTS OF INTEREST

In Chapter 17, we saw how the duty of care attempts to solve the problems that arise when a director does not act in the best interests of the stockholders in her decision-making, even if she does not benefit personally from her decision. In this chapter, we will begin to examine how the duty of loyalty deals with situations in which a director's decision may not be in the best interests of the stockholders precisely because she *does* benefit from that decision. Like the duty of care, the duty of loyalty runs to the corporation and to the stockholders. In the most basic terms, the duty of loyalty requires a director to place the corporation's best interests above her own.

The chapter starts with a roadmap of the issues that will be treated in the succeeding sections and with a discussion of the historical evolution of the duty of loyalty. It then examines the traditional statutory approach to conflict of interest transactions exemplified by the Delaware statute and contrasts that approach with the newer MBCA. Next, we study the elements that courts examine in determining the fairness of a transaction: approval by disinterested decision-makers, full disclosure and fair price. The last section deals with corporate managers' ability to engage in business opportunities that might properly belong to the corporation. Subsequent chapters will consider conflicting loyalties in different contexts: executive compensation (Chapter 18A), transactions by controlling shareholders (Chapter 19), shareholder litigation (Chapter 20), insider trading (Chapter 21) and protection of control (Chapter 22),. The methodology may differ with the context, but the question remains the same: how should a court evaluate the conduct of a director who is faced with what, put broadly, is a conflict of interest?

A director's conflict of interest arises at many levels and in different contexts. Consider, as the paradigm case, a transaction in which a director proposes to sell land that she owns to a corporation of which she is a director. Her conflict is obvious. As the land owner, she would like to receive the highest possible price. As a director, she has a duty to maximize the value of the transaction to the corporation by having the corporation pay the lowest possible price. The law characterizes such a transaction as "self-dealing" because she has an interest on each side of the transaction. The fact that she has conflicting interests does not mean, however, that the consummated transaction will be unfair to the corporation.

> * * * [I]t is important to keep firmly in mind that it is a contingent risk we are dealing with—that an interest conflict is not in itself a crime or a tort or necessarily injurious to others. Contrary to much popular usage, having a "conflict of interest" is not something one is "guilty of"; it is simply a state of affairs. Indeed, in many situations, the corporation and the shareholders may secure major benefits from a transaction despite the presence of a director's conflicting interest. Further, while history is replete with selfish acts, it is also oddly counterpointed by numberless acts taken contrary to self interest.

MBCA Subchapter F, Introductory Comment.

Self-dealing transactions can be both fair and beneficial to a corporation. Were it not so, it would be very easy to formulate a rule proscribing directors from engaging in transactions with their corporations. An "interested" director, however, will frequently be uniquely situated to help the corporation. She may have knowledge about how the corporation will benefit from the transaction and the ability to effectuate the transaction at minimal cost.

Some self-dealing transactions *are* unfair to the corporation. When this occurs the interested director is appropriating the difference between the fair market value of the transaction to the corporation and the payment actually made. Thus, the effect of an unfair self-dealing transaction is no different from the direct diversion of corporate funds or assets. However, self-dealing is apt to be more common than flagrant diversion because the interested director:

> * * * [m]ay more easily rationalize an inflated purchase price than outright stealing. It is frequently possible to identify and exaggerate some reasons why [a corporation] should pay dearly for some particular piece of land or property. That having been done, [the director] may continue to think of himself as a just and honorable man.

Robert Charles Clark, CORPORATE LAW 143 (1986).

But director conflicts of interest are not limited to situations in which the director will directly benefit financially from the transactions. In the paradigm transaction, for example, there may be a director who does not have a financial interest in the sale but whose own position and compensation in the corporation is dependent on the director who does have such an interest. Or a director whose law firm provides services to the corporation where the choice of the law firm is made by the interested director. For each such director, there is a question as to the extent to which her own conflict will interfere with her ability to exercise truly independent judgment when voting on the transaction even if she will not directly benefit financially from the transaction itself. And even if there were no financial interest, consider the personal dimension and the conflict that would arise if a director were a family member or lifelong friend of the interested director.

We must recognize here that the question of a director's ability to exercise independent judgment is not limited to simple self-dealing transactions. We have seen throughout the book that the principal device for enforcing fiduciary duties is the derivative suit, an action brought by a shareholder asserting the corporation's rights against one or more directors for an alleged breach of fiduciary duty. We will study derivative suits in greater detail in Chapter 20 but for purposes of this chapter, it is important to note only that at various points in such a suit, directors may be asked to evaluate the merits of a possible claim against a fellow director for such a breach. The conflict that the directors face in such a situation is behavioral rather than financial. They are being asked to sue someone with whom they share group membership, who they may well have come to trust and respect. How likely is it that they will be able to do so?

As we will see, corporate statutes dealing with director conflicts of interest are generally narrow in scope and in their definitions of who is conflicted in a manner that will affect a court's standard of review of a transaction. Generally, these statutes limit such conflicts to transactions in which a director has a *financial* interest, although commentary to the statutes and some judicial interpretations of the statutory language does take account of some of the behavioral issues described above even when dealing with the paradigmatic sale of land transaction. The major treatment of director "interest" or "independence," however, has come in the broader contexts of shareholder litigation or hostile tender offers and the materials in this chapter should be read with those contexts in mind. We include them here because they seem to be providing the basis on which courts are basing their analyses in narrower settings. Perhaps more important, they inform the broader question with which many of the remaining chapters are concerned: how to evaluate director conduct when one or more directors has, in the broadest sense, a "conflict of interest."

PROBLEM

STARCREST CORPORATION—PART 1

Starcrest Corporation constructs, owns and operates hotels and restaurants throughout the United States. It has built, many of these hotels and restaurants after acquiring the raw land on which they sit. Starcrest is a public company, founded by the Adams family in 1935, whose common stock is listed on the New York Stock Exchange.

In 1955, Starcrest sold 60% of its stock to public investors. Members of the Adams family continue to own the remaining 40%. Elizabeth Adams, the president and chief executive officer, owns 25% and other family members who are not active in the business own the remaining 15%. The board of directors consists of Elizabeth Adams; Paul Baker, the chief financial officer; Robert Crown, the vice-president for sales; Linda Diamond, the general counsel; and Michael Brown, Ruth Grey and Robert White, each of whom is a prominent business executive having no other connections with Starcrest. Baker and Crown have been officers for more than ten years. Diamond joined Starcrest two years ago. Prior to that, she was a senior associate in its principal outside law firm in which she devoted most of her time to Starcrest's work.

Many years ago, Adams inherited a large tract of raw land from a distant uncle. Until recently, she had paid little attention to this land. Now, however, Starcrest is considering building another hotel in this area. Although she knew very little about real estate in the area, conversations with her uncle's lawyer (who specialized in probate work) convinced her that the land was worth $10 million. For the next 30 days, she sought to sell the land privately to sophisticated buyers in the area, none of whom offered more than $5 million. Somewhat daunted, she next listed the land with a real estate broker for a thirty-day period at price of $7.5 million, but received no offers.

In early March, at Adams' request, Patricia Jones, the head of the Corporation's real estate department, appraised the land as a possible site for a new hotel. After examining other sites in the area, none of which seemed as suitable for a new hotel, Jones concluded that the land was worth the $7.5 million Elizabeth was asking. On March 15, Adams offered to sell the land to Starcrest for $7.5 million. She accompanied her offer with a copy of Jones' appraisal. She did not disclose that she had unsuccessfully tried to sell the land before offering it to the Corporation because she did not believe that this information was material to the board of directors in making its decision.

In response to the offer, the board of directors established a committee consisting of Brown, Grey and Diamond to evaluate the offer. Because none of the committee members were experts in real estate, they hired an outside consultant who opined that the land might conceivably be worth $7.5 million but that he wouldn't pay that price. The committee also obtained a formal appraisal from an outside appraiser which valued the land at $5 million.

In June, relying primarily on Jones' appraisal and that of its outside appraiser, the committee recommended that the Corporation offer to purchase the land for $6.5 million, a price that Elizabeth had indicated she was willing to accept. The committee's report set out in detail the procedures it had followed and the basis for the recommendation. Grey dissented from the recommendation on the grounds that there was insufficient evidence to justify paying more than $5 million. The board accepted the committee's recommendation by a vote of 5–1. Grey again dissented and White did not attend the meeting at which the decision was made. Elizabeth did not participate in any of the deliberations of either the committee or the board of directors and did not vote on the transaction.

On Diamond's advice, the Corporation submitted the transaction to the shareholders for ratification at the annual meeting in October. The proxy statement disclosed all the information available to the board of directors and process by which the board reached its decision. At the meeting, the shareholders ratified the transaction with Elizabeth and other Adams family members voting. 54% of the outstanding stock voted in favor; 22% opposed.

It is now one week after the meeting and two days before the parties are scheduled to close the transaction. Grant, a shareholder of the Corporation, learned of the transaction through reading the proxy statement. She believes that the transaction constitutes a windfall to Adams and has consulted you to see what liabilities, if any, Adams and the board of directors may have in connection with the transaction and what remedies, if any, may be available. In advising Grant, answer the following questions, assuming that the applicable law is:

    a) DGCL § 144.

    b) A statute based on former MBCA § 8.31.

    c) MBCA Subchapter F.

1.

    a) Will a court use the business judgment rule or a fairness test to determine whether to enjoin the transaction or impose personal liability on Adams? The board of directors?

    b) Who will have the burden of proof in litigation?

    c) Will the party with the burden of proof be able to establish the fairness or unfairness of the transaction if the court determines that is the applicable standard?

2. Can the shares of the Adams family be counted in determining whether the transaction has been effectively ratified? What effect does shareholder ratification have on any claim for liability?

3. What role does the duty of loyalty play in monitoring directors' performances? To the extent that market mechanisms may be available to reduce the likelihood that directors will engage in self-dealing to the detriment of the corporation, are those mechanisms likely to be effective?

B. AN OVERVIEW OF THE ISSUES

A Review and a Sneak Preview

We start with a review of the manner in which courts treat transactions in which there is no director self-dealing and move to a sneak preview of the analytical framework that courts use when such self-dealing is present.

- In every corporate transaction directors are protected from liability by the business judgment rule which presumes that when making a decision, directors are informed, independent (or are acting in good faith) and have a rational basis for their decision.

- If the plaintiff is able to rebut the presumption of the business judgment rule by showing the directors were not adequately informed or were not independent, the burden will shift to the directors to demonstrate the fairness of the transaction. Under Delaware law, fairness is considered to be "entire fairness" consisting of "fair dealing" and "fair price."

- "Fair price" means that the price is within a range that might have been agreed to by disinterested parties bargaining in an arms-length transaction.

- "Fair dealing" involves the manner in which the transaction was approved by a corporate decision-maker, either the directors or the shareholders. Where the transaction was approved by a majority of disinterested (or independent) directors, under Delaware law, the burden of proof will shift to the plaintiff to demonstrate that the transaction was unfair. There is some Delaware law suggesting that such approval will give the transaction the protection of the business judgment rule and preclude judicial consideration of fairness.

- Where the transaction was approved by a majority of disinterested shareholders, either the burden shifts to the plaintiff to demonstrate that the transaction was unfair or the plaintiff will have to prove that the terms of the transactions constitute waste. Although DGCL § 144 does not refer to "disinterested" shareholders, the courts have interpreted the statute in that way.

- However the transaction has been approved, the decision-maker must be fully informed of all material facts about the transaction and the director's interest. In determining what is "material," the courts appear to have adopted the federal securities laws definition of materiality. If there has not been full disclosure, such lack may either constitute per se unfairness or not permit the burden shifting that would obtain if there had been full disclosure. It is likely that Delaware courts would take the latter view although there is case law to the contrary in other jurisdictions.

C. EVOLVING STANDARDS OF REVIEW

1. THE COMMON LAW STANDARD: 1880–1960

In an extremely influential article, Harold Marsh traces the evolution of the judicial treatment of conflict of interest transactions from the mid-nineteenth century to modern times. Harold Marsh, *Are Directors*

Trustees?, Conflict of Interest and Corporate Morality, 22 BUS.LAW. 35 (1966). In so doing, Marsh demonstrates how corporate law has moved away from a rule of absolute voidability of conflict transactions to a standard of review in which courts will examine the fairness of such transactions.

Marsh argues that in 1880, the general rule was that a director conflict of interest transaction was voidable by the corporation or its shareholders whether or not a majority of disinterested directors had approved it or that the transaction was fair. This absolute voidability stemmed from the courts' belief "that the corporation was entitled to the unprejudiced judgment and advice of all its directors and therefore it did no good to say that the interested director did not participate in the making of the contract on behalf of the corporation." *Id.* at 37.

By 1910, the general rule had changed such that "a contract between a director and his corporation was valid if it was approved by a disinterested majority of his fellow directors and was not found to be unfair or fraudulent by the court if challenged; but that a contract in which a majority of the board was interested was voidable at the instance of the corporation or its shareholders without regard to any question of fairness." *Id.* at 39–40. He attributes the change either to a judicial recognition of the courts' impotence to check the rapid growth of interested director transactions or to the more technical doctrine of trust law which permitted a trustee to deal with his cestui que trust if she made full disclosure and did not take unfair advantage of the cestui.

Marsh suggests that by 1960, the evolution was complete. The general rule had become that "no transaction of a corporation with any or all of its directors was automatically voidable at the suit of a shareholder, whether there was a disinterested majority of the board or not; but that the courts would review such a contract and subject it to rigid and careful scrutiny, and would invalidate the contract if it was found to be unfair to the corporation." *Id.* at 43. He contends that courts basically have ignored earlier decisions and that, through their opinions, they have, explicitly or implicitly, adopted the modern rule. *Id.* at 43–44.

2. CONTEMPORARY STATUTORY APPROACHES

Interested director transactions are now governed by statutes in most states. Most such statutes, such as DGCL. § 144 and former MBCA § 8.31 codify the common law. These statutes have proved difficult to interpret because of the differing stages of development of the case law at the time the statutes were enacted. Many jurisdictions had adopted a general rule that contracts between interested directors would not automatically be invalidated, but had not expressly overruled earlier cases applying an automatic voidability rule. Some jurisdictions retained vestiges of the automatic voidability rule in specific situations, e.g., where the interested director represented both parties to the transaction in the bargaining process, where the interested director was counted for purposes of determining the presence of a quorum, or where the interested director's vote was necessary for approval of the transaction.

Subchapter F of the MBCA was adopted in 1989 to overcome the interpretive problems these statutes posed. Subchapter F utilizes a safe harbor approach. By providing bright line definitions of who is an "interested" director and what constitutes a "conflicting interest transaction," Subchapter F attempts to provide greater prospective certainty and reduce judicial intervention concerning such transactions.

a. *The Traditional Analysis*

In *Remillard Brick Co.*, a disputed transaction was approved by an interested board, who also owned a majority of the voting stock. The defendants asserted that they approved the transaction in their capacity as shareholders (so that a majority of the shareholders had approved the transaction), and therefore the court had no jurisdiction to inquire into the fairness of the transaction. The court disagreed, finding that the good faith preamble to the statute interjected considerations of fairness. This case prompted a change in California's statutory code to disqualify shares being voted by interested directors in a shareholder vote.

REMILLARD BRICK CO. v. REMILLARD–DANDINI CO.

109 Cal.App.2d 405, 241 P.2d 66, 73–77 (1952).

[Stanley and Sturgis controlled a majority of the shares of Remillard–Dandini Co. Remillard–Dandini Co. owned all the shares of San Jose Brick & Tile, Ltd. Stanley and Sturgis controlled the boards of directors of Remillard–Dandini Co. and San Jose Brick & Tile, Ltd. and were executive officers of both corporations and drew salaries from them. The court refers to Remillard–Dandini Co. and San Jose Brick & Tile, Ltd. as the "manufacturing companies." Stanley and Sturgis owned, controlled and operated Remillard–Dandini Sales Corp. which the court refers to as the "sales corporation."

Plaintiff, a minority shareholder of Remillard–Dandini Co., alleged that the majority directors of the manufacturing companies used their power to have the manufacturing companies enter into contracts with the sales corporation, so that the manufacturing companies were stripped of their sales function, and that through the sales corporation, Stanley and Sturgis realized profits which would have gone to the manufacturing companies. Stanley and Sturgis maintained that the minority shareholder and the minority directors of the manufacturing companies were informed of their interests in the contracts. The court invalidated the contracts.]

PETERS, PRESIDING JUSTICE.

It is argued that, since the fact of common directorship was fully known to the boards of the contracting corporations, and because the * * * majority stockholders consented to the transaction, the minority stockholder and directors of the manufacturing companies have no legal cause to complain. In other words, it is argued that if the majority directors and stockholders inform the minority that they are going to mulct the corporation, section 820 of the Corporations Code* constitutes an impervious armor against any attack on the transaction short of actual fraud. If this interpretation of the section were sound, it would be a shocking reflection on the law of California. It would completely disregard the first sentence of section 820 setting forth the elementary rule that "Directors and officers shall exercise their powers in good faith, and with a view to the interests of the corporation", and would mean that if A conniving directors simply disclose their dereliction to the powerless minority, any transaction by which the majority desire to mulct the minority is immune from attack. That is not and cannot be the law.

Section 820 of the Corporations Code is based on former section 311 of the Civil Code, first added to our law in 1931. Stats. of 1931, Chap. 862, p. 1777. Before the adoption of that section it was the law that the mere existence of a common directorate, at least where the vote of the common director was essential to consummate the transaction, invalidated the contract. That rule was changed in 1931 when section 311 was added to the Civil Code, and limited to a greater extent by the adoption of section 820 of the Corporations Code. If the conditions provided for in the section appear, the transaction cannot be set aside simply because there is a common directorate. Here, undoubtedly, there was a literal compliance with subdivision b of the section. The fact of the common directorship was disclosed to the stockholders, and the * * * majority stockholders, did approve the contracts.

---

* Section 820 of the Corporations Code, enacted in 1947 and based on former section 311 of the Civil Code, provided:

Directors and officers shall exercise their powers in good faith, and with a view to the interests of the corporation. No contract or other transaction between a corporation and one or more of its directors, or between a corporation and any corporation, firm, or association in which one or more of its directors are directors or are financially interested, is either void or voidable because such director or directors are present at the meeting of the board of directors or a committee thereof which authorizes or approves the contract or transaction, or because his or their votes are counted for such purpose, if the circumstances specified in any of the following subdivisions exist:

(a) The fact of the common directorship or financial interest is disclosed or known to the board of directors or committee and noted in the minutes, and the board or committee authorizes, approves, or ratifies the contract or transaction in good faith by a vote sufficient for the purpose without counting the vote or votes of such director or directors.

(b) The fact of the common directorship or financial interest is disclosed or known to the shareholders, and they approve or ratify the contract or transaction in good faith by a majority vote or written consent of shareholders entitled to vote.

(c) The contract or transaction is just and reasonable as to the corporation at the time it is authorized or approved.

Common or interested directors may be counted in determining the presence of a quorum at a meeting of the board of directors or a committee thereof which authorizes, approves, or ratifies a contract or transaction.

But neither section 820 of the Corporations Code nor any other provision of the law automatically validates such transactions simply because there has been a disclosure and approval by the majority of the stockholders. That section does not operate to limit the fiduciary duties owed by a director to all the stockholders, nor does it operate to condone acts which, without the existence of a common directorate, would not be countenanced. That section does not permit an officer or director, by an abuse of his power, to obtain an unfair advantage or profit for himself at the expense of the corporation. The director cannot, by reason of his position, drive a harsh and unfair bargain with the corporation he is supposed to represent. If he does so, he may be compelled to account for unfair profits made in disregard of his duty. Even though the requirements of section 820 are technically met, transactions that are unfair and unreasonable to the corporation may be avoided. CALIFORNIA CORPORATION LAWS by Ballantine and Sterling (1949 ed.), p. 102, § 84. It would be a shocking concept of corporate morality to hold that because the majority directors or stockholders disclose their purpose and interest, they may strip a corporation of its assets to their own financial advantage, and that the minority is without legal redress. Here the unchallenged findings demonstrate that Stanley and Sturgis used their majority power for their own personal advantage and to the detriment of the minority stockholder. They used it to strip the manufacturing companies of their sales functions—functions which it was their duty to carry out as officers and directors of those companies. There was not one thing done by them acting as the sales corporation that they could not and should not have done as officers and directors and in control of the stock of the manufacturing companies. It is no answer to say that the manufacturing companies made a profit on the deal, or that Stanley and Sturgis did a good job. The point is that those large profits that should have gone to the manufacturing companies were diverted to the sales corporation. The good job done by Stanley and Sturgis should and could have been done for the manufacturing companies. If Stanley and Sturgis, with control of the board of directors and the majority stock of the manufacturing companies, could thus lawfully, to their own advantage, strip the manufacturing companies of their sales functions, they could just as well strip them of their other functions. If the sales functions could be stripped from the companies in this fashion to the personal advantage of Stanley and Sturgis, there would be nothing to prevent them from next organizing a manufacturing company, and transferring to it the manufacturing functions of these companies, thus leaving the manufacturing companies but hollow shells. This should not, is not, and cannot be the law.

It is hornbook law that directors, while not strictly trustees, are fiduciaries, and bear a fiduciary relationship to the corporation, and to all the stockholders. They owe a duty to all stockholders, including the minority stockholders, and must administer their duties for the common benefit. The concept that a corporation is an entity cannot operate so as to lessen the duties owed to all of the stockholders. Directors owe a duty of highest good faith to the corporation and its stockholders. It is a cardinal principle of corporate law that a director cannot, at the expense of the corporation, make an unfair profit from his position. He is precluded from receiving any personal advantage without fullest disclosure to and consent of *all* those affected. The law zealously regards contracts between corporations with interlocking directorates, will carefully scrutinize all such transactions, and in case of unfair dealing to the detriment of minority stockholders, will grant appropriate relief. Where the transaction greatly benefits one corporation at the expense of another, and especially if it personally benefits the majority directors, it will and should be set aside. In other words, while the transaction is not voidable simply because an interested director participated, it will not be upheld if it is unfair to the minority stockholders. These principles are the law in practically all jurisdictions.

Interpreting an Interested Director Statute

The California statute in *Remillard* is representative of statutes provide that an interested director transaction will not automatically be void or voidable *either* because there has been disclosure to, and approval by, a disinterested decision-maker (directors or shareholders) *or* because the transaction is fair to the corporation. Under such a provision, what role does a court have in determining the fairness of the transaction to the corporation? Because the statute is written in the disjunctive, one possible answer is that there will be judicial consideration of fairness only if there has been no prior approval by a disinterested decision-maker. If this interpretation is correct, it would represent a major reduction in judicial scrutiny (and, hence, potentially less protection for minority shareholders), particularly when compared to the early days of the common law. This approach, however, could be viewed as economically efficient and less costly because it would give prospective certainty to a transaction in which the decisional process has been good, presumably on the theory that good process will lead to substantively fair decisions in most instances.

Alternatively, the statute can be read as removing the absolute bar against interested director transactions but specifying no clear standard in its stead. Support for this reading comes from the language in many statutes that a transaction that satisfies one or more of the tests will not be void or voidable *solely* because of the director's interest. *See, e.g.*, DGCL § 144. Under this construction, the statute relates primarily to the burden of proof in litigation challenging a conflict of interest transaction rather than to the validity of the transaction itself. Thus, the burden of establishing validity initially would be on the interested director but would shift to the shareholder challenging the transaction if there had been full disclosure and approval by a disinterested decision-maker. This interpretation always leaves the question of the transaction's fairness to determine; approval by a disinterested decision-maker only shifts the burden of who must establish fairness or unfairness. While this interpretation can be supported as a means of deterring management self-dealing, it can be read to be inconsistent with the statute's literal language.

The Delaware courts' interpretations of DGCL § 144 illustrate the difficulties of interpretation. In *Fliegler v. Lawrence*, 361 A.2d 218 (Del.Supr.1976), a shareholder brought a derivative suit on behalf of Agau Mines against its officers and directors (including the named defendant Lawrence), and another corporation, United States Antimony Corp. (USAC), which was owned primarily by Lawrence and the other defendants. Lawrence had acquired, in his individual capacity, certain mining properties which he transferred to USAC. Agau later acquired USAC in exchange for 800,000 shares of Agau stock. Fliegler, a minority shareholder of Agau, challenged Agau's acquisition of USAC, claiming it was unfair. The defendants contended that they had been relieved of the burden of proving fairness because the transaction had been ratified by Agau's shareholders pursuant to § 144(a)(2). The court, however, held that the purported ratification did not affect the burden of proof because the majority of shares voted in favor of the acquisition were cast by the defendants in their capacity as Agau stockholders. Only one-third of the disinterested shareholders cast votes. Thus, the *Fliegler* court determined that despite the absence of any provision in § 144(a)(2) requiring *disinterested* shareholder approval of an interested director transaction, it would impose such a requirement before shifting the burden of proof from the interested director to the challenging shareholder.

Having decided the burden of proof question, the court then addressed the proper interpretation of the disjunctive language of § 144. The court rejected the argument that compliance with § 144(a)(2) automatically validated the transaction and concluded that the statute "merely removes an 'interested director' cloud when its terms are met and provides against invalidation of an agreement 'solely' because such a director or officer is involved. Nothing in the statute sanctions unfairness to Agau or removes the transaction from judicial scrutiny." *Id.* at 222.

In *Marciano v. Nakash*, 535 A.2d 400 (Del.1987), the Delaware Supreme Court found a transaction to be fair that, because of a deadlock at both the shareholder and director level, had not been approved by either disinterested shareholders or directors. The court characterized *Fliegler* as having "refused to view § 144 as either completely preemptive of the common law duty of director fidelity of as constituting a grant of broad immunity" and cited with approval *Fliegler*'s "merely removes an 'interested director' cloud" language. *Id.* at 404. In a footnote, however, the court observed:

> Although in this case none of the curative steps afforded under section 144(a) were available because of the director-shareholder deadlock, a non-disclosing director seeking to remove the cloud of interestedness would appear to have the same burden under section 144(a)(3), as under prior case law, of proving the intrinsic fairness of a questioned transaction which had been approved or ratified by the

directors or shareholders. Folk, THE DELAWARE GENERAL CORP. LAW: A COMMENTARY AND ANALYSIS, 86 (1972). On the other hand, approval by fully-informed disinterested directors under section 144(a)(1), or disinterested stockholders under section 144(a)(2), permits invocation of the business judgment rule and limits judicial review to issues of gift or waste with the burden of proof upon the party attacking the transaction.

Id. at 405, n.3. *See also Oberly v. Kirby*, 592 A.2d 445, 467 (Del.1991) ("The key to upholding an interested transaction is the approval of some neutral decision-making body. Under § 144, a transaction will be sheltered from shareholder challenge if approved by either a committee of independent directors, the shareholders, or the courts * * * "). The disjunctive reading in footnote 3 is also consistent with other decisions of the Delaware Supreme Court. *See, e.g., Puma v. Marriott*, 283 A.2d 693 (Del.Ch.1971) (not decided under § 144 but applying business judgment standard of review where disinterested directors approved purchase of corporations from family group including that included inside directors, where terms not dictated by inside directors).

More recent Delaware cases appear to have rejected the view that § 144 imposes disjunctive requirements. In *Kahn v. Lynch Communication Systems, Inc.*, 638 A.2d 1110 (Del.1994), discussing the duties of a controlling shareholder in a transaction not governed by § 144, the court held that fairness was always the standard of review and that approval by a disinterested decision-maker, rather than permitting the application of the business judgment rule, simply shifted the burden of proof from the controlling shareholder to the shareholder-plaintiff. In the *Cinerama* litigation (discussed in Chapter 17), in a different transactional context, Chancellor Allen, cited *Kahn* to support his observation that "as construed by our Supreme Court recently, compliance with the terms of Section 144 does not restore to the board the presumption of the business judgment rule; it simply shifts the burden to plaintiff to prove unfairness." *Cinerama, Inc. v. Technicolor, Inc.*, 663 A.2d 1134, 1154 (Del.Ch.1994). Most recently, Vice–Chancellor (now Chancellor) Chandler, citing both *Cinerama* and *Kahn*, noted:

> * * * [T]he Delaware Supreme Court has, since *Marciano* * * * was decided, more fully developed the standard by which this Court should judge a board's actions when it engages in a transaction with one or more of its own directors * * *. It is now clear that even if a board's action falls within the safe harbor of section 144, the board is not entitled to receive the protection of the business judgment rule. Compliance with section 144 merely shifts the burden to the plaintiffs to demonstrate that the transaction was unfair.

Cooke v. Oolie, 1997 WL 367034, *9 (Del.Ch.1997).

If all this appears confusing, the reason is simple: it is confusing. The courts have done little to make the analysis clear. No Delaware Supreme Court decision squarely decides the issue. *Marciano* contains two different readings of § 144. Later cases either ignore the ambiguity in *Marciano* (*see Citron v. E.I. DuPont de Nemours & Co.*, 584 A.2d 490, 500–01 (Del.Ch.1990) or cite cases that do not directly involve § 144, such as *Kahn*, to support different constructions of § 144 without seeming to consider whether the fact they involve different transactional contexts should lead to different results.

b. *MBCA Subchapter F*

In 1989, the Committee on Corporate Laws of the American Bar Association adopted Subchapter F to replace the then existing § 8.31.[*] The basic provisions of Subchapter F generally are consistent with judicial interpretations of statutes such as DGCL § 144. However, they are designed to preserve the disjunctive force of the word "or" and to provide specific "bright line" definitions of who is an "interested" director and what constitutes a "transaction" to which Subchapter F is applicable. If directors follow the prescribed procedures, the transaction will be reviewed under the business judgment rule and not a fairness standard. To date, thirteen states have adopted some version of Subchapter F.

Sections 8.60 and 8.61 attempt to frame the definition of who is "interested" in a transaction, and what constitutes a "conflict of interest transaction" much more tightly than did § 8.31. The Official Comment to the former § 8.31 stated:

> For purposes of section 8.31 a director should normally be viewed as interested in a transaction if he or the immediate members of his family have a financial interest in the transaction *or a relationship with the other parties to the transaction such that the relationship might reasonably be expected to affect his judgment in the particular matter in a manner adverse to the corporation.* (emphasis added).

The Official Comment to Subchapter F describes the italicized language at best as overly broad and leading to uncertainty by corporate directors, and at worst as vague and destabilizing. Subchapter F takes a markedly different approach.

Section 8.61(a) is a key component in the design of subchapter F. It draws a bright-line circle, declaring that the definitions of section 8.60 wholly occupy and preempt the field of directors' conflicting interest transactions. Of course, outside this circle there is a penumbra of director interests, desires, goals, loyalties, and prejudices that may, in a particular context, run at odds with the best interests of the corporation, but section 8.61(a) forbids a court to ground remedial action on any of them. If a plaintiff charges that a director had a conflict of interest with respect to a transaction of the corporation because the other party was his cousin, the answer of the court should be: "No. A cousin as such and without more, is no conflict of interest transaction. See Chapter 17.

---

[*] Former MBCA 8.31 should not be confused with the present MBCA 8.31 which deals with director liability when there is

not included in section 8.60(3) as a related person—and under section 8.61(a), I have no authority to reach out farther." If a plaintiff contends that the director had a conflict of interest in a corporate transaction because the other party is president of the golf club the director wants desperately to join, the court should respond: "No. The only director's conflicting interest on the basis of which I can set aside a corporate transaction or impose other sanctions is a financial interest as defined by section 8.60."

Official Comment to Section 8.61.

The binary analytic framework of Subchapter F as seen in the bright line approach of §§ 8.60 and 8.61 has been modified by the new § 8.31 (Chapter 17). Under that section, if a person challenging a transaction involving a director can show that a board's approval of a corporate transaction was influenced by a director's relationship with the other party to that transaction, the burden shifts to the director with such a relationship to show that she reasonably believed the challenged transaction was in the corporation's best interests. In effect, § 8.31 creates an intermediate standard of review for a director's transaction that does not involve a "conflicting interest" as defined in § 8.60(1) but that nonetheless may have been influenced by the director's relationship with the other party to that transaction.

Section 8.60's narrowly circumscribed definition of "related person" clearly is intended to leave a number of questionable situations immune from judicial scrutiny on the ground that "the legislative draftsman who chooses to suppress marginal anomalies by resorting to generalized statements of principle will pay a cost in terms of predictability."What factors should be considered in a cost-benefit analysis? Should such an analysis be the basis for the normative judgments found in a statute? If not, on what should such a normative judgment be based?

In many ways, Subchapter F takes the same approach as modern interested director statutes in evaluating substantive fairness (discussed in the next section of the chapter). "[A] 'fair' price is any price in that broad range which an unrelated party might have been willing to pay or willing to accept * * * following a normal arm's-length business negotiation, in the light of the knowledge that would have been reasonably acquired in the course of such negotiations. * * *" Official Comment to § 8.61.

This range of fairness is narrower than the range of discretion to which directors' decisions are entitled under the business judgment standard of Section 8.30. The Official Comment to § 8.61 also points out that courts must consider "whether the transaction was one reasonably likely to yield favorable results * * * from the perspective of furthering the corporation's business activities" in addition to scrutinizing the price and terms of the transaction.

The most important element of fairness in Subchapter F is that Section 8.61(b)(3) appears to provide that a transaction that is "fair" should be upheld, whether or not it was approved by directors or shareholders in compliance with §§ 8.62 and 8.63. However, the Official Comment states:

> * * * [I]n some circumstances, the behavior of the director having the conflicting interest can itself affect the finding and content of "fairness." The most obvious illustration of unfair dealing arises out of the director's failure to disclose fully his interest or hidden defects known to him regarding the transaction. Another illustration could be the exertion of improper pressure by the director upon the other directors. When the facts of such unfair dealing become known, the court should offer the corporation its option as to whether to rescind the transaction on grounds of "unfairness" even if it appears that the terms were "fair" by market standards and the corporation profited from it. * * * Thus, the course of dealing—or process—is a key component to a "fairness" determination under subsection (b)(3).

Official Comment to Section 8.61.

Another part of the Official Comment also suggests that the protection of the business judgment rule may not be as absolute under Subchapter F as it is in other contexts:

> * * * Consider, for example, a situation in which it is established that the board of a manufacturing corporation approved a cash loan to a director where the duration, security and interest terms of the loan were at prevailing commercial rates, but (i) the loan was not made in the course of the corporation's business activities and (ii) the loan required a commitment of limited working capital that would otherwise have been used in furtherance of the corporation's business activities. Such a loan transaction would not be afforded safe-harbor protection by section 8.62(b)(1) since the board did not comply with the requirement in section 8.30(a) that the board's action be, in its reasonable judgment, in the best interests of the corporation—that is, that the action will, as the board judges the circumstances at hand, yield favorable results (or reduce detrimental results) as judged from the perspective of furthering the corporation's business activities.
>
> If a determination is made that the terms of a director's conflicting interest transaction, judged according to the circumstances at the time of commitment, were manifestly unfavorable to the the corporation, that determination would be relevant to an allegation that the directors' action was not taken in good faith and therefore did not comply with section 8.30(a).

Official Comment to Section 8.61.

Does this comment thrust the courts back into determining fairness, notwithstanding Subchapter F's attempt to limit judicial intervention? Or should Subchapter F be read to shield a conflict of interest transaction whose terms are fair by market standards and from which the corporation benefits, even if the interested director failed to disclose material facts about the transaction? This result would overrule those decisions which have held that disclosure is an indispensable element of fairness. Is this a desirable result?

Perhaps because relatively few states have adopted Subchapter F, there has been virtually no litigation to test the interpretative questions that we have seen thus far. What is clear thus far is that the safe harbor provisions of Subchapter F have considerable force. *Fisher* v. *State Mutual Ins. Co.*, 290 F.3d 1256 (11th Cir. 2002) involved a conflict of interest transaction in which the interested directors fully disclosed their interest and did not participate in negotiating or voting on the transaction. The court found that the defendants had fully complied with the safe harbor of the Georgia statute (based on Subchapter F) and affirmed a grant of summary judgment for the directors.

c. *Company Codes: The European Approach*

The European response to corporate conflicts of interest in public companies has been somewhat different from that in the United States. Rather than relying on judicial standards of conduct, the European approach relies on *voluntary* codes of corporate governance. European companies must either adopt (and comply with) these codes or explain their reasons for non-adoption. The focus is on private compliance rather than judicial enforcement.

A recent communication by the European Commission, responding to a report by a "high level group of company law experts" on corporate governance reform in the EU, lays out a series of recommendations to EU Member States. The emphasis is on greater transparency, freedom of companies to adopt what suits them best, and national (rather than pan-European) solutions.

COMMUNICATION FROM THE COMMISSION TO THE COUNCIL AND THE EUROPEAN PARLIAMENT

Modernising Company Law and Enhancing Corporate Governance in the European Union—A Plan to Move Forward (2003)

http://europa.eu.int/comm/internal_market/en/company/company/modern/

Recent financial scandals have prompted a new, active debate on corporate governance, and the necessary restoration of confidence is one more reason for new initiatives at EU level. Investors, large and small, are demanding more transparency and better information on companies, and are seeking to gain more influence on the way the public companies they own operate. Shareholders own companies, not management–yet far too frequently their rights have been trampled on by shoddy, greedy and occasionally fraudulent corporate behavior. A new sense of proportion and fairness is necessary.

[Ensuring adequate protection of members—that is, shareholders—and third parties should be organized along the following lines. First, some new tailored initiatives should be taken with a view to enhancing shareholder rights and clarifying management responsibilities. Second, a proper distinction should be made between categories of companies. A more stringent framework is desirable for listed companies and companies which have publicly raised capital. Third, modern technologies should be utilized to further corporate disclosure and shareholders' ability to exercise their rights.]

Business efficiency and competitiveness, which are crucial components of economic growth and job creation, depend on many factors, one of which is a strong framework of company law. Key to the achievement of this objective is the setting up of a proper balance between actions at EU level an actions at national level. Some company law rules are likely to be best dealt with, and updated, more efficiently at national level, and some competition between national rules may actually be healthy for the efficiency of the single market. [While EU initiatives in the area of company law should certainly address a number of specific cross-border issues (merger or transfer of seat, impediments to the exercise of shareholder rights) flexibility should be available to companies as much as possible. Where systems are deemed to be equivalent, maximum room should be left open to the freedom of the parties involved.]

[There is general agreement that the EU should not devote time and effort to the development of a European corporate governance code. Instead, the European Commission should focus its efforts on the reduction of legal and regulatory barriers to shareholder engagement in cross-border voting as well as the reduction of barriers to shareholder ability to evaluate the governance of companies. There is a remarkable degree of convergence of company law among Member States, and in the rare instances where codes provisions are divergent, the "comply or explain" principle offers a satisfactory solution.]

[To enhance corporate governance disclosure,] listed companies should be required to include in their annual report and accounts a coherent and descriptive statement covering the key elements of their corporate governance structure and practices, which should at least include the following items: [description of the shareholder meeting and shareholder rights; composition and operation of the board and its committees; the shareholders holding major holdings and their rights; the other direct and indirect relationships between these major shareholders and the company, any material transactions with other related parties, and a reference to a code on corporate governance, designed for use at national level, with which the company complies or in relation to which it explains deviations.]

In key areas where executive directors clearly have conflicts of interest decisions in listed companies should be made exclusively by non-executive or supervisory directors who are in the majority independent. With respect to the nomination of directors ... the responsibility for identifying candidates to fill board vacancies should in principle be entrusted to a group composed mainly of executive directors ... Non-executive directors should, nonetheless also be included and specific safeguards should be put in place to deal with conflicts of interest when they arise, for example when a decision has to be made on the reappointment of a director.

These requirements should be enforced by Member States at least on a "comply or explain" basis. Certain minimum standards of what cannot be considered independent should be established at EU level. In view of the recent accounting scandals, special emphasis will be placed on the audit committee (or equivalent body), with a view to fostering the key role it should play in supervising the audit function, [both in its internal and external aspects].

With a view to enhancing directors' responsibilities, the collective responsibility of all board members for financial and key non financial statements should confirmed as a matter of EU law.

The High Level Group made several other recommendations designed to enhance directors responsibilities : a) introduction of a special investigation right, whereby shareholders holding a certain percentage of the share capital should have the right to ask a court or administrative authority to authorise a special investigation into the affairs of the company; b) development of a wrongful trading rule, whereby directors would be held personally accountable for the consequences of the company's failure, if it is foreseeable that the company cannot continue to pay its debts and they don't decide either to rescue the company and ensure payment or to put it into liquidation; c) imposition of directors' disqualification across the EU as a sanction for misleading financial and non-financial statements and other forms of misconduct by directors. The Commission supports these ideas, whose implementation requires further analysis, and therefore intents to present the relevant proposal for a Directive in the medium term.

D. ENTIRE FAIRNESS: FAIR DEALING AND FAIR PRICE

As we have seen, although the validity of an interested director transaction may be subject to review under the business judgment rule in some circumstances, that is not the general rule. Rather, at both common law and under statutes other than those modeled on Subchapter F, the test is whether the transaction was "fair" to the corporation at the time it was entered into. In *Shlensky v. South Parkway Building Corp.*, 19 Ill.2d 268, 166 N.E.2d 793 (1960), the court, in evaluating the fairness of conflict of interest transactions, stated:

> While the concept of "fairness" is incapable of precise definition, courts have stressed such factors as whether the corporation received in the transaction full value in all the commodities purchased; the corporation's need for the property; its ability to finance the

purchase; whether the transaction was at the market price, or below, or constituted a better bargain than the corporation could have otherwise obtained in dealings with others; whether there was a detriment to the corporation as a result of the transaction; whether there was a possibility of corporate gain siphoned off by the directors directly or through corporations they controlled; and whether there was full disclosure—although neither disclosure nor shareholder assent can convert a dishonest transaction into a fair one.

Id. at 801–802

Weinberger v. UOP, Inc., 457 A.2d 701 (Del. 1983) (see Chapter 19), refined the fairness test. Evaluating the fairness of a parent-subsidiary merger, the court held that "entire fairness" was the test and that "entire fairness" had both procedural and substantive elements.

The concept of fairness has two basic aspects: fair dealing and fair price. The former embraces questions of when the transaction was timed, how it was initiated, structured, negotiated, disclosed to the directors, and how the approvals of the directors and the stockholders were obtained. The latter aspect of fairness relates to the economic and financial considerations of the proposed merger, including all relevant factors: assets, market value, earnings, future prospects, and any other elements that affect the intrinsic or inherent value of a company's stock.... However, the test for fairness is not a bifurcated one as between fair dealing and price. All aspects of the issue must be examined as a whole since the question is one of entire fairness.

Id. at 711.

Although *Weinberger* did not involve an interested director transaction, its "entire fairness" approach has now been accepted under Delaware law as the test of the fairness in all conflict of interest transactions. Because of the absence of litigation under Subchapter F, it is not clear whether "fairness" under that statute will be interpreted in the same way.

1. FAIR DEALING (PROCEDURAL FAIRNESS)

a. *Director Approval*

Who Is an Interested or Independent Director?

In determining the validity of a conflict of interest transaction, one of the most often litigated questions is whether the decision-makers are "interested." Corporate statutes make clear that a decision-maker will be interested if she has a direct or indirect financial interest in the transaction. Statutes such as DGCL § 144, however, do not address what kind of non-financial relationship with an interested director will call into question approval by a person who otherwise would be considered disinterested. Official Comment 5 to former MBCA 8.31 suggests that such a person with such a non-financial interest would be considered "interested if he had :

> a relationship with the other parties to the transaction such that the relationship might reasonably be expected to affect his judgment in the particular matter in a manner adverse to the corporation.

In recent decisions, arising in connection with the conduct of derivative suits, courts are examining the concept of the "independence" of a director as well as her "interest." As Chancellor Chandler has recently noted:

> Although interest and independence are two separate and distinct issues, these two attributes are sometimes confused by parties. Many plaintiffs allege facts which they assert establish that the defendant "lacked the disinterest and/or independence" necessary to consider the challenged transaction objectively. The plaintiff then asks the Court to select whichever type of disabling attribute is consistent with the facts alleged and that will support the plaintiff's claim. But it is not for the Court to divine the claims being made. A plaintiff must make clear to the Court the bases upon which his claims rest.
>
> As described above, a disabling "interest," as defined by Delaware common law, exists in two instances. The first is when (1) a director personally receives a benefit (or suffers a detriment), (2) as a result of, or from, the challenged transaction, (3) which is not generally shared with (or suffered by) the other shareholders of his corporation, and (4) that benefit (or detriment) is of such subjective material significance to that particular director that it is reasonable to question whether that director objectively considered the advisability of the challenged transaction to the corporation and its shareholders. The second instance is when a director stands on both sides of the challenged transaction. This latter situation frequently involves the first three elements listed above. As for the fourth element, whenever a director stands on both sides of the challenged transaction he is deemed interested and allegations of materiality have not been required.
>
> "Independence" does not involve a question of whether the challenged director derives a benefit *from the transaction* that is not generally shared with the other shareholders. Rather, it involves an inquiry into whether the director's decision resulted from that director being *controlled* by another. A director can be controlled by another if in fact he is *dominated* by that other party, whether through close personal or familial relationship or through force of will. A director can also be controlled by another if the challenged director is *beholden* to the allegedly controlling entity. A director may be considered beholden to (and thus controlled by) another when the allegedly controlling entity has the unilateral power (whether direct or indirect through control over other decision makers), to decide whether the challenged director continues to

receive a benefit, financial or otherwise, upon which the challenged director is so dependent or is of such subjective material importance to him that the threatened loss of that benefit might create a reason to question whether the controlled director is able to consider the corporate merits of the challenged transaction objectively.

Confusion over whether specific facts raise a question of interest or independence arises from the reality that similar factual circumstances may implicate *both* interest and independence, one but not the other, or neither. By way of example, consider the following: Director A is both a director and officer of company X. Company X is to be merged into company Z. Director A's vote in favor of recommending shareholder approval of the merger is challenged by a plaintiff shareholder.

Scenario One. Assume that one of the terms of the merger agreement is that director A was to be an officer in surviving company Z, *and* that maintaining his position as a corporate officer in the surviving company was material to director A. That fact might, when considered in light of *all* of the facts alleged, lead the Court to conclude that director A had a disabling interest.

Scenario Two. Assume that director C is both a director and the majority shareholder of company X. Director C had the power plausibly to threaten director A's position as officer of corporation X should director A vote against the merger. Assume further that director A's position as a corporate officer is material to director A. Those circumstances, when considered in light of *all* of the facts alleged, might lead the Court to question director A's independence from director C, because it could reasonably be assumed that director A was controlled by director C, since director A was beholden to director C for his position as officer of the corporation. Confusion over whether to label this disability as a disqualifying "interest" or as a "lack of independence" may stem from the fact that, colloquially, director A was "interested" in keeping his job as a corporate officer. Scenario Two, however, raises only a question as to director A's independence since there is nothing that suggests that director A would receive something *from the transaction* that might implicate a disabling interest.

If a plaintiff's allegations combined all facts described in both Scenario One *and* Scenario Two, it might be reasonable to question *both* director A's interest and independence. Conversely, if all the facts in both scenarios were alleged *except* for the materiality of Director A's position as a corporate officer (perhaps because director A is a billionaire and his officer's position pays $20,000 per year and is not even of prestige value to him) then *neither* director A's interest nor his independence would be reasonably questioned. The key issue is not simply whether a particular director receives a benefit from a challenged transaction not shared with the other shareholders, or solely whether another person or entity has the ability to take some benefit away from a particular director, but whether the possibility of gaining some benefit or the fear of losing a benefit is likely to be of such importance to that director that it is reasonable for the Court to question whether valid business judgment or selfish considerations animated that director's vote on the challenged transaction.

Orman v. *Cullman*, 794 A.2d 5, 25–6, *n*.50 (Del.Ch. 2002)

As you read the following cases, consider whether the concepts they examine in connection with derivative suits also should be applied to the review of the fairness of a self-dealing transaction.

IN RE THE WALT DISNEY COMPANY DERIVATIVE LITIGATION

731 A.2d 342 (Del.Ch.1998), *aff'd in part, rev'd in part sub nom. Brehm v. Eisner*, 746 A.2d 244 (Del.2000).

CHANDLER, CHANCELLOR.

[Plaintiffs allege that the defendant Directors' breached their fiduciary duties of loyalty, good faith, and due care by entering into the Employment Agreement with Michael Ovitz and then by terminating Ovitz without cause, i.e., a Non–Fault Termination. Plaintiffs further assert the employment contract constituted corporate waste.]

III. BACKGROUND FACTS

In September 1995, Michael D. Eisner, chairman of the board and chief executive officer of Disney, recruited and hired his friend, Michael S. Ovitz, to serve as Disney's president. On October 1, 1995, Ovitz and Eisner signed a five-year employment contract (the "Employment Agreement" or the "Agreement") which the Disney Board approved unanimously. Thereafter, Ovitz was nominated and elected to serve as a director on Disney's Board.

Pursuant to the Employment Agreement, Ovitz was to receive an annual salary of $1 million, a discretionary bonus, and options to purchase five million shares of Disney common stock. * * *

Of particular significance to this case, under the Employment Agreement, if Disney terminated Ovitz's employment without good cause or if Ovitz resigned from Disney with the consent of the Company (referred to in the Employment Agreement as a "Non–Fault Termination"), three million of Ovitz's options would vest immediately upon his separation from the Company, and Ovitz would be entitled to wait until the later of September 30, 2002, or twenty-four months after the date of separation to exercise these options. The Employment Agreement also provided for Ovitz to receive a lump payment of $10,000,000 if he were terminated without cause prior to September 30, 2002. In addition, if Ovitz were terminated without cause, he would receive an additional payment equal to the present value of the remaining salary payments due under the Agreement through September 30, 2000, as well as the product of $7.5

million times the number of fiscal years remaining under the Agreement (i.e., Ovitz's approximate foregone bonuses).

Ovitz's employment with Disney did not work out well, and it was widely known that Ovitz was seeking alternative employment elsewhere. Plaintiffs allege that in September 1996, Ovitz sent Eisner a letter stating his desire to leave Disney. That letter notwithstanding, on December 11, 1996, only fourteen months after Ovitz joined Disney, Eisner consented to Ovitz's request for a Non–Fault Termination. The following day, Disney announced that Ovitz's employment with the Company would be terminated. Thereafter, the Disney Board approved Ovitz's Non–Fault Termination.

* * *

V. Breach of Fiduciary Duty and Waste Claims

[In order to proceed with their derivative claims, Plaintiffs must set forth in their complaint particularized facts that create a reasonable doubt that (1) a majority of the members of Disney's board of directors are disinterested and independent or (2) the challenged transaction was otherwise the product of a valid exercise of business judgment.]

In order to create a reasonable doubt that a director is disinterested, a derivative plaintiff must plead particular facts to demonstrate that a director "will receive a personal financial benefit from a transaction that is not equally shared by the stockholders" or, conversely, that "a corporate decision will have a materially detrimental impact on a director, but not on the corporation and the stockholders." In these situations, a director cannot be expected to act "without being influenced by the ... personal consequences" flowing from the decision. At the other end of the spectrum, a board member is considered to be disinterested when he or she neither stands to benefit financially nor suffer materially from the decision whether to pursue the claim sought in the derivative plaintiff's demand.

B. * * * *Independence and Absence of Self–Interest*

* * * Plaintiffs attack the former Board's decision to enter into the Employment Agreement. * * * Plaintiffs offer several reasons for their assertion that the Board is not independent. Chief among them is Plaintiffs' assertion that Eisner dominates and controls the Board. Plaintiffs argue that at least twelve of the fifteen members of the Disney Board * * * had such strong ties to Eisner that they would not have been able to make an impartial decision * * *. In order to prove domination and control by Eisner, Plaintiffs must demonstrate first that Eisner was personally interested in obtaining the Board's approval of the Employment Agreement and, second, that a majority of the Board could not exercise business judgment independent of Eisner in deciding whether to approve the Employment Agreement.

1. Eisner's Alleged Interest in Ovitz's Compensation

Plaintiffs offer two grounds for finding that Eisner was interested in the Employment Agreement. First, Plaintiffs suggest that Eisner's long-time personal relationship with Ovitz caused him to be interested in obtaining the Board's approval of the Employment Agreement. The fact that Eisner has long-standing personal and business ties to Ovitz cannot overcome the presumption of independence that all directors, including Eisner, are afforded.

Second, Plaintiffs allege that Eisner, by providing his second-in-command a lucrative compensation package, set a high baseline from which he could negotiate upward for increased compensation for himself. Plaintiffs' allegation cannot reasonably be inferred. At all times material to this litigation, Eisner owned several million options to purchase Disney stock. Therefore, it would not be in Eisner's economic interest [to allow Ovitz to leave Disney without good cause and] to cause the Company to issue millions of additional options unnecessarily and at considerable cost. * * *

2. Eisner's Alleged Domination of the Board

I turn now to the Disney directors whom Plaintiffs allege were under Eisner's control, to consider whether they could have exercised their business judgment independently of Eisner.

* * * While the issues at times present close calls, ultimately I am not persuaded that the allegations with regard to nine of the following twelve Board members survive * * *.

a. Disney, Litvack, and Nunis

Plaintiffs allege that directors Roy E. Disney, Sanford M. Litvack, and Richard A. Nunis were unable to exercise independent business judgment with respect to a demand because they were Disney executive employees who reported to and were accountable to Eisner at the time Plaintiffs commenced this litigation. I note at the outset the general Delaware rule that "the fact that they hold positions with the company [controlled by Eisner] . . . is no more disqualifying than is the fact that he designated them as directors."

I begin my analysis with Mr. Disney, who earns a substantial salary and receives numerous, valuable options on Disney stock. As a top executive, his compensation is set by the Board, not solely by Eisner. Furthermore, Mr. Disney, along with his family, owns approximately 8.4 million shares of Disney stock. At today's prices these shares are worth $2.1 billion. The only reasonable inference that I can draw about Mr. Disney is that he is an economically rational individual whose priority is to protect the value of his Disney shares, not someone who would intentionally risk his own and his family's interests in order to placate Eisner. Nothing in Plaintiffs' pleadings suggest that Mr. Disney would place Eisner's interests over Mr. Disney's own and over those of the Company in derogation of his fiduciary duties as a Disney director.

With respect to Nunis and Litvack, contrary to Plaintiffs' allegations, these directors do not necessarily lose their ability to exercise independent business judgment merely by virtue of their being officers of Disney and Disney's subsidiaries. Moreover, there is no merit in Plaintiffs' highly speculative argument that Litvack and Nunis were interested in the Employment Agreement because they had a personal financial interest in establishing a heightened compensation level throughout the Company. Plaintiffs, however, have pleaded with some particularity that there is at least a reasonable doubt as to Litvack and Nunis's ability to vote independently of Eisner. Their salaries are presumably also set by the Board, but they do not hold the same level of shares as Roy E. Disney and his family, and so there is a reasonable possibility they are more beholden to Eisner. Since, as a matter of law, Plaintiffs are unable to show a reasonable doubt as to Eisner's absence of self-interest, his potential domination over these two directors is inconsequential.

* * *

f. O'Donovan

Plaintiffs also allege that Father Leo J. O'Donovan, involved only in the decision to honor the Employment Agreement, is incapable of rendering independent business judgment. O'Donovan is the president of Georgetown University, the alma mater of one of Eisner's sons and the recipient of over $1 million of donations from Eisner since 1989. Accordingly, Plaintiffs allege that O'Donovan would not act contrary to Eisner's wishes.

The closest parallel to O'Donovan's situation faced by this Court occurred in *Lewis v. Fuqua*. Any reliance by Plaintiffs on that case, however, would be misplaced. In *Lewis*, the allegedly disinterested director, Sanford, was the President of Duke University. Duke was the recipient of a $10 million pledge from the dominant board member, Fuqua. Nevertheless, several differences exist that serve to distinguish that matter from the present one. First and foremost, Sanford had "numerous political and financial dealings" with Fuqua, while Plaintiffs here have not alleged any such relationship between Eisner and O'Donovan. Secondly, Fuqua and Sanford served as directors together both on the Board whose actions were being challenged and on the Duke University Board of Trustees. Such an interlocking directorship, a situation that would likely lead to a reasonable doubt of O'Donovan's independence, does not exist here, as Eisner has no formal relationship with Georgetown University. These two differences are sufficient to demonstrate that *Lewis* does not apply here.

The question, then, is whether Eisner exerted such an influence on O'Donovan that O'Donovan could not exercise independent judgment as a director. Plaintiffs do not allege any personal benefit received by O'Donovan—in fact, they admit that O'Donovan is forbidden, as a Jesuit priest, from collecting any director's fee. Plaintiffs cite the case of *Kahn v. Tremont Corp*. "Eisner's philanthropic largess to Georgetown is no less disqualifying than the financial arrangements enjoyed by the special committee members in *Kahn*." In that case, however, two of the three special committee members received a direct, personal financial benefit from their affiliation with the interested party, and the third sought membership on the boards of other entities controlled by the interested party. The distinction between *Kahn* and this matter then is clear, and I do not believe that Plaintiffs have presented a reasonable doubt as to the independence of O'Donovan.

g. Bowers

Director Reveta F. Bowers is the principal of the elementary school that Eisner's children once attended. Plaintiffs suggest that because Bowers' salary as a teacher is low compared to her director's fees and stock options, "only the most rigidly formalistic or myopic analysis" would view Bowers as not beholden to Eisner.

Plaintiffs fail to recognize that the Delaware Supreme Court has held that "such allegations [of payment of director's fees], without more, do not establish any financial interest." To follow Plaintiffs' urging to discard "formalistic notions of interest and independence in favor of a realistic approach" expressly would be to overrule the Delaware Supreme Court.

Furthermore, to do so would be to discourage the membership on corporate boards of people of less-than extraordinary means. Such "regular folks" would face allegations of being dominated by other board members, merely because of the relatively substantial compensation provided by the board membership compared to their outside salaries. I am especially unwilling to facilitate such a result. Without more, Plaintiffs have failed to allege facts that lead to a reasonable doubt as to the independence of Bowers.

* * *

i. Russell

Director Irwin E. Russell is an entertainment lawyer who serves as Eisner's personal counsel and has a long history of personal and business ties to Eisner. As a result, Plaintiffs allege Russell is unable to exercise independent business judgment.

In addition to being Eisner's personal counsel: Russell's law office is listed as the mailing address for Eisner's primary residence; Russell is the registered agent for several entities in which Eisner is involved; Russell has represented Eisner in connection with Eisner's negotiation of the Eisner Compensation Agreement in 1996 and early 1997 (during which negotiation he recused himself from his Board role); and, Plaintiffs assert, Russell practices in a small firm for which the fees derived from Eisner likely represent a large portion of the total amount of fees received by the firm. Accordingly, it appears Plaintiffs have raised a reasonable doubt as to Russell's independence of Eisner's influence for the purpose of considering a demand.

IN RE ORACLE CORP. DERIVATIVE LITIGATION
824 A.2d 917 (Del. Ch. 2003).

STRINE, VICE CHANCELLOR.

In this opinion, I address the motion of the special litigation committee ("SLC") of Oracle Corporation to terminate this action, "the Delaware Derivative Action," and other such actions pending in the name of Oracle against certain Oracle directors and officers. These actions allege that these Oracle directors engaged in insider trading while in possession of material, non-public information showing that Oracle would not meet the earnings guidance it gave to the market for the third quarter of Oracle's fiscal year 2001. The SLC bears the burden of persuasion on this motion and must convince me that there is no material issue of fact calling into doubt its independence. This requirement is set forth in *Zapata Corp. v. Maldonado* and its progeny.

The question of independence "turns on whether a director is, *for any substantial reason,* incapable of making a decision with only the best interests of the corporation in mind." That is, the independence test ultimately "focus[es] on impartiality and objectivity." In this case, the SLC has failed to demonstrate that no material factual question exists regarding its independence.

During discovery, it emerged that the two SLC members—both of whom are professors at Stanford University—are being asked to investigate fellow Oracle directors who have important ties to Stanford, too. Among the directors who are accused by the derivative plaintiffs of insider trading are: (1) another Stanford professor, who taught one of the SLC members when the SLC member was a Ph.D. candidate and who serves as a senior fellow and a steering committee member alongside that SLC member at the Stanford Institute for Economic Policy Research or "SIEPR"; (2) a Stanford alumnus who has directed millions of dollars of contributions to Stanford during recent years, serves as Chair of SIEPR's Advisory Board and has a conference center named for him at SIEPR's facility, and has contributed nearly $600,000 to SIEPR and the Stanford Law School, both parts of Stanford with which one of the SLC members is closely affiliated; and (3) Oracle's CEO, who has made millions of dollars in donations to Stanford through a personal foundation and large donations indirectly through Oracle, and who was considering making donations of his $100 million house and $170 million for a scholarship program as late as August 2001, at around the same time period the SLC members were added to the Oracle board. Taken together, these and other facts cause me to harbor a reasonable doubt about the impartiality of the SLC.

It is no easy task to decide whether to accuse a fellow director of insider trading. For Oracle to compound that difficulty by requiring SLC members to consider accusing a fellow professor and two large benefactors of their university of conduct that is rightly considered a violation of criminal law was unnecessary and inconsistent with the concept of independence recognized by our law. The possibility that these extraneous considerations biased the inquiry of the SLC is too substantial for this court to ignore. I therefore deny the SLC's motion to terminate.

I. FACTUAL BACKGROUND

A. *Summary of the Plaintiffs' Allegations*

The Delaware Derivative Complaint centers on alleged insider trading by four members of Oracle's board of directors—Lawrence Ellison, Jeffrey Henley, Donald Lucas, and Michael Boskin (collectively, the "Trading Defendants"). Each of the Trading Defendants had a very different role at Oracle.

Ellison is Oracle's Chairman, Chief Executive Officer, and its largest stockholder, owning nearly twenty-five percent of Oracle's voting shares. By virtue of his ownership position, Ellison is one of the wealthiest men in America. By virtue of his managerial position, Ellison has regular access to a great deal of information about how Oracle is performing on a week-to-week basis.

Henley is Oracle's Chief Financial Officer, Executive Vice President, and a director of the corporation. Like Ellison, Henley has his finger on the pulse of Oracle's performance constantly.

Lucas is a director who chairs Oracle's Executive Committee and its Finance and Audit Committee. * * *

Boskin is a director, Chairman of the Compensation Committee, and a member of the Finance and Audit Committee. * * *

B. *The Plaintiffs' Claims in the Delaware Derivative Action*

The plaintiffs make two central claims in their amended complaint in the Delaware Derivative Action. First, the plaintiffs allege that the Trading Defendants breached their duty of loyalty by misappropriating inside information and using it as the basis for trading decisions. This claim rests its legal basis on the venerable case of *Brophy v. Cities Service Co.* Its factual foundation is that the Trading Defendants were aware (or at least possessed information that should have made them aware) that the company would miss its December guidance by a wide margin and used that information to their advantage in selling at artificially inflated prices.

Second, as to the other defendants—who are the members of the Oracle board who did not trade—the plaintiffs allege a *Caremark* violation, in the sense that the board's indifference to the deviation between the company's December guidance and reality was so extreme as to constitute subjective bad faith.

D. *The Formation of the Special Litigation Committee*

On February 1, 2002, Oracle formed the SLC in order to investigate the Delaware Derivative Action and to determine whether Oracle should press the claims raised by the plaintiffs, settle the case, or terminate it. Soon after its formation, the SLC's charge was broadened to give it the same mandate as to all the pending derivative actions, wherever they were filed.

The SLC was granted full authority to decide these matters without the need for approval by the other members of the Oracle board.

E. *The Members of the Special Litigation Committee*

Two Oracle board members were named to the SLC. Both of them joined the Oracle board on October 15, 2001, more than a half a year after Oracle's 3Q FY 2001 closed. The SLC members also share something else: both are tenured professors at Stanford University.

Professor Hector Garcia–Molina is Chairman of the Computer Science Department at Stanford and holds the Leonard Bosack and Sandra Lerner Professorship in the Computer Science and Electrical Engineering Departments at Stanford. A renowned expert in his field, Garcia–Molina was a professor at Princeton before coming to Stanford in 1992. Garcia–Molina's appointment at Stanford represented a homecoming of some sort, because he obtained both his undergraduate and graduate degrees from Stanford.

The other SLC member, Professor Joseph Grundfest, is the W.A. Franke Professor of Law and Business at Stanford University. He directs the University's well-known Directors' College[8] and the Roberts Program in Law, Business, and Corporate Governance at the Stanford Law School. Grundfest is also the principal investigator for the Law School's Securities Litigation Clearinghouse. Immediately before coming to Stanford, Grundfest served for five years as a Commissioner of the Securities and Exchange Commission. Like Garcia–Molina, Grundfest's appointment at Stanford was a homecoming, because he obtained his law degree and performed significant post-graduate work in economics at Stanford.

As will be discussed more specifically later, Grundfest also serves as a steering committee member and a senior fellow of the Stanford Institute for Economic Policy Research, and releases working papers under the "SIEPR" banner.

For their services, the SLC members were paid $250 an hour, a rate below that which they could command for other activities, such as consulting or expert witness testimony. Nonetheless, during the course of their work, the SLC members became concerned that (arguably scandal-driven) developments in the evolving area of corporate governance as well as the decision in *Telxon v. Meyerson,* might render the amount of their compensation so high as to be an argument against their independence. Therefore, Garcia–Molina and Grundfest agreed to give up any SLC-related compensation if their compensation was deemed by this court to impair their impartiality.

---

8. In the interests of full disclosure, I spoke at the Directors' College in spring 2002.

H. *The SLC's Investigation and Report*

The SLC's investigation was, by any objective measure, extensive. The SLC reviewed an enormous amount of paper and electronic records. SLC counsel interviewed seventy witnesses, some of them twice. SLC members participated in several key interviews, including the interviews of the Trading Defendants.

Importantly, the interviewees included all the senior members of Oracle's management most involved in its projection and monitoring of the company's financial performance, including its sales and revenue growth. These interviews combined with a special focus on the documents at the company bearing on these subjects, including e-mail communications.

The SLC also asked the plaintiffs in the various actions to identify witnesses the Committee should interview. The Federal Class Action plaintiffs identified ten such persons and the Committee interviewed all but one, who refused to cooperate. The Delaware Derivative Action plaintiffs and the other derivative plaintiffs declined to provide the SLC with any witness list or to meet with the SLC.

During the course of the investigation, the SLC met with its counsel thirty-five times for a total of eighty hours. In addition to that, the SLC members, particularly Professor Grundfest, devoted many more hours to the investigation.

In the end, the SLC produced an extremely lengthy Report totaling 1,110 pages (excluding appendices and exhibits) that concluded that Oracle should not pursue the plaintiffs' claims against the Trading Defendants or any of the other Oracle directors serving during the 3Q FY 2001. * * *

III. THE APPLICABLE PROCEDURAL STANDARD

In order to prevail on its motion to terminate the Delaware Derivative Action, the SLC must persuade me that: (1) its members were independent; (2) that they acted in good faith; and (3) that they had reasonable bases for their recommendations. If the SLC meets that burden, I am free to grant its motion or may, in my discretion, undertake my own examination of whether Oracle should terminate and permit the suit to proceed if I, in my oxymoronic judicial "business judgment," conclude that procession is in the best interests of the company. This two-step analysis comes, of course, from *Zapata*.

As I understand it, this standard requires me to determine whether, on the basis of the undisputed factual record, I am convinced that the SLC was independent, acted in good faith, and had a reasonable basis for its recommendation. If there is a material factual question about these issues causing doubt about any of these grounds, I read *Zapata* and its progeny as requiring a denial of the SLC's motion to terminate.[20]

---

20. *See Lewis v. Fuqua*, 502 A.2d 962, 966 (Del.Ch.1985); *Kaplan v. Wyatt*, 484 A.2d 501, 506–08 (Del.Ch.1984), *aff'd*, 499 A.2d 1184 (Del.1985). Importantly, the

IV. IS THE SLC INDEPENDENT?

A. *The Facts Disclosed in the Report*

In its Report, the SLC took the position that its members were independent. In support of that position, the Report noted several factors including:

- the fact that neither Grundfest nor Garcia–Molina received compensation from Oracle other than as directors;
- the fact that neither Grundfest nor Garcia–Molina were on the Oracle board at the time of the alleged wrongdoing;
- the fact that both Grundfest and Garcia–Molina were willing to return their compensation as SLC members if necessary to preserve their status as independent;
- the absence of any other material ties between Oracle, the Trading Defendants, and any of the other defendants, on the one hand, and Grundfest and Garcia–Molina, on the other; and
- the absence of any material ties between Oracle, the Trading Defendants, and any of the other defendants, on the one hand, and the SLC's advisors, on the other.

Noticeably absent from the SLC Report was any disclosure of several significant ties between Oracle or the Trading Defendants and Stanford University, the university that employs both members of the SLC. In the Report, it was only disclosed that:

- defendant Boskin was a Stanford professor;
- the SLC members were aware that Lucas had made certain donations to Stanford; and
- among the contributions was a donation of $50,000 worth of stock that Lucas donated to Stanford Law School after Grundfest delivered a speech to a venture capital fund meeting in response to Lucas's request. It happens that Lucas's son is a partner in the fund and that approximately half the donation was allocated for use by Grundfest in his personal research.

B. *The "Stanford" Facts that Emerged During Discovery*

In view of the modesty of these disclosed ties, it was with some shock that a series of other ties among Stanford, Oracle, and the Trading Defendants emerged during discovery. Although the plaintiffs have embellished these ties considerably beyond what is reasonable, the plain facts are a striking departure from the picture presented in the Report.

granting of the SLC's motion using the Rule 56 standard does not mean that the court has made a determination that the claims the SLC wants dismissed would be subject to termination on a summary judgment motion, only that the court is satisfied that there is no material factual dispute that the SLC had a reasonable basis for its decision to seek termination. *See Kaplan v. Wyatt*, 484 A.2d 501, 519 (Del.Ch.1984) ("[I]t is the Special Litigation Committee which is under examination at this first-step stage of the proceedings, and not the merits of the plaintiff's cause of action."), *aff'd*, 499 A.2d 1184 (Del.1985).

Before discussing these facts, I begin with certain features of the record—as I read it—that are favorable to the SLC. Initially, I am satisfied that neither of the SLC members is compromised by a fear that support for the procession of this suit would endanger his ability to make a nice living. Both of the SLC members are distinguished in their fields and highly respected. Both have tenure, which could not have been stripped from them for making a determination that this lawsuit should proceed.

Nor have the plaintiffs developed evidence that either Grundfest or Garcia–Molina have fundraising responsibilities at Stanford. Although Garcia–Molina is a department chairman, the record is devoid of any indication that he is required to generate contributions. And even though Grundfest heads up Stanford's Directors' College, the plaintiffs have not argued that he has a fundraising role in that regard. For this reason, it is important to acknowledge up front that the SLC members occupy positions within the Stanford community different from that of the University's President, deans, and development professionals, all of whom, it can be reasonably assumed, are required to engage heavily in the pursuit of contributions to the University.

This is an important point of departure for discussing the multitude of ties that have emerged among the Trading Defendants, Oracle, and Stanford during discovery in this case. In evaluating these ties, the court is not faced with the relatively easier call of considering whether these ties would call into question the impartiality of an SLC member who was a key fundraiser at Stanford[21] or who was an untenured faculty member subject to removal without cause. Instead, one must acknowledge that the question is whether the ties I am about to identify would be of a material concern to two distinguished, tenured faculty members whose current jobs would not be threatened by whatever good faith decision they made as SLC members.

1. *Boskin*

Defendant Michael J. Boskin is the T.M. Friedman Professor of Economics at Stanford University. During the Administration of President George H.W. Bush, Boskin occupied the coveted and important position of Chairman of the President's Council of Economic Advisors.

---

21. *Compare In re The Limited, Inc. S'holders Litig.*, 2002 WL 537692, at *6–*7 (Del.Ch. Mar. 27, 2002) (concluding that a university president who had solicited a $25 million contribution from a corporation's President, Chairman, and CEO was not independent of that corporate official in light of the sense of "owingness" that the university president might harbor with respect to the corporate official), *and Lewis v. Fuqua*, 502 A.2d 962, 966–67 (Del.Ch.1985) (finding that a special litigation committee member was not independent where the committee member was also the president of a university that received a $10 million charitable pledge from the corporation's CEO and the CEO was a trustee of the university), *with In re Walt Disney Co. Derivative Litig.*, 731 A.2d 342, 359 (Del.Ch. 1998) (deciding that the plaintiffs had not created reasonable doubt as to a director's independence where a corporation's Chairman and CEO had given over $1 million in donations to the university at which the director was the university president and from which one of the CEO's sons had graduated), *aff'd in part, rev'd in part sub nom. Brehm v. Eisner*, 746 A.2d 244 (Del. 2000).

He returned to Stanford after this government service, continuing a teaching career there that had begun many years earlier.

During the 1970s, Boskin taught Grundfest when Grundfest was a Ph.D. candidate. Although Boskin was not Grundfest's advisor and although they do not socialize, the two have remained in contact over the years, speaking occasionally about matters of public policy.

Furthermore, both Boskin and Grundfest are senior fellows and steering committee members at the Stanford Institute for Economic Policy Research, which was previously defined as "SIEPR." According to the SLC, the title of senior fellow is largely an honorary one. According to SIEPR's own web site, however, "[s]enior fellows actively participate in SIEPR research and participate in its governance."

Likewise, the SLC contends that Grundfest went MIA as a steering committee member, having failed to attend a meeting since 1997. The SIEPR web site, however, identifies its steering committee as having the role of "advising the director [of SIEPR] and guiding [SIEPR] on matters pertaining to research and academics." Because Grundfest allegedly did not attend to these duties, his service alongside Boskin in that capacity is, the SLC contends, not relevant to his independence.

That said, the SLC does not deny that both Boskin and Grundfest publish working papers under the SIEPR rubric and that SIEPR helps to publicize their respective works. Indeed, as I will note later in this opinion, Grundfest, in the same month the SLC was formed, addressed a meeting of some of SIEPR's largest benefactors—the so-called "SIEPR Associates." The SLC just claims that the SIEPR affiliation is one in which SIEPR basks in the glow of Boskin and Grundfest, not the other way around, and that the mutual service of the two as senior fellows and steering committee members is not a collegial tie of any significance.

2. *Lucas*

As noted in the SLC Report, the SLC members admitted knowing that Lucas was a contributor to Stanford. They also acknowledged that he had donated $50,000 to Stanford Law School in appreciation for Grundfest having given a speech at his request. About half of the proceeds were allocated for use by Grundfest in his research.

But Lucas's ties with Stanford are far, far richer than the SLC Report lets on. To begin, Lucas is a Stanford alumnus, having obtained both his undergraduate and graduate degrees there. By any measure, he has been a very loyal alumnus.

Lucas's connections with Stanford as a contributor go beyond [a foundation of which Lucas is Chairman] however. From his own personal funds, Lucas has contributed $4.1 million to Stanford, a substantial percentage of which has been donated within the last half-decade. Notably, Lucas has, among other things, donated $424,000 to SIEPR and approximately $149,000 to Stanford Law School. Indeed, Lucas is not only a major contributor to SIEPR, he is the Chair of its Advisory Board.

At SIEPR's facility at Stanford, the conference center is named the Donald L. Lucas Conference Center

From these undisputed facts, it is inarguable that Lucas is a very important alumnus of Stanford and a generous contributor to not one, but two, parts of Stanford important to Grundfest: the Law School and SIEPR.

With these facts in mind, it remains to enrich the factual stew further, by considering defendant Ellison's ties to Stanford.

3. *Ellison*

There can be little doubt that Ellison is a major figure in the community in which Stanford is located. The so-called Silicon Valley has generated many success stories, among the greatest of which is that of Oracle and its leader, Ellison. One of the wealthiest men in America, Ellison is a major figure in the nation's increasingly important information technology industry. Given his wealth, Ellison is also in a position to make—and, in fact, he has made—major charitable contributions.

[Vice-ChancellorStrine details Ellisado Contributors' to Stanford]

Taken together, these facts suggest that Ellison (when considered as an individual and as the key executive and major stockholder of Oracle) had, at the very least, been involved in several endeavors of value to Stanford.

C. *The SLC's Argument*

The SLC contends that even together, these facts regarding the ties among Oracle, the Trading Defendants, Stanford, and the SLC members do not impair the SLC's independence. In so arguing, the SLC places great weight on the fact that none of the Trading Defendants have the practical ability to deprive either Grundfest or Garcia–Molina of their current positions at Stanford. Nor, given their tenure, does Stanford itself have any practical ability to punish them for taking action adverse to Boskin, Lucas, or Ellison—each of whom, as we have seen, has contributed (in one way or another) great value to Stanford as an institution. As important, neither Garcia–Molina nor Grundfest are part of the official fundraising apparatus at Stanford; thus, it is not their on-the-job duty to be solicitous of contributors, and fundraising success does not factor into their treatment as professors.

In so arguing, the SLC focuses on the language of previous opinions of this court and the Delaware Supreme Court that indicates that a director is not independent only if he is dominated and controlled by an interested party, such as a Trading Defendant. The SLC also emphasizes that much of our jurisprudence on independence focuses on economically consequential relationships between the allegedly interested party and the directors who allegedly cannot act independently of that director. Put another way, much of our law focuses the bias inquiry on whether there are economically material ties between the interested party and the director whose impartiality is questioned, treating the possible effect on one's personal wealth as the key to the independence inquiry. Putting a point on this, the SLC cites certain decisions of Delaware courts concluding that directors who are personal friends of an interested party were not, by virtue of those personal ties, to be labeled non-independent.

More subtly, the SLC argues that university professors simply are not inhibited types, unwilling to make tough decisions even as to fellow professors and large contributors. What is tenure about if not to provide professors with intellectual freedom, even in non-traditional roles such as special litigation committee members? No less ardently—but with no record evidence that reliably supports its ultimate point—the SLC contends that Garcia–Molina and Grundfest are extremely distinguished in their fields and were not, in fact, influenced by the facts identified heretofore. Indeed, the SLC argues, how could they have been influenced by many of these facts when they did not learn them until the post-Report discovery process? If it boils down to the simple fact that both share with Boskin the status of a Stanford professor, how material can this be when there are 1,700 others who also occupy the same position?

E. *The Court's Analysis of the SLC's Independence*

Having framed the competing views of the parties, it is now time to decide.

I begin with an important reminder: the SLC bears the burden of proving its independence. It must convince me.

But of what? According to the SLC, its members are independent unless they are essentially subservient to the Trading Defendants—*i.e.,* they are under the "domination and control" of the interested parties. If the SLC is correct and this is the central inquiry in the independence determination, they would win. Nothing in the record suggests to me that either Garcia–Molina or Grundfest are dominated and controlled by any of the Trading Defendants, by Oracle, or even by Stanford.

But, in my view, an emphasis on "domination and control" would serve only to fetishize much-parroted language, at the cost of denuding the independence inquiry of its intellectual integrity. Take an easy example. Imagine if two brothers were on a corporate board, each successful in different businesses and not dependent in any way on the other's beneficence in order to be wealthy. The brothers are brothers, they stay in touch and consider each other family, but each is opinionated and strong-willed. A derivative action is filed targeting a transaction involving one of the brothers. The other brother is put on a special litigation committee to investigate the case. If the test is domination and control, then one brother could investigate the other. Does any sensible person think that is our law? I do not think it is.

And it should not be our law. Delaware law should not be based on a reductionist view of human nature that simplifies human motivations on the lines of the least sophisticated notions of the law and economics movement. *Homo sapiens* is not merely *homo economicus*. We may be thankful that an array of other motivations exist that influence human behavior; not all are any better than greed or avarice, think of envy, to name just one. But also think of motives like love, friendship, and collegiality, think of those among us who direct their behavior as best they can on a guiding creed or set of moral values.

Nor should our law ignore the social nature of humans. To be direct, corporate directors are generally the sort of people deeply enmeshed in social institutions. Such institutions have norms, expectations that, explicitly and implicitly, influence and channel the behavior of those who participate in their operation. Some things are "just not done," or only at a cost, which might not be so severe as a loss of position, but may involve a loss of standing in the institution. In being appropriately sensitive to this factor, our law also cannot assume—absent some proof of the point—that corporate directors are, as a general matter, persons of unusual social bravery, who operate heedless to the inhibitions that social norms generate for ordinary folk.

For all these reasons, this court has previously held that the Delaware Supreme Court's teachings on independence can be summarized thusly:

> At bottom, the question of independence turns on whether a director is, *for any substantial reason,* incapable of making a decision with only the best interests of the corporation in mind. That is, the Supreme Court cases ultimately focus on impartiality and objectivity.

This formulation is wholly consistent with the teaching of *Aronson,* which defines independence as meaning that "a director's decision is based on the corporate merits of the subject before the board rather than extraneous considerations or influences." As noted by Chancellor Chandler recently, a director may be compromised if he is beholden to an interested person. Beholden in this sense does not mean just owing in the financial sense, it can also flow out of "personal or other relationships" to the interested party.

Without backtracking from these general propositions, it would be less than candid if I did not admit that Delaware courts have applied these general standards in a manner that has been less than wholly consistent. Different decisions take a different view about the bias-producing potential of family relationships, not all of which can be explained by mere degrees of consanguinity. Likewise, there is admittedly case law that gives little weight to ties of friendship in the independence inquiry. In this opinion, I will not venture to do what I believe to be impossible: attempt to rationalize all these cases in their specifics.[55] Rather, I undertake what I understand to be my duty and what is

---

55. I readily concede that the result I reach is in tension with the specific outcomes of certain other decisions. But I do not believe that the result I reach applies a new definition of independence; rather, it recognizes the importance (*i.e.,* the materiality) of other bias-creating factors other than fear that acting a certain way will invite economic retribution by the interested directors.

possible: the application of the independence inquiry that our Supreme Court has articulated in a manner that is faithful to its essential spirit.

1. *The Contextual Nature of the Independence Inquiry Under Delaware Law*

In examining whether the SLC has met its burden to demonstrate that there is no material dispute of fact regarding its independence, the court must bear in mind the function of special litigation committees under our jurisprudence. Under Delaware law, the primary means by which corporate defendants may obtain a dismissal of a derivative suit is by showing that the plaintiffs have not met their pleading burden under the test of *Aronson v. Lewis,* or the related standard set forth in *Rales v. Blasband.* In simple terms, these tests permit a corporation to terminate a derivative suit if its board is comprised of directors who can impartially consider a demand.

In evaluating the independence of a special litigation committee, this court must take into account the extraordinary importance and difficulty of such a committee's responsibility. It is, I daresay, easier to say no to a friend, relative, colleague, or boss who seeks assent for an act (*e.g.,* a transaction) that has not yet occurred than it would be to cause a corporation to sue that person. This is admittedly a determination of so-called "legislative fact," but one that can be rather safely made. Denying a fellow director the ability to proceed on a matter important to him may not be easy, but it must, as a general matter, be less difficult than finding that there is reason to believe that the fellow director has committed serious wrongdoing and that a derivative suit should proceed against him.

The difficulty of making this decision is compounded in the special litigation committee context because the weight of making the moral judgment necessarily falls on less than the full board. A small number of directors feels the moral gravity—and social pressures—of this duty alone.

For all these reasons, the independence inquiry is critically important if the special litigation committee process is to retain its integrity, a quality that is, in turn, essential to the utility of that process.

* * *

In assessing the independence of the Oracle SLC, I necessarily examine the question of whether the SLC can independently make the difficult decision entrusted to it: to determine whether the Trading Defendants should face suit for insider trading-based allegations of breach of fiduciary duty. An affirmative answer by the SLC to that question would have potentially huge negative consequences for the Trading Defendants, not only by exposing them to the possibility of a large damage award but also by subjecting them to great reputational harm. To have Professors Grundfest and Garcia–Molina declare that Oracle should press insider trading claims against the Trading Defendants would have been, to put it mildly, "news." Relatedly, it is reasonable to think that an SLC determination that the Trading Defendants had likely engaged in insider trading would have been accompanied by a recommendation that they step down as fiduciaries until their ultimate culpability was decided.

Therefore, I necessarily measure the SLC's independence contextually, and my ruling confronts the SLC's ability to decide impartially whether the Trading Defendants should be pursued for insider trading. This contextual approach is a strength of our law, as even the best minds have yet to devise across-the-board definitions that capture all the circumstances in which the independence of directors might reasonably be questioned. By taking into account all circumstances, the Delaware approach undoubtedly results in some level of indeterminacy, but with the compensating benefit that independence determinations are tailored to the precise situation at issue.

2. *The SLC Has Not Met Its Burden to Demonstrate the Absence of a Material Dispute of Fact About Its Independence*

Using the contextual approach I have described, I conclude that the SLC has not met its burden to show the absence of a material factual question about its independence. I find this to be the case because the ties among the SLC, the Trading Defendants, and Stanford are so substantial that they cause reasonable doubt about the SLC's ability to impartially consider whether the Trading Defendants should face suit. The concern that arises from these ties can be stated fairly simply, focusing on defendants Boskin, Lucas, and Ellison in that order, and then collectively.

As SLC members, Grundfest and Garcia–Molina were already being asked to consider whether the company should level extremely serious accusations of wrongdoing against fellow board members. As to Boskin, both SLC members faced another layer of complexity: the determination of whether to have Oracle press insider trading claims against a fellow professor at their university. Even though Boskin was in a different academic department from either SLC member, it is reasonable to assume that the fact that Boskin was also on faculty would—to persons possessing typical sensibilities and institutional loyalty—be a matter of more than trivial concern. Universities are obviously places of at-times intense debate, but they also see themselves as communities. In fact, Stanford refers to itself as a "community of scholars." To accuse a fellow professor—whom one might see at the faculty club or at inter-disciplinary presentations of academic papers—of insider trading cannot be a small thing—even for the most callous of academics.

As to Boskin, Grundfest faced an even more complex challenge than Garcia–Molina. Boskin was a professor who had taught him and with whom he had maintained contact over the years. Their areas of academic interest intersected, putting Grundfest in contact if not directly with Boskin, then regularly with Boskin's colleagues. Moreover, although I am told by the SLC that the title of senior fellow at SIEPR is an honorary one, the fact remains that Grundfest willingly accepted it and was one of a select number of faculty who attained that status. And, they both just happened to also be steering committee members. Having these ties, Grundfest would have more difficulty objectively determining whether Boskin engaged in improper insider trading than would a person who was not a fellow professor, had not been a student of Boskin, had not kept in touch with Boskin over the years, and who was not a senior fellow and steering committee member at SIEPR.

In so concluding, I necessarily draw on a general sense of human nature. It may be that Grundfest is a very special person who is capable of putting these kinds of things totally aside. But the SLC has not provided evidence that that is the case. In this respect, it is critical to note that I do not infer that Grundfest would be less likely to recommend suit against Boskin than someone without these ties. Human nature being what it is, it is entirely possible that Grundfest would in fact be tougher on Boskin than he would on someone with whom he did not have such connections. The inference I draw is subtly, but importantly, different. What I infer is that a person in Grundfest's position would find it difficult to assess Boskin's conduct without pondering his own association with Boskin and their mutual affiliations. Although these connections might produce bias in either a tougher or laxer direction, the key inference is that these connections would be on the mind of a person in Grundfest's position, putting him in the position of either causing serious legal action to be brought against a person with whom he shares several connections (an awkward thing) or not doing so (and risking being seen as having engaged in favoritism toward his old professor and SIEPR colleague).

The same concerns also exist as to Lucas. For Grundfest to vote to accuse Lucas of insider trading would require him to accuse SIEPR's Advisory Board Chair and major benefactor of serious wrongdoing—of conduct that violates federal securities laws. Such action would also require Grundfest to make charges against a man who recently donated $50,000 to Stanford Law School after Grundfest made a speech at his request.

And, for both Grundfest and Garcia–Molina, service on the SLC demanded that they consider whether an extremely generous and influential Stanford alumnus should be sued by Oracle for insider trading. Although they were not responsible for fundraising, as sophisticated professors they undoubtedly are aware of how important large contributors are to Stanford, and they share in the benefits that come from serving at a university with a rich endowment. A reasonable professor giving any thought to the matter would obviously consider the effect his decision might have on the University's relationship with Lucas, it being (one hopes) sensible to infer that a professor of reasonable collegiality and loyalty cares about the well-being of the institution he serves.

In so concluding, I give little weight to the SLC's argument that it was unaware of just how substantial Lucas's beneficence to Stanford has been. I do so for two key reasons. Initially, it undermines, rather than inspires, confidence that the SLC did not examine the Trading Defendants' ties to Stanford more closely in preparing its Report. The Report's failure to identify these ties is important because it is the SLC's burden to show independence. In forming the SLC, the Oracle board should have undertaken a thorough consideration of the facts bearing on the independence of the proposed SLC members from the key objects of the investigation.

The purported ignorance of the SLC members about all of Lucas's donations to Stanford is not helpful to them for another reason: there were too many visible manifestations of Lucas's status as a major contributor for me to conclude that Grundfest, at the very least, did not understand Lucas to be an extremely generous benefactor of Stanford. * * * Combined with the other obvious indicia of Lucas's large contributor status (including the $50,000 donation Lucas made to Stanford Law School to thank Grundfest for giving a speech) and Lucas's obviously keen interest in his alma mater, Grundfest would have had to be extremely insensitive to his own working environment not to have considered Lucas an extremely generous alumni benefactor of Stanford, and at SIEPR and the Law School in particular.

In concluding that the facts regarding Lucas's relationship with Stanford are materially important, I must address a rather odd argument of the SLC's. The argument goes as follows. Stanford has an extremely large endowment. Lucas's contributions, while seemingly large, constitute a very small proportion of Stanford's endowment and annual donations. Therefore, Lucas could not be a materially important contributor to Stanford and the SLC's independence could not be compromised by that factor.

But missing from that syllogism is any acknowledgment of the role that Stanford's solicitude to benefactors like Lucas might play in the overall size of its endowment and campus facilities. Endowments and buildings grow one contribution at a time, and they do not grow by callous indifference to alumni who (personally and through family foundations) have participated in directing contributions of the size Lucas has. Buildings and conference centers are named as they are as a recognition of the high regard universities have for donors (or at least, must feign convincingly). The SLC asks me to believe that what universities like Stanford say in thank you letters and public ceremonies is not in reality true; that, in actuality, their contributors are not materially important to the health of those academic institutions. This is a proposition that the SLC has not convinced me is true, and that seems to contradict common experience.

Nor has the SLC convinced me that tenured faculty are indifferent to large contributors to their institutions, such that a tenured faculty member would not be worried about writing a report finding that a suit by the corporation should proceed against a large contributor and that there was credible evidence that he had engaged in illegal insider trading. The idea that faculty members would not be concerned that action of that kind might offend a large contributor who a university administrator or fellow faculty colleague (*e.g.*, Shoven at SIEPR) had taken the time to cultivate strikes me as implausible and as resting on an narrow-minded understanding of the way that collegiality works in institutional settings.

In view of the ties involving Boskin and Lucas alone, I would conclude that the SLC has failed to meet its burden on the independence question. The tantalizing facts about Ellison merely reinforce this conclusion. The SLC, of course, argues that Ellison is not a large benefactor of Stanford personally, that Stanford has demonstrated its independence of him by rejecting his child for admission, and that, in any event, the SLC was ignorant of any negotiations between Ellison and Stanford about a large contribution. For these reasons, the SLC says, its ability to act independently of Ellison is clear.

I find differently. The notion that anyone in Palo Alto can accuse Ellison of insider trading without harboring some fear of social awkwardness seems a stretch. That being said, I do not mean to imply that the mere fact that Ellison is worth tens of billions of dollars and is the key force behind a very important social institution in Silicon Valley disqualifies all persons who live there from being independent of him. Rather, it is merely an acknowledgement of the simple fact that accusing such a significant person in that community of such serious wrongdoing is no small thing.

[T]he SLC [also] contends that neither SLC member was aware of Ellison's relationship with Stanford until after the Report was completed. Thus, this relationship, in its various facets, could not have compromised their independence. Again, I find this argument from ignorance to be unavailing. An inquiry into Ellison's connections with Stanford should have been conducted before the SLC was finally formed and, at the very least, should have been undertaken in connection with the Report. In any event, given how public Ellison was about his possible donations it is difficult not to harbor troublesome doubt about whether the SLC members were conscious of the possibility that Ellison was pondering a large contribution to Stanford. In so concluding, I am not saying that the SLC members are being untruthful in saying that they did not know of the facts that have emerged, only that these facts were in very prominent journals at the time the SLC members were doing due diligence in aid of deciding whether to sign on as Oracle board members. The objective circumstances of Ellison's relations with Stanford therefore generate a reasonable suspicion that seasoned faculty members of some sophistication—including the two SLC members—would have viewed Ellison as an active and prized target for the University. The objective circumstances also require a finding that Ellison was already, through his personal Foundation and Oracle itself, a benefactor of Stanford.

Taken in isolation, the facts about Ellison might well not be enough to compromise the SLC's independence. But that is not the relevant inquiry. The pertinent question is whether, given *all* the facts, the SLC has met its independence burden.

When viewed in that manner, the facts about Ellison buttress the conclusion that the SLC has not met its burden. Whether the SLC members had precise knowledge of all the facts that have emerged is not essential, what is important is that by any measure this was a social atmosphere painted in too much vivid Stanford Cardinal red for the SLC members to have reasonably ignored it. Summarized fairly, two Stanford professors were recruited to the Oracle board in summer 2001 and soon asked to investigate a fellow professor and two benefactors of the University. On Grundfest's part, the facts are more substantial, because his connections—through his personal experiences, SIEPR, and the Law School—to Boskin and to Lucas run deeper.

It seems to me that the connections outlined in this opinion would weigh on the mind of a reasonable special litigation committee member deciding whether to level the serious charge of insider trading against the Trading Defendants. As indicated before, this does not mean that the SLC would be less inclined to find such charges meritorious, only that the connections identified would be on the mind of the SLC members in a way that generates an unacceptable risk of bias. That is, these connections generate a reasonable doubt about the SLC's impartiality because they suggest that material considerations other than the best interests of Oracle could have influenced the SLC's inquiry and judgments.

Before closing, it is necessary to address two concerns. The first is the undeniable awkwardness of opinions like this one. By finding that there exists too much doubt about the SLC's independence for the SLC to meet its *Zapata* burden, I make no finding about the subjective good faith of the SLC members, both of whom are distinguished academics at one of this nation's most prestigious institutions of higher learning. Nothing in this record leads me to conclude that either of the SLC members acted out of any conscious desire to favor the Trading Defendants or to do anything other than discharge their duties with fidelity. But that is not the purpose of the independence inquiry.

That inquiry recognizes that persons of integrity and reputation can be compromised in their ability to act without bias when they must make a decision adverse to others with whom they share material affiliations. To conclude that the Oracle SLC was not independent is not a conclusion that the two accomplished professors who comprise it are not persons of good faith and moral probity, it is solely to conclude that they were not situated to act with the required degree of impartiality. *Zapata* requires independence to ensure that stockholders do not have to rely upon special litigation committee members who must put aside personal considerations that are ordinarily influential in daily behavior in making the already difficult decision to accuse fellow directors of serious wrongdoing.

Finally, the SLC has made the argument that a ruling against it will chill the ability of corporations to locate qualified independent directors in the academy. This is overwrought. If there are 1,700 professors at Stanford alone, as the SLC says, how many must there be on the west coast of the United States, at institutions without ties to Oracle and the Trading Defendants as substantial as Stanford's? Undoubtedly, a corporation of Oracle's market capitalization could have found prominent academics willing to serve as SLC members, about whom no reasonable question of independence could have been asserted.

Rather than form an SLC whose membership was free from bias-creating relationships, Oracle formed a committee fraught with them. As a result, the SLC has failed to meet its *Zapata* burden, and its motion to terminate must be denied. Because of this reality, I do not burden the reader with an examination of the other *Zapata* factors. In the absence of a finding that the SLC was independent, its subjective good faith and the reasonableness of its conclusions would not be sufficient to justify termination. Without confidence that the SLC was impartial, its findings do not provide the assurance our law requires for the dismissal of a derivative suit without a merits inquiry.

How Far Does Oracle *Reach?*

The Delaware Supreme Court appears undecided on how far *Oracle*'s behavioral analysis should reach. On one hand, *Oracle* might be seen applying only to directorial independence on a special litigation committee. Or, on the other, the decision might be seen as applying generally to judicial measurement of board independence, including in such contexts as whether a pre-suit demand on the board would be futile (see Chapter 20). In *Beam ex. rel. Martha Stewart Living Omnimedia, Inc.* v. *Stewart*, 845 A.2d 1040 (Del. 2004), the court both limited *Oracle* to the specific context of the independence of a special litigation committee and suggested that specific allegations of friendship might affect the determination of independence when considering demand futility.

In *Beam*, the plaintiff had alleged that Martha Stewart breached her duties of loyalty and care by selling ImClone stock and making misleading statements to the media thereafter. Relying on *Oracle*, the plaintiff contended that demand was futile because social and business connections created a reasonable doubt as to the independence of a majority of the board of directors. The Court of Chancery held that demand was required because the plaintiff had been unable to allege specific facts to demonstrate a lack of independence, and the Delaware Supreme Court affirmed.

Addressing the question of personal friendship, the Delaware Supreme Court returned to earlier jurisprudence (recall that in *Oracle*, Vice–Chancellor Strine noted that his decision was inconsistent with some Delaware opinions), stating:

A variety of motivations, including friendship, may influence the demand futility inquiry. But, to render a director unable to consider demand, a relationship must be of a bias-producing nature. Allegations of mere personal friendship or a mere outside business relationship, standing alone, are insufficient to raise a reasonable doubt about a director's independence. In this connection, we adopt as our own the Chancellor's analysis in this case:

> [S]ome professional or personal friendships, which may border on or even exceed familial loyalty and closeness, may raise a reasonable doubt whether a director can appropriately consider demand. This is particularly true when the allegations raise serious questions of either civil or criminal liability of such a close friend. Not all friendships, or even most of them, rise to this level and the Court cannot make a *reasonable* inference that a particular friendship does so without specific factual allegations to support such a conclusion. [833 A.2d at 979 (footnotes omitted).]

The facts alleged by Beam regarding the relationships between Stewart and these other members of MSO's board of directors largely boil down to a "structural bias" argument, which presupposes that the professional and social relationships that naturally develop among members of a board impede independent decisionmaking.

Critics will charge that [by requiring the independence of only a majority of the board] we are ignoring the structural bias common to corporate boards throughout America, as well as the other unseen socialization processes cutting against independent discussion and decisionmaking in the boardroom. The difficulty with structural bias in a demand futile case is simply one of establishing it in the complaint for purposes of Rule 23.1. We are satisfied that discretionary review by the Court of Chancery of complaints alleging specific facts pointing to bias on a particular board will be sufficient for determining demand futility.

In the present case, the plaintiff attempted to plead affinity beyond mere friendship between Stewart and the other directors, but her attempt is not sufficient to demonstrate demand futility. Even if the alleged friendships may have preceded the directors' membership on MSO's board and did not necessarily arise out of that membership, these relationships are of the same nature as those giving rise to the structural bias argument.

Allegations that Stewart and the other directors moved in the same social circles, attended the same weddings, developed business relationships before joining the board, and described each other as "friends," even when coupled with Stewart's 94% voting power, are insufficient, without more, to rebut the presumption of independence. They do not provide a sufficient basis from which reasonably to infer that Martinez, Moore and Seligman may have been beholden to Stewart. Whether they arise before board membership or later as a result of collegial relationships among the board of directors, such affinities—standing alone—will not render presuit demand futile.

That is not to say that personal friendship is always irrelevant to the independence calculus. But, for presuit demand purposes, friendship must be accompanied by substantially more in the nature of serious allegations that would lead to a reasonable doubt as to a director's independence. That a much stronger relationship is necessary to overcome the presumption of independence at the demand futility stage becomes especially compelling when one considers the risks that directors would take by protecting their social acquaintances in the face of allegations that those friends engaged in misconduct. To create a reasonable doubt about an outside director's independence, a plaintiff must plead facts that would support the inference that because of the nature of a relationship or additional circumstances other than the interested director's stock ownership or voting power, the non-interested director would be more willing to risk his or her reputation than risk the relationship with the interested director.

Id. at 1050–2.

The Delaware Supreme Court (in a separate section titled "A Word About the Oracle Case") addressed specifically the meaning of *Oracle*.

> In his opinion, the Chancellor referred several times to the Delaware Court of Chancery decision in *In re Oracle Corp. Derivative Litigation*. Indeed, the plaintiff relies on the *Oracle* case in this appeal. *Oracle* involved the issue of the independence of the Special Litigation Committee (SLC) appointed by the Oracle board to determine whether or not the corporation should cause the dismissal of a corporate claim by stockholder-plaintiffs against directors. The Court of Chancery undertook a searching inquiry of the relationships between the members of the SLC and Stanford University in the context of the financial support of Stanford by the corporation and its management. The Vice Chancellor concluded, after considering the SLC Report and the discovery record, that those relationships were too close for purposes of the SLC analysis of independence.
>
> We need not decide whether the substantive standard of independence in an SLC case differs from that in a presuit demand case. As a practical matter, the procedural distinction relating to the diametrically-opposed burdens and the availability of discovery into independence may be outcome-determinative on the issue of independence. Moreover, because the members of an SLC are vested with enormous power to seek dismissal of a derivative suit brought against their director-colleagues in a setting where presuit demand is already excused, the Court of Chancery must exercise careful oversight of the bona fides of the SLC and its process. Aside from the procedural distinctions, the Stanford connections in *Oracle* are factually distinct from the relationships present here.

Id. at 1054–55.

While thus seeming to limit *Oracle*, the Delaware Supreme Court continued to reiterate a consistent theme found in its other demand futility opinions: the usefulness of inspection rights afforded by Section 220 to obtain facts that might create a reasonable doubt as to directorial independence:

> Beam's failure to plead sufficient facts to support her claim of demand futility may be due in part to her failure to exhaust all

reasonably available means of gathering facts. As the Chancellor noted, had Beam first brought a Section 220 action seeking inspection of MSO's books and records, she might have uncovered facts that would have created a reasonable doubt. For example, irregularities or "cronyism" in MSO's process of nominating board members might possibly strengthen her claim concerning Stewart's control over MSO's directors. A books and records inspection might have revealed whether the board used a nominating committee to select directors and maintained a separation between the director-selection process and management. A books and records inspection might also have revealed whether Stewart unduly controlled the nominating process or whether the process incorporated procedural safeguards to ensure directors' independence. Beam might also have reviewed the minutes of the board's meetings to determine how the directors handled Stewart's proposals or conduct in various contexts. Whether or not the result of this exploration might create a reasonable doubt would be sheer speculation at this stage. But the point is that it was within the plaintiff's power to explore these matters and she elected not to make the effort.

Id. at 1056–57.

Together with the court's observation that personal friendships are not "always irrelevant to the independence calculus," it is possible that the court is leaving open a broader concept of independence. On the other hand, the court also indicated that it might revisit *Oracle* in the future, noting that "[i]n *Oracle* we declined to accept an interlocutory appeal last year. That matter may come before us at some time in the future. *Id.* at 1055, n.44. *See also*, Paul K. Rowe and Trevor S. Norwitz, *Delaware Affirms That Director Independence Can Coexist with Social Ties and "Friendship" with Management*, 12 CORP. GOVERNANCE ADVISOR No.3, p.31 (May/June 2004) ("*Beam* represents an important restatement of the fundamental principle of corporate governance—the presumption that non-management directors are independent (even if they occasionally play golf with the CEO or attend his child's wedding) unless there is real evidence to the contrary.")

The Attorney as Director

We have already considered the question of whether a lawyer should be a director of her client's corporation. One risk of doing so, as the discussion of Russell in *Disney* makes clear, is that the lawyer-director's independence is likely to be called into question when there is a conflict of interest transaction on which she is asked to vote. The problem is particularly acute when the lawyer is an employee of the corporation but it is also difficult when the lawyer is outside counsel.

In *Gries Sports Enterprises, Inc. v. Cleveland Browns Football Co., Inc.*, 26 Ohio St.3d 15, 496 N.E.2d 959 (1986), the court found that both the outside and inside counsel (Berick and Bailey) were "interested" directors "because they had received a personal financial benefit from the challenged transaction" which was not equally shared by the stockholders. The court also held that under Delaware case law, Berick was dominated because it was his job to do what Modell (the principal stockholder, president and CEO) requested.

One justice dissented. In analyzing the position of Berick and Bailey, he questioned what he called "the majority's simplistic analysis that merely because Berick was an officer in the Browns, and functioned accordingly, that he was not an independent director."

Berick's disinterest is * * * attacked by asserting that he, as outside legal counsel through his law firm, planned and prepared both transactions. As a matter of law, the presence of outside directors enhances the presumption of validity attributable to a director's actions. *See, e.g., Puma v. Marriott*, 283 A.2d 693 (Del.Ch. 1971). In this case, the fee ultimately paid to Berick's firm for legal services was approximately twenty to twenty-five thousand dollars, which is asserted by appellants to be a financial interest in the outcome of the transaction. It is also asserted that because Modell offered to buy Berick's shares of Browns stock, that Berick was dominated by Modell.

However, the fee for services paid to Berick's firm was not at all dependent on the transactions at issue. Payment was owed and would have been made, despite the outcome of the board's vote. Nor was the law firm dependent on the Browns, since the Browns constituted less than one percent of that firm's business. Also, Berick refused to sell his shares of stock to Modell. Although Berick was enthusiastic concerning the acquisition of CSC, nothing about his opinion indicates anything other than a personal viewpoint. The fact that Berick sits as a director on the boards of a number of corporations, public and private, indicates a professional attitude. Thus, there was no dominance or tainting self-interest in his vote.

The majority fully misstates the law of Delaware by its statement that "Bailey's dual positions as an officer and general counsel for both corporations make him an 'interested' director." There are no Delaware cases which support this view. In fact, the cases utilized by the majority would agree that an interested director is one who is on both sides of the transaction, and who somehow wrongfully receives a benefit.

Bailey, who is in-house counsel to the Browns, is said to be an interested director because he helped to structure the two transactions. It was also alleged that Modell dominated him because he was presented to the board by Modell for the position of director and, at times, Modell sent Bailey to negotiate for him.

The law of Delaware makes it clear that positional relationships, without more, do not rise to disqualification of the director's vote. In the view of the Delaware Supreme Court, "it is not enough to charge that a director was nominated by or elected at the behest of those controlling the outcome of a corporate election. That is the usual way a person becomes a corporate director. It is the care, attention and sense of individual responsibility to the performance of one's duties, not the method of election, that generally touches on independence." [*Aronson v. Lewis*, 473 A.2d 805 (Del.1984).] "Such contentions do not support any claim under Delaware law that * * * directors lack independence." *Id.* at 815. Instead, it must be demonstrated that the directors "through personal or other relationships * * * are beholden to the controlling person." *Id.*

Because of Bailey's position, he would naturally have negotiated for the Browns and, consequently, Modell. He was approved as a director by the entire board, including Gries. At no time was there proof of any self-dealing by Bailey. He personally believed the Browns should acquire CSC so as to control the team's playing facilities. Mere like-mindedness on issues hardly rises to the level of domination or self-interest.

Id. at 977–78.

Are you persuaded by this analysis? Why was it written in dissent?"

Can Directors Be Truly Independent?

Professor Charles Elson questions whether most directors can truly be independent.

> There are three problems with a management-appointed board that leads to ineffective oversight. First, personal and psychic ties to the individuals who are responsible for one's appointment to a board make it difficult to engage in necessary confrontation. It is always tough to challenge a fiend, particularly when the challenging party may one day, as an officer of another enterprise, end up in the same position. Second, conflicts with a manager who is also a member of one's own board may lead to future retribution on one's own turf, thus reducing the incentive to act. Third, and most important, when one owes one's own board position to the largesse of management, any action taken that is inimical to management may result in a failure to be renominated to the board, which-given the large fees paid to directors (and the great reputational advantage of board membership)-malfunction as an effective club to stifle dissension. This is why the development of substantial director compensation, a consequence of management control, has acted to stifle board oversight of management, and has, in fact, enhanced management domination.

Charles M. Elson, *Director Compensation*, 50 S.M.U.L. Rev. 127, 161–162 (1996). See also, James D. Cox & Harry Munsinger, *Bias in the Boardroom: Psychological Foundations and Legal Implications of Corporate Cohesion*," Law and Contemp. Probs., Summer 1985, at 83, 98–99).

Recall the discussion in Chapter 16 of how independence is defined in the new NYSE and NASDAQ listing standards. To what extent are those standards likely to have an impact on courts' determinations of when a director is independent?

b. *Shareholder Approval*

An interested director transaction can also be found to be procedurally fair if it has been approved or subsequently ratified by shareholder vote provided that the material facts as to the transaction and the director's interest were disclosed to the shareholders. At common law, many cases held that if the terms of the transaction were substantively fair, the shares of the interested director could be voted in favor of ratification. Other decisions held that such shares could not be voted because interested directors could not ratify their own contracts with the corporation. Courts were divided as to whether a majority of informed shareholders could ratify a fraudulent transaction, or whether such ratification required unanimous approval. Where those issues did not arise, shareholder ratification created a presumption that the transaction was fair. Thus, some courts indicated that shareholder ratification has the effect of shifting the burden of proof to the party challenging the transaction to show that the terms were so unequal as to amount to waste. See *Gottlieb v. Heyden Chemical Corp.*, 91 A.2d 57 (Del.Ch.1952); *Eliasberg v. Standard Oil Co.*, 92 A.2d 862 (Ch.Div.1952), *aff'd* 97 A.2d 437 (N.J.1953). Where, however, the interested directors own a majority of the shares, shareholder ratification generally does not shift the burden of proving unfairness to the challenging party. See *Brundage v. New Jersey Zinc Co.*, 226 A.2d 585 (N.J.1967); *Pappas v. Moss*, 393 F.2d 865 (3d Cir.1968); *David J. Greene & Co. v. Dunhill International, Inc.*, 249 A.2d 427 (Del.Ch.1968).

It appears that the shareholder approval provision of the interested director statutes codify the common law. Thus an interested director transaction is not void or voidable if the director's interest is disclosed to the shareholders and the shareholders approve the transaction. However, technical compliance with the statutory procedures will not immunize a transaction from scrutiny for fairness where the interested directors are also majority shareholders who vote in favor of the transaction. *Remillard Brick Co. v. Remillard-Dandini Co.*, 241 P.2d 66 (Cal.App. 1952).

To avoid the uncertainty of whether shareholder approval is valid if the interested directors vote their shares, it is now common to obtain "majority of the minority" shareholder approval as a condition of the transaction, particularly in controlled mergers. See *Weinberger, supra*. Calif.Corp.Code § 310(a)(1)) adopts the "majority of the minority" approach in transactions in which the directors have a material financial interest.

In this connection, Harold Marsh has written:

> The rule [permitting shareholder approval of an interested director transaction after full disclosure] has been justified on the basis that where there is shareholder ratification the case is precisely analogous to that of a trustee dealing with his cestui que trust after full disclosure, and is not at all a case of a trustee dealing with

himself. However, the validity of this analogy may be seriously questioned. When a trustee deals with his cestui que trust who is an individual that is sui juris, after full disclosure, then the cestui que trust is able to negotiate for himself and there is no more danger of fraud or over-reaching than in any other business transaction. However, when the shareholders of a Publicly-held company are asked to ratify a transaction with interested directors they cannot as a practical matter *negotiate* for the corporation. They are, they must be, limited to rejecting or accepting the deal formulated by the interested directors. Even if it be assumed that the deal is fair, that is not what the shareholders are entitled to. They are entitled to have someone negotiate the best deal obtainable for their corporation, fair or unfair. This the interested directors cannot do. As the New Hampshire court said, it is "impossible for common directors to procure the lowest rates for one party and the highest rates for the other. * * * They were not arbitrators, called in to adjust conflicting claims. * * * "

Harold Marsh, *Are Directors Trustees? Conflict of Interest and Corporate Morality*, 22 Bus.Law. 35, 48–49 (1966).

Consider former Chancellor Allen's explication of the effect of shareholder ratification on interested director transactions and the previous discussion of the effect of director approval on such transactions.

LEWIS v. VOGELSTEIN

699 A.2d 327 (Del.Ch.1997).

ALLEN, CHANCELLOR.

This shareholders' suit challenges a stock option compensation plan for the directors of Mattel, Inc., which was approved or ratified by the shareholders of the company at its 1996 Annual Meeting of Shareholders ["1996 Plan" or "Plan"]

* * *

I.

The facts as they appear in the pleading are as follows. The Plan was adopted in 1996 and ratified by the company's shareholders at the 1996 annual meeting. It contemplates two forms of stock option grants to the company's directors: a one-time grant of options on a block of stock and subsequent, smaller annual grants of further options.

With respect to the one-time grant, the Plan provides that each outside director will qualify for a grant of options on 15,000 shares of Mattel common stock at the market price on the day such options are granted (the "one-time options"). The one-time options are alleged to be exercisable immediately upon being granted although they will achieve economic value, if ever, only with the passage of time. It is alleged that if not exercised, they remain valid for ten years.

With respect to the second type of option grant, the Plan qualifies each director for a grant of options upon his or her re-election to the board each year (the "Annual Options"). The maximum number of options grantable to a director pursuant to the annual options provision depends on the number of years the director has served on the Mattel board. Those outside directors with five or fewer years of service will qualify to receive options on no more than 5,000 shares, while those with more than five years service will qualify for options to purchase up to 10,000 shares. Once granted, these options vest over a four year period, at a rate of 25% per year. When exercisable, they entitle the holder to buy stock at the market price on the day of the grant. According to the complaint, options granted pursuant to the annual options provision also expire ten years from their grant date, whether or not the holder has remained on the board.

When the shareholders were asked to ratify the adoption of the Plan, as is typically true, no estimated present value of options that were authorized to be granted under the Plan was stated in the proxy solicitation materials.

II.

As the presence of valid shareholder ratification of executive or director compensation plans importantly affects the form of judicial review of such grants, it is logical to begin an analysis of the legal sufficiency of the complaint by analyzing the sufficiency of the attack on the disclosures made in connection with the ratification vote.

A. DISCLOSURE OBLIGATION:

[The court rejected plaintiff's claim that defendants had a duty to disclose the estimated present value of the stock option grants to which directors might become entitled under the 1996 Plan.]

III.

* * * I turn to the motion to dismiss the complaint's allegation to the effect that the Plan, or grants under it, constitute a breach of the directors' fiduciary duty of loyalty. As the Plan contemplates grants to the directors that approved the Plan and who recommended it to the shareholders, we start by observing that it constitutes self-dealing that would ordinarily require that the directors prove that the grants involved were, in the circumstances, entirely fair to the corporation. However, it is the case that the shareholders have ratified the directors' action. That ratification is attacked only on the ground just treated. Thus, for these purposes I assume that the ratification was effective. The question then becomes what is the effect of informed shareholder ratification on a transaction of this type (i.e., officer or director pay).

A. SHAREHOLDER RATIFICATION UNDER DELAWARE LAW:

What is the effect under Delaware corporation law of shareholder ratification of an interested transaction? The answer to this apparently simple question appears less clear than one would hope or indeed expect. Four possible effects of shareholder ratification appear logically available: **First**, one might conclude that an effective shareholder ratification acts as a complete defense to any charge of breach of duty. **Second**, one might conclude that the effect of such ratification is to shift the substantive test on judicial review of the act from one of fairness that would otherwise be obtained (because the transaction is an interested one) to one of waste. **Third**, one might conclude that the ratification shifts the burden of proof of unfairness to plaintiff, but leaves that shareholder-protective test in place. **Fourth**, one might conclude (perhaps because of great respect for the collective action disabilities that attend shareholder action in public corporations) that shareholder ratification offers no assurance of assent of a character that deserves judicial recognition. Thus, under this approach, ratification on full information would be afforded no effect. Excepting the fourth of these effects, there are cases in this jurisdiction that reflect each of these approaches to the effect of shareholder voting to approve a transaction.

In order to state my own understanding I first note that by shareholder ratification I do not refer to every instance in which shareholders vote affirmatively with respect to a question placed before them. I exclude from the question those instances in which shareholder votes are a necessary step in authorizing a transaction. Thus the law of ratification as here discussed has no direct bearing on shareholder action to amend a certificate of incorporation or bylaws. * * * [N]or does that law bear on shareholder votes necessary to authorize a merger, a sale of substantially all the corporation's assets, or to dissolve the enterprise. For analytical purposes one can set such cases aside.

1. *Ratification generally*: I start with principles broader than those of corporation law. Ratification is a concept deriving from the law of agency which contemplates the ex post conferring upon or confirming of the legal authority of an agent in circumstances in which the agent had no authority or arguably had no authority. To be effective, of course, the agent must fully disclose all relevant circumstances with respect to the transaction to the principal prior to the ratification. Beyond that, since the relationship between a principal and agent is fiduciary in character, the agent in seeking ratification must act not only with candor, but with loyalty. Thus an attempt to coerce the principal's consent improperly will invalidate the effectiveness of the ratification.

Assuming that a ratification by an agent is validly obtained, what is its effect? One way of conceptualizing that effect is that it provides, after the fact, the grant of authority that may have been wanting at the time of the agent's act. Another might be to view the ratification as consent or as an estoppel by the principal to deny a lack of authority. In either event the effect of informed ratification is to validate or affirm the act of the agent as the act of the principal.

Application of these general ratification principles to shareholder ratification is complicated by three other factors. **First**, most generally, in the case of shareholder ratification there is of course no single individual acting as principal, but rather a class or group of divergent individuals—the class of shareholders. This aggregate quality of the principal means that decisions to affirm or ratify an act will be subject to collective action disabilities; that some portion of the body doing the ratifying may in fact have conflicting interests in the transaction; and some dissenting members of the class may be able to assert more or less convincingly that the "will" of the principal is wrong, or even corrupt and ought not to be binding on the class. In the case of individual ratification these issues won't arise, assuming that the principal does not suffer from multiple personality disorder. Thus the collective nature of shareholder ratification makes it more likely that following a claimed shareholder ratification, nevertheless, there is a litigated claim on behalf of the principal that the agent lacked authority or breached its duty. The **second**, mildly complicating factor present in shareholder ratification is the fact that in corporation law the "ratification" that shareholders provide will often not be directed to lack of legal authority of an agent but will relate to the consistency of some authorized director action with the equitable duty of loyalty. Thus shareholder ratification sometimes acts not to confer legal authority—but as in this case—to affirm that action taken is consistent with shareholder interests. **Third**, when what is "ratified" is a director conflict transaction, the statutory law—in Delaware Section 144 of the Delaware General Corporation Law—may bear on the effect.

2. Shareholder ratification: These differences between shareholder ratification of director action and classic ratification by a single principal, do lead to a difference in the effect of a valid ratification in the shareholder context. The principal novelty added to ratification law generally by the shareholder context, is the idea—no doubt analogously present in other contexts in which common interests are held—that, in addition to a claim that ratification was defective because of incomplete information or coercion, shareholder ratification is subject to a claim by a member of the class that the ratification is ineffectual (1) because a majority of those affirming the transaction had a conflicting interest with respect to it or (2) because the transaction that is ratified constituted a corporate waste. As to the second of these, it has long been held that shareholders may not ratify a waste except by a unanimous vote. The idea behind this rule is apparently that a transaction that satisfies the high standard of waste constitutes a gift of corporate property and no one should be forced against their will to make a gift of their property. In all events, informed, uncoerced, disinterested shareholder ratification of a transaction in which corporate directors have a material conflict of interest has the effect of protecting the transaction from judicial review except on the basis of waste.

B. THE WASTE STANDARD:

The judicial standard for determination of corporate waste is well developed. Roughly, a waste entails an exchange of corporate assets for consideration so disproportionately small as to lie beyond the range at which any reasonable person might be willing to trade. Most often the claim is associated with a transfer of corporate assets that serves no corporate purpose; or for which no consideration at all is received. Such a transfer is in effect a gift. If, however, there is *any substantial* consideration received by the corporation, and if there is a *good faith judgment* that in the circumstances the transaction is worthwhile, there should be no finding of waste, even if the fact finder would conclude *ex post* that the transaction was unreasonably risky. Any other rule would deter corporate boards from the optimal rational acceptance of risk. * * * Courts are ill-fitted to attempt to weigh the "adequacy" of consideration under the waste standard or, ex post, to judge appropriate degrees of business risk.

[The court concluded that plaintiff's complaint should not be dismissed because the one time option grants to the directors were sufficiently unusual as to require further inquiry into whether they constituted waste. This portion of the court's opinion is set forth in Chapter 18A.]

HARBOR FINANCE PARTNERS v. HUIZENGA
751 A.2d 879 (Del. Ch. 1999).

STRINE, VICE CHANCELLOR.

This matter involves a challenge to the acquisition of AutoNation, Incorporated by Republic Industries, Inc. A shareholder plaintiff contends that this acquisition (the "Merger") was a self-interested transaction effected for the benefit of Republic directors who owned a substantial block of AutoNation shares, that the terms of the transaction were unfair to Republic and its public stockholders, and that stockholder approval of the transaction was procured through a materially misleading proxy statement (the "Proxy Statement").

* * *

The Rule 12(b)(6) motion: The complaint fails to state a claim that the disclosures in connection with the Merger were misleading or incomplete. The affirmative stockholder vote on the Merger was informed and uncoerced, and disinterested shares constituted the overwhelming proportion of the Republic electorate. As a result, the business judgment rule standard of review is invoked and the Merger may only be attacked as wasteful. As a matter of logic and sound policy, one might think that a fair vote of disinterested stockholders in support of the transaction would dispose of the case altogether because a waste claim must be supported by facts demonstrating that "no person of ordinary sound business judgment" could consider the merger fair to Republic and because many disinterested and presumably rational Republic stockholders voted for the Merger. But under an unbroken line of authority dating from early in this century, a non-unanimous, although overwhelming, free and fair vote of disinterested stockholders does not extinguish a claim for waste. The waste vestige does not aid the plaintiff here, however, because the complaint at best alleges that the Merger was unfair and does not plead facts demonstrating that no reasonable person of ordinary business judgment could believe the transaction advisable for Republic. Thus I grant the defendants' motion to dismiss under Chancery Court Rule 12(b)(6).

* * *

II. Legal Analysis

4. Why Doesn't A Fully Informed, Uncoerced Vote Of Disinterested Stockholders Foreclose A Waste Claim?

Although I recognize that our law has long afforded plaintiffs the vestigial right to prove that a transaction that a majority of fully informed, uncoerced independent stockholders approved by a non-unanimous vote was wasteful, I question the continued utility of this "equitable safety valve."

The origin of this rule is rooted in the distinction between voidable and void acts, a distinction that appears to have grown out of the now largely abolished ultra vires doctrine. Voidable acts are traditionally held to be ratifiable because the corporation can lawfully accomplish them if it does so in the appropriate manner. Thus if directors who could not lawfully effect a transaction without stockholder approval did so anyway, and the requisite approval of the stockholders was later attained, the transaction is deemed fully ratified because the subsequent approval of the stockholders cured the defect.

In contrast, void acts are said to be non-ratifiable because the corporation cannot, in any case, lawfully accomplish them. Such void acts are often described in conclusory terms such as "ultra vires" or "fraudulent" or as "gifts or waste of corporate assets." Because at first blush it seems it would be a shocking, if not theoretically impossible, thing for stockholders to be able to sanction the directors in committing illegal acts or acts beyond the authority of the corporation, it is unsurprising that it has been held that stockholders cannot validate such action by the directors, even on an informed basis.

One of the many practical problems with this seemingly sensible doctrine is that its actual application has no apparent modern day utility insofar as the doctrine covers claims of waste or gift, except as an opportunity for Delaware courts to second-guess stockholders. There are several reasons I believe this to be so.

First, the types of "void" acts susceptible to being styled as waste claims have little of the flavor of patent illegality about them, nor are they categorically ultra vires. Put another way, the oft-stated proposition that "waste cannot be ratified" is a tautology that, upon close examination, has little substantive meaning. I mean, what rational person would ratify "waste"? Stating the question that way, the answer is, of course, no one. But in the real world stockholders are not asked to ratify obviously wasteful transactions. Rather than lacking any plausible business rationale or being clearly prohibited by statutory or common law, the transactions attacked as waste in Delaware courts are ones that are quite ordinary in the modern business world. Thus a review of the Delaware cases reveals that our courts have reexamined the merits of stockholder votes approving such transactions as: stock option plans; the fee agreement between a mutual fund and its investment advisor; corporate mergers; the purchase of a business in the same industry as the acquiring corporation; and the repurchase of a corporate insider's shares in the company. These are all garden variety transactions that may be validly accomplished by a Delaware corporation if supported by sufficient consideration, and what is sufficient consideration is a question that fully informed stockholders seem as well positioned as courts to answer. That is, these transactions are neither per se ultra vires or illegal; they only become "void" upon a determination that the corporation received no fair consideration for entering upon them.

Second, the waste vestige is not necessary to protect stockholders and it has no other apparent purpose. While I would hesitate to permit stockholders to ratify a blatantly illegal act—such as a board's decision to indemnify itself against personal liability for intentionally violating applicable environmental laws or bribing government officials to benefit the corporation—the vestigial exception for waste has little to do with corporate integrity in the sense of the corporation's responsibility to society as a whole. Rather, if there is any benefit in the waste vestige, it must consist in protecting stockholders. And where disinterested stockholders are given the information necessary to decide whether a transaction is beneficial to the corporation or wasteful to it, I see little reason to leave the door open for a judicial reconsideration of the matter.

The fact that a plaintiff can challenge the adequacy of the disclosure is in itself a substantial safeguard against stockholder approval of waste. If the corporate board failed to provide the voters with material information undermining the integrity or financial fairness of the transaction subject to the vote, no ratification effect will be accorded to the vote and the plaintiffs may press all of their claims. As a result, it is difficult to imagine how elimination of the waste vestige will permit the accomplishment of unconscionable corporate transactions, unless one presumes that stockholders are, as a class, irrational and that they will rubber stamp outrageous transactions contrary to their own economic interests.

In this regard, it is noteworthy that Delaware law does not make it easy for a board of directors to obtain "ratification effect" from a stockholder vote. The burden to prove that the vote was fair, uncoerced, and fully informed falls squarely on the board. Given the fact that Delaware law imposes no heightened pleading standards on plaintiffs alleging material nondisclosures or voting coercion and given the pro-plaintiff bias inherent in Rule 12(b)(6), it is difficult for a board to prove ratification at the pleading stage. If the board cannot prevail on a motion to dismiss, the defendant directors will be required to submit to discovery and possibly to a trial.

Nor is the waste vestige necessary to protect minority stockholders from oppression by majority or controlling stockholders. Chancellor Allen recently noted that the justification for the waste vestige is "apparently that a transaction that satisfies the high standard of waste constitutes a gift of corporate property and no one should be forced against their will to make a gift of their property." This justification is inadequate to support continued application of the exception. As an initial matter, I note that property of the corporation is not typically thought of as personal property of the stockholders, and that it is common for corporations to undertake important value-affecting transactions over the objection of some of the voters or without a vote at all.

In any event, my larger point is that this solicitude for dissenters' property rights is already adequately accounted for elsewhere in our corporation law. Delaware fiduciary law ensures that a majority or controlling stockholder cannot use a stockholder vote to insulate a transaction benefiting that stockholder from judicial examination. Only votes controlled by stockholders who are not "interested" in the transaction at issue are eligible for ratification effect in the sense of invoking the business judgment rule rather than the entire fairness form of review. That is, only the votes of those stockholders with no economic incentive to approve a wasteful transaction count.

Indeed, it appears that a corporation with a controlling or majority stockholder may, under current Delaware law, never escape the exacting entire fairness standard through a stockholder vote, even one expressly conditioned on approval by a "majority of the minority." Because of sensitivity about the structural coercion that might be thought to exist in such circumstances, our law limits an otherwise fully informed, uncoerced vote in such circumstances to having the effect of making the plaintiffs prove that the transaction was unfair. Doubtless defendants appreciate this shift, but it still subjects them to a proceeding in which the substantive fairness of their actions comes under close scrutiny by the court—the type of scrutiny that is inappropriate when the business judgment rule's presumption attaches to a decision.

Third, I find it logically difficult to conceptualize how a plaintiff can ultimately prove a waste or gift claim in the face of a decision by fully informed, uncoerced, independent stockholders to ratify the transaction. The test for waste is whether any person of ordinary sound business judgment could view the transaction as fair.

If fully informed, uncoerced, independent stockholders have approved the transaction, they have, it seems to me, made the decision that the transaction is "a fair exchange." As such, it is difficult to see the utility of allowing litigation to proceed in which the plaintiffs are permitted discovery and a possible trial, at great expense to the corporate defendants, in order to prove to the court that the transaction was so devoid of merit that each and every one of the voters comprising the majority must be disregarded as too hopelessly misguided to be considered a "person of ordinary sound business judgment." In this day and age in which investors also have access to an abundance of information about corporate transactions from sources other than boards of directors, it seems presumptuous and paternalistic to assume that the court knows better in a particular instance than a fully informed corporate electorate with real money riding on the corporation's performance.

Finally, it is unclear why it is in the best interests of disinterested stockholders to subject their corporation to the substantial costs of litigation in a situation where they have approved the transaction under attack. Enabling a dissident who failed to get her way at the ballot box in a fair election to divert the corporation's resources to defending her claim on the battlefield of litigation seems, if anything, contrary to the economic well-being of the disinterested stockholders as a class. Why should the law give the dissenters the right to command the corporate treasury over the contrary will of a majority of the disinterested stockholders? The costs to corporations of litigating waste claims are not trifling.

Although there appears to be a trend in the other direction, binding case law still emphasizes the ease with which a plaintiff may state a waste claim and the difficulty of resolving such a claim without a trial. As in this case, proxy statements and other public filings often contain facts that, if true, would render waste claims wholly without merit. Plaintiffs' lawyers (for good reason) rarely put such facts in their complaints and it is doubtful that the court can look to them to resolve a motion to dismiss a waste claim even where the plaintiff has not pled that the facts in the public filings are not true. Given this reality and the teaching of prior cases, claims with no genuine likelihood of success can make it to discovery and perhaps to trial. To the extent that there is corporate waste in such cases, it appears to be some place other than in the corporate transactions under scrutiny.

For all these reasons, a reexamination of the waste vestige would seem to be in order. Although there may be valid reasons for its continuation, those reasons should be articulated and weighed against the costs the vestige imposes on stockholders and the judicial system. Otherwise, inertia alone may perpetuate an outdated rule fashioned in a very different time.

c. *Disclosure*

Procedural fairness requires full disclosure of the existence of a conflict, and of other "material" information concerning the substance of the transaction, to the disinterested directors or to the shareholders from whom approval of the transaction is sought. Indeed, some cases have suggested that the failure to make full disclosure constitutes per se unfairness. Although that is not the general rule, as we saw in Chapter 15, the duty of disclosure has taken on increasingly greater significance in evaluating a transaction.

The importance of disclosure in conflict transactions antedates modern statutes. *Globe Woolen Co. v. Utica Gas & Electric Co.*, 224 N.Y. 483,

121 N.E. 378 (1918) involved a contract between Globe Woolen and Utica Gas, a utility company. Maynard, the president of Globe Woolen also was a controlling shareholder of, and the dominant figure on the Utica Gas board. He had negotiated the challenged contract which had proved to be disastrously disadvantageous to Utica Gas. The court found that Maynard dominated the Utica Gas board and that he was "interested" in the transaction. Although his refusal to vote gave the transaction the form and presumption of propriety, the court held that the transaction unfair and voidable by Utica Gas. Judge Cardozo wrote:

* * * [As a result of the contract, Utica Gas has] supplied the plaintiff with electric current for nothing, and owes, if the contract stands, about $11,000 for the privilege. These elements of unfairness, Mr. Maynard must have known, if indeed his knowledge be material. He may not have known how great the loss would be. He may have trusted to the superior technical skill of Mr. Greenidge [an employee of Utica Gas] to compute with approximate accuracy the comparative cost of steam and electricity. But he cannot have failed to know that he held a one-sided contract, which left the defendant at his mercy. He was not blind to the likelihood that in a term of ten years there would be changes in the business. The swiftness with which some of the changes followed permits the inference that they were premeditated. * * * But whether these and other changes were premeditated or not, at least they were recognized as possible. With that recognition, no word of warning was uttered to Greenidge or to any of the defendant's officers. There slumbered within these contracts a potency of profit which the plaintiff neither ignored in their making nor forgot in their enforcement.

It is no answer to say that this potency, if obvious to Maynard, ought also to have been obvious to other members of the committee. They did not know, as he did, the likelihood or the significance of changes in the business. There was need, too, of reflection and analysis before the dangers stood revealed. For the man who framed the contracts there was opportunity to consider and to judge. His fellow members, hearing them for the first time, and trustful of his loyalty, would have no thought of latent peril. That they had none is sufficiently attested by the fact that the contracts were approved. There was inequality, therefore, both in knowledge and in the opportunity for knowledge. It is not important in such circumstances whether the trustee foresaw the precise evils that developed. The inference that he did, might not be unsupported by the evidence. But the indefinite possibilities of hardship, the opportunity in changing circumstances to wrest unlooked-for profits and impose unlooked-for losses, these must have been foreseen. Foreseen or not, they were there, and their presence permeates the contracts with oppression and inequity.

We hold, therefore, that the refusal to vote does not nullify as of course an influence and predominance exerted without a vote. We hold that the constant duty rests on a trustee to seek no harsh advantage to the detriment of his trust, but rather to protest and renounce if through the blindness of those who treat with him he gains what is unfair. And because there is evidence that in the making of these contracts, that duty was ignored, the power of equity was fittingly exercised to bring them to an end.

121 N.E. at 380–8.

In *State ex rel. Hayes Oyster Co. v. Keypoint Oyster Co.*, 391 P.2d 979 (Wash. 1964), the president, a director and substantial shareholder, arranged for the sale of corporate properties to another corporation in which he was to have an interest. The transaction was submitted to the shareholders for their approval, but without disclosure of the director's interest. The director voted a majority of the stock, including his own, in favor of the sale. In invalidating the transaction, the court stated:

> * * * [T]his court has abolished the mechanical rule whereby any transaction involving corporate property in which a director has an interest is voidable at the option of the corporation. Such a contract cannot be voided if the director or officer can show that the transaction was fair to the corporation. However, non-disclosure by an interested director or officer is, in itself, unfair. This wholesome rule can be applied automatically without any of the unsatisfactory results which flowed from a rigid bar against any self-dealing.
>
> * * *
>
> * * * [The] shareholders and directors had the right to know of Hayes' interest in [the properties] in order to intelligently determine the advisability of retaining Hayes as president and manager under the circumstances, and to determine whether or not it was wise to enter into the contract at all, in view of Hayes' conduct. In all fairness, they were entitled to know that their president and director might be placed in a position where he must choose between the interest[s of the two corporations in conducting their business with one another.]

Id. at 984.

Although this language suggests that only the existence of the director's interest in the transaction need be disclosed, the court also said that the director was obligated to disclose fully all relevant or material information concerning the transaction to the directors and shareholders. This statement reflects the views of most common law courts.

2. FAIR PRICE (SUBSTANTIVE FAIRNESS)

Notwithstanding the emphasis that courts give to fair dealing, it is important to keep in mind the substantive element of a fairness analysis. If it is impossible to obtain approval by a disinterested decision-maker (as was true in *Marciano*), the court will turn to substantive fairness to determine the validity of the transaction. Similarly, as we have seen, in Delaware, it would appear that when a transaction *has* been approved by disinterested directors or shareholders, the court will still examine the substantive fairness of the transaction but the burden of proving unfairness will have shifted to the complaining shareholder.

The elements of substantive fairness set out in *Shlensky* stress a comparison of the fair market value of the transaction to the price the corporation actually paid, as well as the corporation's need for and ability to consummate the transaction. The test often has been articulated as "whether the proposition submitted would have commended itself to an independent corporation." *International Radio Telegraph Co. v. Atlantic Communication Co.*, 290 Fed. 698 (2d Cir.1923). To the extent that this formulation contemplates independent arms-length negotiation as providing the basis for fair market value, a range of prices could satisfy the test of substantive fairness. Consider the Official Comment to MBCA Subchapter F:

> (1) *Terms of the Transaction*. If the issue in a transaction is the "fairness" of a price, "fair" is not to be taken to imply that there is a single "fair" price, all others being "unfair." It has long been settled that a "fair" price is any price in that broad range which an unrelated party might have been willing to pay or willing to accept, as the case may be, for the property, following a normal arm's-length business negotiation, in the light of the knowledge that would have been reasonably acquired in the course of such negotiations, any result within that range being "fair" The same statement applies not only to price but to any other key term of the deal.
>
> Although the "fair" criterion applied by the court is a range rather than a point, the width of that range is only a segment of the full spectrum of the directors' discretion associated with the exercise of business judgment under section 8.30(a). That is to say, the scope of decisional discretion that a court would have allowed to the directors if they had acted and had complied with section 8.30(a) is wider than the range of fairness" contemplated for judicial determination where section 8.61(b)(3) is the governing provision.
>
> (2) *Benefit to the Corporation*. In considering the "fairness" of the transaction, the court will in addition be required to consider not only the market fairness of the terms of the deal, but also, as the board would have been required to do, whether the transaction was one that was reasonably likely to yield favorable results (or reduce detrimental results) from the perspective of furthering corporation's business activities. Thus, if a manufacturing company that is short of working capital allocates some of its scarce funds to purchase a sailing yacht owned by one of its directors, it will not be easy to persuade the court that the transaction is "fair" in the sense that it was reasonably made to further the business interests of the corporation; the fact that the price paid for the yacht was stipulated to be a "fair" market price will not be enough alone to uphold the transaction. See also the discussion above regarding section 8.30(a).

Because of the difficulty of determining substantive fairness, courts often appear to be influenced in their determination by whether there were procedural irregularities in the interested director's efforts to validate the transaction. In such a case, the presence or absence of procedural safeguards may lead to the inference of substantive fairness or unfairness in the transaction. At the same time, as *Weinberger* suggests, in the absence of fraud, fair price may be more important than fair dealing. *See Kahn* v. *Lynch*, Chapter 19.

E. CORPORATE OPPORTUNITY

The corporate opportunity doctrine is a "default mechanism for allocating property rights between a corporation and those who manage it." Eric Talley, *Turning Servile Opportunities to Gold: A Strategic Analysis of the Corporate Opportunities Doctrine*, 108 YALE L.J. 277, 280 (1998). Analyzed under the duty of loyalty, the doctrine forbids a director, officer, or managerial employee from diverting to herself a business opportunity that "belongs" to the corporation. As the court noted in *Guth v. Loft*, 5 A.2d 503, 511 (Del.1939), noted, a corporate fiduciary cannot take a business opportunity for herself if it is one that the corporation can financially undertake; is within the line of the corporation's business and is advantageous to the corporation; and is one in which the corporation has an interest or a reasonable expectancy.

As with so much else in the duty of loyalty, the proposition is relatively simple to state and difficult to apply. The problem is to separate "opportunities" that should be turned over to the corporation from those that can properly be exploited by the individual. The issue arises because a corporation can only act through its agents, some of whom may have interests outside the corporation. When a business opportunity is presented to such a person (usually a director or officer), is she free to accept it for herself, or must she first offer it to the corporation? And which opportunities that belong to the corporation may she nevertheless take because the corporation, for some reason, is unable to do so?

To answer these questions, one must balance a number of interests. First, the corporation must ensure that its managers and its resources are directed to furthering its own legitimate business interests. Those in positions of trust and confidence cannot be permitted to abuse their positions to further their own economic interests at the expense of their employers. On the other hand, by cordoning off a class of business opportunities as belonging to the corporation, the doctrine effectively prohibits managers from competing with the corporation by using those opportunities, even in the absence of an explicit non-competition agreement. Larger social interests, therefore, are implicated as well. Society benefits when the party best able to take advantage of an opportunity is permitted to pursue it. If the definition of a corporate opportunity is too broad, society suffers because competition is chilled. Those with specialized abilities to recognize entrepreneurial opportunities will be forced by artificial pressures to forego exploiting them.

The corporate opportunity doctrine differs from other types of fiduciary duties with respect to the harm that the corporation suffers. In every other breach of fiduciary duty, actual harm to the corporation must be shown. With a corporate opportunity, however, the harm to the corporation is not actual; the breach arises because the corporate manager took the opportunity for herself and failed to present it to the corporation. Had she presented it, the corporation might have rejected it; had the corporation accepted it, the opportunity might not have been profitable. This last aspect of the doctrine is most relevant in determining the appropriate remedy for the unlawful taking of a corporate opportunity.

PROBLEM

STARCREST CORPORATION—PART 2

A little over a year ago, Starcrest Corporation, which constructs, owns and operates hotels and restaurants throughout the United States, began to discuss the possibility of buying or building a gambling casino. After a management presentation to the directors on the advantages and disadvantages of such a step, the board authorized the officers to begin an active search for specific prospects. Management's initial investigations in the United States turned up nothing that seemed appropriate.

Robert White, a director of Starcrest, has extensive personal investments in a variety of fields, including substantial real estate holdings. He is also the president and chairman of the board of Petro Investments, Inc., a holding company whose assets are invested primarily in real estate. Shortly after the board meeting at which the directors of Starcrest were informed of management's initial investigations, White met an old business acquaintance while on a trip to the Bahamas. White's friend told him that a casino there had just come on the market at what the friend said was a very attractive price. The friend further advised White that if he acted quickly the seller would take $10 million in cash for the casino. White immediately called the real estate broker who was handling the casino, and within two days signed a contract on behalf of Petro to purchase it. Twelve months later, Petro resold the casino at a $6 million profit.

Beatrice Parker, a Starcrest shareholder, has recounted essentially these facts and has asked you about the possibility of success of a derivative suit against White. How should you advise her under the traditional corporate opportunity doctrine? The ALI's version of the corporate opportunity doctrine? What additional information would you need to know?

1. TRADITIONAL CORPORATE OPPORTUNITY DOCTRINE

FARBER v. SERVAN LAND COMPANY, INC.
662 F.2d 371 (5th Cir.1981).

[In 1959, Charles Serianni and other investors formed Servan Land Company,(Servan) to build and operate a golf course and country club near Fort Lauderdale, Florida. Serianni and A.I. Savin owned a majority of the stock and were Servan's principal officers. There were eight other stockholders, including Jack Farber, the plaintiff in this action. Servan acquired 160 acres of land on which to build the course and, shortly thereafter acquired an additional twenty acres abutting the course.

At the 1968 annual stockholders' meeting, a Servan director and stockholder said that James Farquhar, the vendor of the twenty acre tract, was willing to sell another 160 acres of abutting land to the corporation that was suitable for use as an additional golf course. After some discussion, the stockholders took no action to authorize the purchase of the land. In March 1969, Serianni and Savin, in their individual capacities, bought the 160 acres that had been discussed at the stockholders' meeting.

There was no discussion of the purchase at the 1969 annual stockholders' meeting, held in April 1969. In 1970, Farber learned of the purchase from a third party, and at the annual stockholders' meeting, he inquired about it. Savin and Serianni acknowledged the purchase, but there is conflicting evidence as to whether the stockholders ratified the purchase.

In 1973, Serianni, Savin and the corporation entered into an agreement with a purchaser to sell as a package the corporation's assets and the 160 acres of adjoining land Serianni and Savin had bought; each contract of sale was conditioned upon execution of the other. Of the aggregate sales price, the defendants allocated $5,000,000 to the corporation and $3,353,700 to Savin and Serianni, though this division was not based on any appraisal of the respective properties.

At a special directors' and stockholders' meeting, all the stockholders except Farber approved the sale and voted to liquidate Servan. After the sale was completed Farber brought a derivative suit alleging that Savin and Serianni's purchase constituted the taking of a corporate opportunity. Farber also sought appointment of an appraiser to determine the proper allocation of the purchase price.

The district court found that Serianni had been the "driving force" of Servan from its inception. The court also found that, although there was a possibility of real estate development, such development was not one of the purposes for which Servan had been formed. After reviewing the events of the 1968 stockholders' meeting, the court said that Serianni and Savin should have called a special stockholders' meeting to give the stockholders the opportunity to have the corporation purchase the land before Serianni and Savin did so individually. The court noted, however, that the corporation benefitted from their purchase because the entire package was worth more when the assets and real estate were sold in 1973. Finally, the court found that Farber was entitled to an appraisal to determine whether the corporation should have received a larger portion of the total sale price of the properties than the $5 million allocated by Serianni and Savin.

The appraiser subsequently valued the corporation's properties at $4,065,915, and the Serianni–Savin property at $3,950,925. Thus Serianni and Savin had allotted to the corporation a greater percentage of the proceeds of the sale than would have been allocated using the appraiser's figures.

After the appraisal, the district court issued a memorandum opinion which set forth its earlier findings and incorporated the results of the appraisal. The court again noted that Servan had profited from the purchase by Serianni and Savin. It also found that the acreage did not constitute a corporate opportunity because the property bore no substantial relationship to Servan's primary purpose of operating a golf course. Thus the purchase was not "antagonistic to any significant corporate purpose."]

TJOFLAT, CIRCUIT JUDGE:

I

* * *

Farber appealed the district court's decision, and this court vacated and remanded it for clarification, stating: "if, as seems to be clearly expressed, there was no corporate opportunity, why should, as is three times stated, Serianni and Savin have offered the 160 adjacent acres to the corporation? The holdings are inconsistent." *Farber v. Servan Land Co., Inc.*, 541 F.2d 1086, 1088 (5th Cir.1976). * * * We stated:

> If the corporate opportunity doctrine is otherwise applicable it is not made inapplicable by the realization of a substantial gain from a fortuitous sale of its assets at the same time as the sale of the property asserted to be a corporate opportunity to a lone buyer who would not have bought either property without the other. If a corporate opportunity existed the corporation and its stockholders would have been entitled to the profits from the sale of both parcels.

Id.

On remand, the district court failed to explain why it found that Serianni and Savin had a duty to offer the opportunity to purchase the 160 acres to the corporation, but it reaffirmed its finding that "Seriani (sic) and Savin had satisfactorily sustained the burden of establishing the propriety of the transaction." * * *

Farber appeals once again.

II

In reviewing the district court's decision we must evaluate its resolution of four key issues: whether a corporate opportunity existed; whether the stockholders declined the opportunity by failing to act; whether the stockholders ratified Serianni and Savin's purchase; and whether the subsequent benefit the corporation received in selling its assets in conjunction with Serianni and Savin's 160 acres rectifies any wrong it might have suffered through the defendants' initial purchase of the land.

A. THE EXISTENCE OF A CORPORATE OPPORTUNITY

In Florida, a corporate director or officer "occupies a quasi-fiduciary relation to the corporation and the existing stockholders. He is bound to act with fidelity and the utmost good faith." *Flight Equipment & Engineering Corp. v. Shelton*, 103 So.2d 615, 626 (Fla.1958). Because he "occupies a fiduciary relationship to the corporation, (he) will not be allowed to act in hostility to it by acquiring for his own benefit any intangible assets of the corporation * * *. He cannot make a private profit from his position or, while acting in that capacity, acquire an interest adverse to that of the corporation * * *." *Pruyser v. Johnson*, 185 So.2d 516, 521 (Fla.App.1966).

If one occupying a fiduciary relationship to a corporation acquires, "in opposition to the corporation, property in which the corporation has an interest or tangible expectancy or which is essential to its existence," he violates what has come to be known as the "doctrine of 'corporate opportunity'." * * * Florida has long recognized the doctrine of corporate opportunity, and has described a corporate opportunity as a business opportunity in which the corporation has an interest for a "valid and significant corporate purpose." *Pan American Trading & Trapping v. Crown Paint, Inc.*, 99 So.2d 705, 706 (Fla.1957). The opportunity need not be "of the utmost importance to the welfare of the corporation," *Pan American*, 99 So.2d at 706, to be protected from preemption by the corporation's directors and officers. As we elaborated in the first appeal of this case, however, the opportunity must "fit into the present activities of the corporation or fit into an established corporate policy which the acquisition of the opportunity would forward." *Farber*, 541 F.2d at 1088.

In its initial opinion the district court found that no corporate opportunity existed:

> The court finds the possibility of real estate development was contemplated by the stockholders. For example, Mr. Forman testified, via deposition, that scarcely a meeting of the stockholders occurred without discussing the acquiring of additional property from Mr. Farquhar. However, the possibility of real estate development would always be in the minds of a group of affluent businessmen. This does not mean that real estate development was actually part of the corporate purpose and the court specifically finds that

real estate development was not a purpose for which the corporation was formed * * *.

The mere fact that the land was adjacent to the corporate land in itself does not support a conclusion that therefore the acreage was a corporate opportunity. The property had no substantial relation to the corporation's primary purpose of operating a golf course and the individual purpose was not antagonistic to any significant corporate purpose and thus the facts do not fall within the general proposition that an officer of a corporation cannot acquire title to or an interest in property prejudicial to the corporation.

Farber v. Servan Land Co., Inc., 393 F.Supp. at 635, 638. We find that the district court's findings of fact do not support its legal conclusion that the opportunity to buy Farquhar's 160 acres was not a corporate opportunity.

It should be noted that the district court not only found that the stockholders frequently discussed acquisition of Mr. Farquhar's land at their meetings; it also found that the stockholders had discussed this matter at the last meeting, just shortly before Serianni and Savin made their purchase, and that they had "indicated a sense of approval to the idea of acquiring abutting land from Mr. Farquhar." Further, the court heard testimony that the corporation needed the land on the perimeter of the golf course, and evidence that the corporation had bought additional land from Mr. Farquhar in the past and that it had bought and operated a lodge located on part of that land. These facts make it clear that the opportunity to acquire the Farquhar land was an advantageous one that fit into a present, significant corporate purpose, as well as an ongoing corporate policy, and that the corporation had an active interest in it. Accordingly, the opportunity to buy the land constituted a corporate opportunity.

B. Whether the Stockholders Declined the Opportunity

In addition to finding that no corporate opportunity existed, the district court found that if one did exist, "it was rejected by the corporation." The court apparently reached this conclusion because after deciding at their annual meeting that the opportunity to purchase the land should be investigated, the stockholders did not vote, at that meeting, to commit the funds available from the refinancing to purchase the Farquhar property. We find that this failure does not indicate a decision to refrain from pursuing the opportunity to purchase. Indeed, since the stockholders apparently lacked specific information about Mr. Farquhar's terms of sale, it would have been illogical to make a commitment of funds at that time. It is true that there is no evidence to indicate that the stockholders undertook formal investigation of the potential purchase between the time of the meeting and the time of Serianni and Savin's purchase. It should be noted, however, that Serianni was the president of the corporation and the only active director. The other stockholders customarily relied upon him to exercise the executive powers of the corporation, since most of them resided in other states. Because the other stockholders relied upon Serianni to initiate the investigation on the corporation's behalf, he may not now translate his own inaction into a corporate rejection of the opportunity, thus allowing him to buy the land personally. The district court's finding that the corporation rejected the opportunity is clearly erroneous.

C. Ratification of the Purchase

As another ground for its decision, the district court held that the stockholders ratified Serianni and Savin's purchase at their May 9, 1970 meeting. Farber attacks this finding on two grounds. First, he argues that it was clearly erroneous to rely on the corporate minutes, which indicated a vote to ratify, rather than on his court reporter's transcript of the meeting, which indicates no ratification attempt.

The district court received adequate evidence that the corporate minutes were valid and reliable. This left it with an issue of credibility, and this court, on appeal, cannot say that the district judge's decision to rely on the corporate minutes was clearly erroneous. This is especially so since official minutes of corporate meetings are generally considered the best evidence of corporate business transacted.

Farber also argues that even if the ratification vote did take place, it cannot be used to prohibit his derivative action. We agree. When ratification is possible and the proceedings are proper, stockholders may sanction the act of a corporate officer or director and thus abolish any cause of action that the corporation might have against that individual. Not all acts may be ratified, and the Florida courts have not indicated whether stockholders are capable of ratifying a director or officer's breach of fiduciary duty. We do not need to decide whether ratification was possible here, however, because even if it was, the manner of ratification in this case renders the ratification a nullity.

According to the corporate minutes, all of the directors present at the annual meeting, except the plaintiff, voted to ratify the land purchase. Both of the purchasing directors were present, and between the two of them, they held four-sevenths of the stock. While it is true that directors ordinarily may vote their stock on measures in which they have a personal interest, most authorities agree that " '(t)he violation of their duty by corporate directors cannot be ratified by the action of those who were guilty of participation in the wrongful acts, even though they constitute a majority of the directors or of the stockholders.' "*Chesapeake Construction Corp. v. Rodman*, 256 Md. 531, 537, 261 A.2d 156, 159 (Md.App.1970) (quoting 19 C.J.S. Corporations § 763(b) at p. 112). Thus, Serianni and Savin may not bind Farber by ratifying their own inappropriate acts. Farber is entitled to bring a derivative action.

D. The Effect of Benefit to the Corporation

Finally, in finding in favor of the defendants, the district court relied heavily on the notion that by valuing the two properties favorably for the corporation when they were sold jointly, and by selling the properties together, thus raising the value of each, Serianni and Savin benefitted the corporation. This benefit, according to the court, precluded any recovery for breach of fiduciary duty in obtaining the Farquhar acres in the first place.

As we stated in the first appeal, however:

> If the corporate opportunity doctrine is otherwise applicable it is not made inapplicable by the realization of a substantial gain from a fortuitous sale of its assets at the same time as the sale of the property asserted to be a corporate opportunity to a lone buyer who would not have bought either property without the other. *If a corporate opportunity existed the corporation and its stockholders would have been entitled to the profits from the sale of both parcels.*
>
> *Farber*, 541 F.2d at 1088 (emphasis added).

Further, it has already been established that Serianni and Savin apportioned the proceeds of the joint sale without the benefit of an appraisal of the individual properties. While it may be to their credit that they overvalued the corporate property in the apportionment, they have not contended, nor has the district court found, that this overvaluation constituted a deliberate settlement between the parties for damages incurred in the defendants' acquisition of the Farquhar property. Despite the undervaluation of their own property relative to the corporation's assets, Serianni and Savin made a handsome profit on the sale. The two directors must hold those profits in trust for the corporation.

III

We find that the opportunity to buy Mr. Farquhar's 160 acres constituted a corporate opportunity and that the defendants, Serianni and Savin, breached their fiduciary duties to the corporation by preempting that opportunity. We also find that the attempted ratification of the preemption does not preclude Farber from bringing a derivative suit on behalf of the corporation.

The corporation is entitled to the profits of the directors' subsequent sale of the 160 acres. We remand the case to the district court to determine the proper amount of damages and the appropriate method for distributing those damages.

2. WHAT IS A CORPORATE OPPORTUNITY?

Courts have traditionally used one or more tests to determine whether a corporate opportunity exists: (1) interest or expectancy; (2) line of business; and (3) fairness.

a. *Interest or Expectancy*

The interest or expectancy analysis is the earliest judicial test. *See, e.g., Lagarde v. Anniston Lime & Stone Co.*, 28 So. 199 (Ala.1900). The concept underlying "interest or expectancy" appears to be "something much less tenable than ownership—less than a legal right to exclude independent third parties from acquiring the project; and less even contingent contractual claims." Victor Brudney and Robert Charles Clark, *A New Look at Corporate Opportunities*, 94 HARV.L.REV. 997, 1013–14 (1981) ("Brudney & Clark"). Clearly the test is difficult to apply. In *Litwin v. Allen*, 25 N.Y.S.2d 667, 686 (Sup.Ct.1940) the court suggested how to discern whether the corporation has an interest or expectancy:

> This corporate right or expectancy, this mandate upon directors to act for the corporation, may arise from various circumstances, such as, for example, the fact that directors had undertaken to negotiate in the field on behalf of the corporation, or that the corporation was in need of the particular business opportunity to the knowledge of the directors, or that the business opportunity was seized and developed at the expense, and with the facilities of the corporation. It is noteworthy that in cases which have imposed this type of liability upon fiduciaries, the thing determined by the court to be the subject of the trust was a thing of special and unique value to the [beneficiary]; for example, real estate, a proprietary formula valuable to the corporation's business, patents indispensable or valuable to its business, a competing enterprise or one required for the growth and expansion of the corporation's business or the like.

b. Line of Business

Under the line of business test, a corporation has a prior claim to a business opportunity presented to an officer or director that falls within the firm's particular line of business. The test is closely related to the "interest or expectancy" standard, but includes a practicality assessment of the corporations ability to take on the business opportunity. In *Guth v. Loft*, 23 Del.Ch. 255, 5 A.2d 503, 514 (1939), the court explained the concept as follows:

> * * * The phrase is not within the field of precise definition, nor is it one that can be bounded by a set formula. It has a flexible meaning, which is to be applied reasonably and sensibly to the facts and circumstances of the particular case. Where a corporation is engaged in a certain business, and an opportunity is presented to it embracing an activity as to which it has fundamental knowledge, practical experience and ability to pursue, which, logically and naturally is adaptable to its business having regard for its financial position, and is one that is consonant with its reasonable needs and aspirations for expansion, it may be properly said that the opportunity is in the line of the corporation's business.

Thus, if a business proposition would require a corporation to modify its operating infrastructure beyond a certain threshold, the business opportunity would be found to be outside the corporation's line of business. Courts will typically apply the test to extend beyond a corporation's existing operations. The rationale for such an application is simple. Courts recognize that corporations are dynamic entities. Furthermore, shareholders reasonably expect that a corporation will go beyond the status quo and take advantage of highly profitable, but safe, opportunities. Note, *When Opportunity Knocks: An Analysis of the Brudney and Clark and ALI Principles of Corporate Governance Proposals for Deciding Corporate Opportunity Claims*, 11 J.Corp.L. 255, 258 (1986).

The difficulties involved in applying the line of business test are exacerbated when a director or officer holds positions in two or more corporations or is a corporate manager in one corporation and a substantial shareholder in another and dominates the latter through her ability to select its officers and directors. See Comment, *Corporate Opportunity*, 74 Harv.L.Rev. 765, 770–771 (1961). Potential conflicts are exacerbated in venture capital, where the venture capitalist will sit on several boards of corporations in similar lines of business. Note, *The Venture Capitalist's Corporate Opportunity Problem*, 2001 Colum. Bus. L. Rev. 473 (2001).

In *Johnston v. Greene*, 121 A.2d 919 (Del.Ch.1956), Odlum, a financier, who was an officer and director of numerous corporations, was offered, in his individual capacity, the chance to acquire the stock of Nutt–Shel, a corporation 100% owned by Hutson, and several patents pertaining to its business. The business of Nutt–Shel had no close relation to the business of Airfleets, Inc., of which Odlum was president. Odlum turned over to Airfleets the opportunity to buy the stock of Nutt–Shel, but purchased the patents for his friends and associates and, to a limited extent, for himself. Airfleets, a corporation with a large amount of cash, possessed the financial capability to buy the patents. The board of Airfleets, dominated by Odlum, voted to buy only the stock. In a shareholders' derivative action against Odlum and the directors. the Delaware Supreme Court found that Odlum had not breached his duty in the sale of the patents. In discussing the problem of multiple conflicting loyalties, the court stated:

> * * * At the time when the Nutt–Shel business was offered to Odlum, his position was this: He was the part-time president of Airfleets. He was also president of Atlas—an investment company. He was a director of other corporations and a trustee of foundations interested in making investments. If it was his fiduciary duty, upon being offered any investment opportunity, to submit it to a corporation of which he was a director, the question arises, Which corporation? Why Airfleets instead of Atlas? Why Airfleets instead of one of the foundations? So far as appears, there was no specific tie between the Nutt–Shel business and any of these corporations or foundations. Odlum testified that many of his companies had money to invest, and this appears entirely reasonable. How, then, can it be said that Odlum was under any obligation to offer the opportunity to one particular corporation? And if he was not under such an obligation, why could he not keep it for himself?
>
> Plaintiff suggests that if Odlum elects to assume fiduciary relationships to competing corporations he must assume the obligations that are entailed by such relationships. So he must, but

what are the obligations? The mere fact of having funds to invest does not ordinarily put the corporations "in competition" with each other, as that phrase is used in the law of corporate opportunity. There is nothing inherently wrong in a man of large business and financial interests serving as a director of two or more investment companies, and both Airfleets and Atlas (to mention only two companies) must reasonably have expected that Odlum would be free either to offer to any of his companies any business opportunity that came to him personally, or to retain it for himself—provided always that there was no tie between any of such companies and the new venture or any specific duty resting upon him with respect to it.

It is clear to us that the reason why the Nutt–Shel business was offered to Airfleets was because Odlum, having determined that he did not want it for himself, chose to place the investment in that one of his companies whose tax situation was best adapted to receive it. He chose to do so, although he could probably have sold the stock to an outside company at a profit to himself. If he had done so, who could have complained? If a stockholder of Airfleets could have done so, why not a stockholder of Atlas as well?

Id. at 924–25.

c. *Fairness*

A few courts have adopted a fairness test, either by itself or in combination with other standards. In *Durfee v. Durfee & Canning, Inc.*, 80 N.E.2d 522, 529 (Mass.1948), the court stated:

* * * [T]he true basis of the governing doctrine [of corporate opportunity] rests fundamentally on the unfairness in the particular circumstances of a director, whose relation to the corporation is fiduciary, taking advantage of an opportunity * * * when the interests of the corporation justly call for protection. This calls for the application of ethical standards of what is fair and equitable * * * [in] particular sets of facts.

The fairness test is premised on removing the temptation for officers and directors to breach their fiduciary duty by making such breaches profitless. *Id.* at 528–29. However, an amorphous fairness test produces uncertainty in application and unpredictability in result. Thus, the test does not provide a reliable guide to an officer or director concerning the scope of her duty to offer a specific opportunity to the corporation.

As a consequence of this uncertainty, some courts have attempted to combine the line of business doctrine with the fairness test. In *Miller v. Miller*, 222 N.W.2d 71, 81 (Minn.1974), the court first determined when an opportunity was a corporate opportunity under the line of business test. If this test was satisfied, then under the second test, the officer or director would be liable unless she could sustain the burden of showing she did not violate her duties of good faith, loyalty, and fair dealing. The court stated that the following factors would be relevant in determining whether the taking of an opportunity was fair to the corporation:

> * * * [T]he nature of the officer's relationship to the management and control of the corporation; whether the opportunity was presented to him in his official or individual capacity; his prior disclosure of the opportunity to the board of directors or shareholders and their response; whether or not he used or exploited corporate facilities, assets, or personnel in acquiring the opportunity; whether his acquisition harmed or benefited the corporation; and all other facts and circumstances bearing on an officer's good faith and whether he exercised the diligence, devotion, care and fairness toward the corporation which ordinarily prudent men would exercise under similar circumstances in like position.

Id. at 81–82.

The *Miller* approach appears to give an officer or director who may have usurped a corporate opportunity another line of defense under the fairness rubric. Commentators have criticized the *Miller* approach as "add[ing] only a new layer of confusion to an already murky area of the law, without forwarding the analysis in any significant fashion." Brudney & Clark, 94 HARV.L.REV. at 999 n.2. Because of the multitude of factors a trier of fact considers in determining "fairness", particularly whether an individual's usurpation of the opportunity harmed the corporation, the *Miller* test is not useful as a planning vehicle or litigation predictor. *Cf. Southeast Consultants, Inc. v. McCrary Engineering Corp.*, 273 S.E.2d 112 (Ga.1980) (substituting interest or expectancy test for line of business test in first step of the *Miller* analysis).

3. WHEN CAN A MANAGER TAKE A CORPORATE OPPORTUNITY?

a. *Financial or Economic Capacity*

The [economic] capacity inquiry, derived from the financial ability prong of the *Guth* analysis, examines the corporation-proposition-fiduciary nexus in economic terms. The general rule seems to be that if a corporation is financially incapable of exploiting a business proposition, that proposition cannot be said to "belong" to the corporation. Thus, at this stage of the decision-making process, a fiduciary who correctly determines that a proposition is beyond her corporation's financial means cannot be said to have appropriated a corporate opportunity if she later exploits it for herself. The capacity inquiry seems to have underpinnings in economic efficiency. Courts would apparently prefer to see a business proposition developed rather than allow it to languish because of economic constraints. At the capacity-inquiry waypoint, therefore, the integrity of the fiduciary relationship is trumped by a preference for vigorous economic competition.

DeLarme R. Landes, *Economic Efficiency and the Corporate Opportunity Doctrine: In Defense of a Contextual Disclosure Rule*, 74 TEMP. L. REV. 837, 850 (2001).

Courts differ in their willingness to consider whether usurpation occurred solely because the corporation is financially unable to take advantage of the opportunity either because of financial difficulty or a lack of liquid assets. In *Irving Trust Co. v. Deutsch*, 73 F.2d 121, 124 (2d Cir.1934), *rev'g in part* 2 F.Supp. 971 (S.D.N.Y.1932), *cert. denied* 294 U.S. 708, 55 S.Ct. 405, 79 L.Ed. 1243 (1935), the court stated:

> * * * Nevertheless, [these facts which raise some question whether the corporation actually lacked the funds or credit necessary for carrying out a contract] tend to show the wisdom of a rigid rule forbidding directors of a solvent corporation to take over for their own profit a corporate contract on the plea of the corporation's financial inability to perform. If the directors are uncertain whether the corporation can make the necessary outlays, they need not embark it upon the venture; if they do, they may not substitute themselves for the corporation any place along the line and divert possible benefits into their own pockets.

Id. at 124.

Other courts are less rigid. Some allow corporate managers to retain an opportunity if the corporation did not then "have the liquid funds available" to take advantage of it. Corporate managers must use their best efforts to uncover the financing needed by their corporation to acquire an opportunity. A director or officer, however, need not advance funds to enable a corporation to take advantage of a business opportunity. *See, A.C. Petters Co. v. St. Cloud Enterprises, Inc.*, 222 N.W.2d 83 (1974). See also *Gauger v. Hintz*, 55 N.W.2d 426 (1952).

With respect to the relevance of corporate inability to undertake an opportunity, Brudney and Clark conclude:

> There is no reason to allow the diverters to exploit opportunities that they claim the corporation is unable to exploit, if the claimed inability may be feasibly eliminated. To permit claims of disability to become the subject of judicial controversy when they can only be disproved by outsiders with great difficulty and at considerable expense is to tempt participants to actions whose impropriety is visible but rarely subject to effective challenge. Availability of the defense of corporate incapacity reduces the incentive to solve corporate financing and other problems.
>
> The argument against the defense of incapacity or disability may be less forceful for close corporations than for public corporations because of the greater familiarity of the participants with the affairs of the firm, their better access to relevant information, and the relative manageability of the problems. But the arguments against the defense are not without power in the close corporation context as well, as several courts have noted. Moreover, the possibili-

ty of obtaining consent to non-pro rata participation in a venture that the corporation appears unable to exploit should remove the seeming harshness of a rule that does not allow the defense of corporate incapacity. Indeed, rejection by the other participants of a request to assist in curing the incapacity might occur in circumstances that imply consent to the requesting person's taking the opportunity.

Brudney & Clark, 94 Harv.L.Rev. at 1022.

Is it possible that if the corporation is simply in serious financial difficulty or lacks liquid assets but is still a going concern, "the very existence of a prospective profitmaking venture may generate additional financial backing and may convince creditors to be less importunate in their demands." Comment, *Corporate Opportunity*, 74 Harv.L.Rev. 765, 772–73 (1961).

b. *Corporate Rejection of an Opportunity*

i. *Fairness and the Role of Disclosure*

Even if a manager has taken a corporate opportunity, her conduct may not constitute a breach of duty to the corporation if she can demonstrate that the corporation was precluded from taking advantage of the opportunity; that the offer came to her in her personal capacity rather than as a manager of the corporation; or that the corporation rejected the opportunity.

What is important is whether the opportunity has been offered to and rejected by an independent board of directors after full disclosure. *Gaynor v. Buckley*, 203 F.Supp. 620 (D.Or.1962), *aff'd on other grounds* 318 F.2d 432 (9th Cir.1963). As a prerequisite to developing an opportunity personally, an officer or director must generally tender the opportunity to the corporation. *See, e.g., Kerrigan v. Unity Savings Ass'n*, 317 N.E.2d 39, 43–44 (Ill.1974). After an officer or director has tendered an opportunity to the corporation, it may accept or reject the opportunity. By accepting the opportunity, the corporation precludes an officer or director from developing it individually. Rejection of an opportunity by a disinterested board usually is dispositive of a subsequent claim that the officer or director usurped a corporate opportunity.

The taking of an opportunity which has been rejected by a controlled board may be validated if the rejection is otherwise fair to the corporation. See, e.g., *Johnston v.* Greene, *supra*. However, should an officer or director be allowed to prevail on a showing of fairness? One commentator has stated:

> Allowing the fiduciary to attempt to show the fairness of the diversion in these circumstances gives undeserved weight to board action that bears no resemblance to a rejection based on unfettered business judgment. Moreover, an inability to establish board domination which in fact existed would cloak the rejection with the protection of the business judgment rule. * * * Given the difficulty

of proving that the board is dominated, the rejection of an opportunity by a dominated board may give the diverting party the protection of the business judgment rule. If the board is shown to be interested or dominated, the director still has the opportunity to prove the fairness of the diversion. Because of the amorphous nature of the fairness test, the diverting fiduciary may prevail even when the corporation's interests cry out for protection.

Note, *When Opportunity Knocks: An Analysis of the Brudney & Clark and ALI Principles of Corporate Governance for Deciding Corporate Opportunity Claims*, 11 J.Corp.L. 255, 272–73 (1986).

Section 5.05 of the ALI Principles of Corporate Governance provides that a corporate manager may not take a corporate opportunity unless she has made full disclosure of her conflict of interest and the corporation has rejected the opportunity. In addition, the rejection either must be fair to the corporationor, if made in advance, must be made by disinterested directors or shareholders. If the rejection is made by disinterested directors, it must meet the standards of the business judgment rule. If the rejection is made by disinterested shareholders, it must not constitute a waste of corporate assets.

The central feature of ALI § 5.05 is the strict requirement of full disclosure prior to taking advantage of any corporate opportunity. To date, two courts have explicitly adopted the ALI approach. The Maine Supreme Judicial Court noted:

> * * * The disclosure-oriented approach provides a clear procedure whereby a corporate officer may insulate herself through prompt and complete disclosure from the possibility of a legal challenge. The requirement of disclosure recognizes the paramount importance of the corporate fiduciary's duty of loyalty. At the same time it protects the fiduciary's ability pursuant to the proper procedure to pursue her own business ventures free from the possibility of a lawsuit.

Northeast Harbor Golf Club, Inc. v. Harris, 661 A.2d 1146, 1152 (Me. 1995). See also, *Klinicki v. Lundgren*, 695 P.2d 906 (Or.1985) (adopting an earlier version of § 5.05 which remained unchanged).

Other courts have not been willing to make disclosure an absolute pre-requisite to the validity of the taking. In *Broz v. Cellular Information Systems, Inc.*, 673 A.2d 148 (Del.1996), the Delaware Supreme Court held that Broz, a director of Cellular Information Systems (CIS), did not usurp a corporate opportunity by acquiring a cellular telephone license for a corporation of which he was the sole shareholder. CIS itself lacked an interest in the license and did not have the financial ability to make the acquisition. It was, however, the subject of a potential acquisition by a corporation that would have wanted to acquire the license. The court found that the acquisition had come to Broz individually rather than in his capacity as a director of CIS and that he had ascertained from CIS' top management and some of its directors that CIS did not wish to acquire the license for itself. The court noted that although a director might be be shielded from liability had the director formally offered the opportunity to the corporation, there was no legal requirement that the director do so. The court recognized that the manner in which Broz had discussed the issue with the other directors did not constitute formal board assent. Nevertheless, given Broz' attempts to determine whether CIS might be interested, the court concluded that his failure to present the opportunity formally did not result in the improper usurpation of a corporate opportunity. The court declined to impose "a new requirement onto the law of corporate opportunity, *viz.*, the requirement of formal presentation under circumstances where the corporation does not have an interest, expectancy or financial ability." *Id.* at 157.

Ostrowski v. Avery, 703 A.2d 117 (Conn.1997) involved an alleged usurpation of a corporate opportunity by the son of the majority shareholder who consented to the development of a business venture at a time when the corporation's board had exhibited some interest in the same type of venture. The Connecticut Supreme Court found that because of the familial relationship, the consenting director could not have been considered "disinterested" and thus could not have authorized the son's pursuit of the opportunity. The court thus concluded that there had not been appropriate disclosure sufficient to justify the son's conduct.

In addressing the consequences of the failure to make adequate disclosure, the court recognized the appeal of the ALI approach and the importance of disclosure but declined to adopt § 5.05 because it offered "no opportunity to differentiate among the variety of financial circumstances in which an alleged usurpation of a corporate opportunity may arise." *Id.* at 126. Rather, the court adopted:

> * * * [T]wo major propositions of law decided by *Broz*. We agree with the principle that adequate disclosure of a corporate opportunity is an absolute defense to fiduciary liability for alleged usurpation of such a corporate opportunity. A corporate fiduciary who avails himself or herself of such a safe harbor should not be held accountable subsequently for opportunities embraced or forgone. * * * We also agree that, without prior adequate disclosure, a corporate fiduciary still may prove bona fides by clear and convincing evidence, by establishing that his or her conduct has not harmed the corporation. We add, however, that, in assessing such harm, the trier of fact must give special weight to the effect of nondisclosure on the corporation's entrepreneurial opportunities.

Id. at 128.

It also may be significant if the opportunity has been presented to and rejected by the shareholders after full disclosure. In the context of the publicly held corporation, Brudney and Clark argue that the proxy process usually will not result in truly informed consent. They maintain that "consent to the officer's taking a corporate opportunity approaches the kind of waste for which unanimous stockholder approval is traditionally required." Brudney & Clark, 94 Harv.L.Rev. at 1033. Thus, they conclude that all officers and directors, except outside directors, of public corporations should be precluded from taking any active, outside business opportunities. Several justifications are advanced for this rule. A strict rule would protect the usually powerless shareholders in public corporations from diversions of corporate assets. The scope of opportunities of public corporations suitable for exploitation is greater than in close corporations. The pursuit of active, outside business interests would distract full-time officers from corporate affairs. However, as to outside directors, a corporate opportunity would exist only when such a director has used corporate resources in acquiring or developing an opportunity. The narrower duty rests on the basis of the more limited responsibilities and remuneration of outside directors. *Id.* at 1023–25, 1042–1044. Alternatively, if "lawmakers decide that a safety valve is needed for the rare case in which genuine corporate consent [to a diversion] is available in the public corporation context, after the board rejects an opportunity, the shareholders would be required to approve the rejection before an officer or director could exploit the opportunity." *Id.* at 1035.

However, Brudney and Clark urge a more flexible approach for close corporations in light of the basically contractual nature of the venture. They reason:

> * * * Investors in public corporations are usually passive and widely scattered contributors of money to be managed by preselected officers to whom they effectively delegate full decision making power over operating matters. In contrast, investors in private ventures are fairly small in number and tend to know one another. They make more conscious choices when selecting managers from among themselves. They are likely to be active participants rather than merely passive contributors of funds. And they can consent in a more meaningful way to diversions of corporate assets by fellow participants, either when they form or join enterprises, or on the occasion of the diversion. Accordingly, such investors have less need of categorical strictures on such diversions.

Id. at 1003.

Implicit in Brudney and Clark's argument is the recognition that 5.05 may be an awkward fit for close corporations because, as you will see in Chapter 23, informal decision-making by the principal participants in the venture rather than formal board action is often the norm.

ii. The Delaware Statutory Approach

In 2000, Delaware enacted a statutory provision, DGCL 122 (17), which is directed to the question of when a manager may exploit a corporate opportunity and which grants to every corporation the power to:

> Renounce, in its certificate of incorporation or by action of its board of directors, any interest or expectancy of the corporation in, or in being offered an opportunity to participate in, specified business

opportunities or specified classes or categories of business opportunities that are presented to the corporation or one or more of its officers, directors or stockholders.

The official comment to the new section states that a corporation or board of directors can choose to identify "classes or categories of business opportunities" by line or type of business, identity of originator, identity of the party or parties to or having an interest in the business opportunity, identity of the recipient of the business opportunity, periods of time, or geographical location. The comment further specifies that this subsection "does not change the level of judicial scrutiny that will apply to the renunciation of an interest or expectancy of the corporation in a business opportunity, which will be determined by the common law of fiduciary duty, including the duty of loyalty."

The possibility of including such a provision in a corporation's certification of incorporation is likely to be of particular interest to potential investors, such as venture capitalists, who take positions in numerous companies in the same or related industries and who are interested in being represented on portfolio corporations' boards of directors. The availability of the power granted by § 122(17) also poses at least two interesting questions: First, should the absence of a renunciation permitted by this provision increase the likelihood that a court will find the corporation has an interest or expectancy in an opportunity that arguably belongs both to that corporation and to a second corporation on whose board one of its directors also serves? As you will see in Chapter 23, with respect to protecting the interests of minority shareholders in close corporations, Delaware courts have held that the availability of a statutory provision providing special protections may preclude creation of judicial rules providing similar protections. *See Nixon v. Blackwell*, infra.

Second, what will be the standard of review of a board decision to renounce specific business opportunities or classes or categories of business opportunities? Will the court use a business judgment rule standard on the ground that such a determination is simply ordinary business or, because corporate opportunities, by definition, involve the duty of loyalty, will the court employ a fairness standard? Will it matter whether the renunciation is made in a provision in the corporation's certificate of incorporation or in a resolution adopted by its board of directors?

4. REMEDIES FOR USURPING A CORPORATE OPPORTUNITY

In general, the remedy for any completed breach of fiduciary duty is the award of damages in the amount of the harm the corporation suffered from the breach. When dealing with the taking of a corporate opportunity, however, the problem of the appropriate remedy is somewhat more complex. Recall that the original harm in such a case is that the corporate manager took the opportunity for herself and failed to present it to the corporation. Had she presented it, the corporation might have rejected it; had the corporation accepted it, there is no evidence as to how successful the corporation would have been in developing and using it. Thus the gain realized by the offending manager is not necessarily co-extensive with the actual harm suffered by the corporation. Indeed, to establish a breach of duty for taking a corporate opportunity, unlike any other breach of fiduciary duty, it is not necessary to show that the corporation suffered *actual* harm from the taking. The harm is that the corporation was deprived of the right to take the opportunity for itself.

One possible remedy is to assess damages in the amount of the profits realized by the usurping manager on the theory of unjust enrichment. Profit is generally easy to measure if the manager has already sold the opportunity, although as *Farber* illustrates, valuation problems may arise. This is all the more true if the manager's profit results from reselling the opportunity to the corporation from which she took it.

The traditional remedy is the imposition of a constructive trust upon the manager's new business. This approach eliminates messy valuation problems and effectively permits the corporation to recover any lost profits which it might otherwise have realized. The offending manager, however, is entitled to expenditures she have made in pursuing the opportunity, including her reasonable compensation. *See generally Phoenix Airline Services, Inc. v. Metro Airlines, Inc.*, 390 S.E.2d 219, 227 (Ga.App.1989) (Pope, J. concurring), *rev'd on other grounds*, 397 S.E.2d 699 (Ga.1990).

F. EXECUTIVE COMPENSATION

Replace pages 771–781 (section "F") with the following, which is added at the end of Chapter 18 at page 803:

Chapter 18A

EXECUTIVE COMPENSATION

Executive compensation is at the heart of the problem of (and answer to) agency costs in the modern corporation. It is the principal device by which managers extract returns from the business, and it is the principal means of aligning manager interests with those of shareholders. In other words, even though compensation of managers through salary or stock options reduces shareholder returns, well-designed compensation can induce managers to maximize returns.

How is the right balance best achieved? Answers pour in from all directions. State corporate statutes empower the board of directors to set executive compensation; state judges generally defer to board-set compensation, particularly if approved by shareholders; federal securities law requires public companies to disclose the details of their top executives' compensation, and prohibits public companies from giving personal loans to their executives; federal tax law limits the deductibility of compensation above $1 million, unless it is linked to corporate performance and the stock exchanges mandate the tasks and composition of the board's compensation committee of listed companies.

This chapter begins with an overview of executive compensation—its different forms, the mechanics of approval, and the debate surrounding whether current pay levels in public companies are defensible. Next it considers the standard of review of executive compensation under state corporate law, a standard in Delaware that appears to be in flux. Finally, we summarize how federal law over the last several years has increasingly regulated the form, disclosure and liability surrounding executive pay—a significant federalization of corporate governance.

PROBLEM

STARCREST CORPORATION—PART 2A

Remember Starcrest Corporation from Chapter 18—the hotel and restaurant company listed on the New York Stock Exchange. As you recall, 40% of the company's stock is held by the Adams family, the remaining 60% by public investors. The company's CEO Elizabeth Adams has decided to retire, and the Adams family wants Linda Diamond, the company's talented general counsel and board member, to succeed Elizabeth.

The Starcrest board approves Diamond as the new CEO, and delegates full authority to the board's compensation committee to negotiate a pay package with Diamond. The members of the compensation committee are the board's three outside directors: Michael Brown, Ruth Grey and Robert White, each a prominent business executive with no other connections with Starcrest.

You have been hired as counsel to the compensation committee to assist in their deliberations. Brown, Grey and Ruth are aware of the rethinking in the United States of executive compensation over the last couple years, as stories of executive misdeeds and "pay without performance" have spread across the business news. The committee has also hired a compensation consultant, who has prepared a report recommending the types of compensation to be included in Diamond's pay package, the benchmarks against which to measure her performance, the terms of a stock option plan under which options would be granted to her, the nature of her severance package, and the perks that should be given to her. The consultant also summarizes the level of pay of CEOs in companies similar in business and size to Starcrest.

Assuming Starcrest is incorporated in Delaware, please advise the committee before negotiations begin with Diamond on the following questions:

- What standard of judicial review will be applied to Diamond's pay package? Will the review vary according to the type of compensation granted?
- What procedure must the committee follow in approving Diamond's pay? Will the committee members be exculpated from personal liability under DGCL § 102(b)(7) if they follow these procedures?
- Must the committee submit the pay package (or particular aspects of it) to a shareholder vote? Even if not required, would shareholder approval be useful nonetheless? How should the committee deal with the risk that institutional shareholders might vote against the package?
- The stock option plan contains two provisions that seem troublesome—
    - any options granted pursuant to the plan are to have an exercise price equal to the current Starcrest stock price, but may later be re-priced if "circumstances warrant." Is the re-pricing clause valid?
    - the company will lend to the executive, on a short-term basis, sufficient cash to purchase the underlying shares when she

exercises her stock options. After selling the shares, the executive will then be able to repay the loans. Are these loans valid?

A. THE COMPENSATION PUZZLE

1. FORMS OF EXECUTIVE COMPENSATION

Compensation of corporate executives takes many forms. A typical package includes salary, bonuses, stock options, stock-based plans, deferred compensation (pension) plans, and fringe benefits (or "perks").

The Tyco story. Consider the compensation paid in 2001 to Dennis Kozlowski, the CEO of Tyco International, as described in the company's proxy statement filed with the SEC. Although somewhat higher than average, the components of the pay package are typical of most U.S. public companies—particularly in the emphasis on stock-based compensation:

Annual Compensation				Long-term compensation		All other compensation
Salary	Cash Bonus (3)	Stock bonus	Other annual compensation	Restricted stock award (4)	Shares underlying stock options	
$1,650,000	$4,000,000	--	$219,543	$30,398,880	1,439,135	$4,313,553

The notes to Tyco's compensation table explained that "other compensation" includes company contributions to Kozlowski's retirement plans ($13,600 under the company's qualified plan and $397,450 under its non-qualified plan), payment of life insurance premiums and related tax gross up of $3,827,503, and director's fees of $75,000.

In another table, the company described the stock options granted Kozlowski, which represented about 3.4% of the total options granted Tyco employees in 2001. Assuming a 26.6% rise in stock value before being exercised, the options were determined to have a present value of $21,800,000. The stock options granted Kozlowski in 2001 were in addition to earlier-granted options. All told, he held (as of 2001) the option to acquire a total of 11,236,737 shares of Tyco—the options worth roughly $200,000,000.

Kozlowski also participated in retirement plans maintained by Tyco that promised him a fixed lifetime benefit of $343,112/month when he retired at age 65. In 2001, the company entered into a retention agreement with Kozlowski that required him to stay as Tyco's CEO through 2008 and then remain as a consultant for life. Under the agreement, Kozlowski would receive an award of 800,000 shares of restricted stock in 2002 and, on retirement, a lump sum payment of three times his annual base salary plus the highest annual incentive compensation earned within the prior 8 years. He would continue to receive other benefits comparable to those provided prior to retirement—such as use of corporate homes and the corporate jet.

The board's compensation committee summarized its philosophy:

> Tyco's philosophy is to hire and retain the best executive talent. Tyco believes in competitive pay to keep and continually motivate exceptionally talented executives—if such pay is merited by performance. Tyco generally employs entrepreneurial executives, those that are willing to have a significant amount of their pay tied to performance and the equity of the Company. Tyco's executive compensation program reflects this focus. It offers the executive significant financial rewards when Tyco and the executive achieve excellent results.

Was Kozlowski worth it? The company's proxy statement compared the results of Tyco to the results of leading stock market indicators by assuming an investment of $100 in each as of 1993, the year that Kozlowski became Tyco's CEO:

	1993	1994	1995	1996	1997	1998	1999	2000	2001
Tyco International	100	112	133	202	376	551	1031	1037	910
S&P 500	100	101	128	161	217	254	325	368	270
Dow Jones Industrial	100	101	126	177	256	289	429	530	391

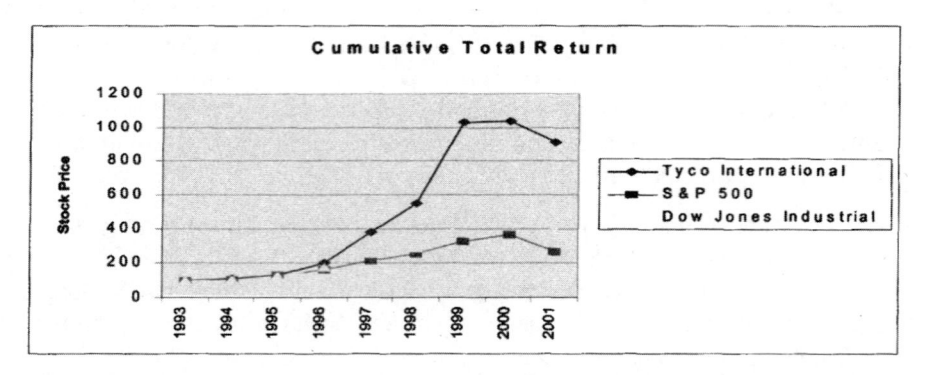

The story for Dennis Kozlowski, however, does not end happily. In 2002, questions began to circulate about Tyco's accounting and bookkeeping practices, resulting in a 19 percent drop in its stock price. A few months later, Kozlowski resigned as CEO (for "personal reasons") when a criminal investigation began into his evasion of state sales tax on art purchases, some made using corporate money.

Things have gotten worse. Soon after his resignation, the SEC filed civil charges against Kozlowski (and two other Tyco executives) for failing to disclose loans from the company, alleging that Kozlowski's improper and undisclosed loans totaled $315 million. The company announced soon afterward its own claims seeking a return of Kozlowski's income and benefits since 1997, totaling $250 million, and the forfeiture of his severance pay. A New York prosecutor then brought charges of conspiracy and grand larceny against Kozlowski and two other Tyco executives, the charges carrying individual jail sentences of up to 25 years, for taking unauthorized bonuses, abusing company loan programs, and pumping up Tyco stock prices to dump their shares on the inflated market—all told, costing Tyco shareholders $600 million. (In June 2005, Kozlowski and Tyco's former CFO Mark Swartz were found guilty by a jury of grand larceny, falsifying business records, and securities fraud. They each face up to 30 years in prison. Most of the other legal proceedings are still pending.)

Stock options. In the 1990s commentators and consultants urged corporations to attempt to align executives' interests with those of shareholders by offering executives highly contingent, long-term incentive compensation tied to the price of their corporation's stock. Economists pointed out that managers compensated with cash salaries were too risk-averse—stock options would encourage them "to think like shareholders." Corporations responded by implementing generous stock option plans that in many instances constituted 75% of the total compensation package.

A quick reminder: stock options give the executive the right—but not the obligation—to buy shares of the company. The possibility that the company's stock price will rise creates value for the option holder. Options have a special terminology:

- The right to buy shares is a *call option*; the right to sell is a *put option*.
- The price specified in an option contract is the *strike price* or *exercise price*.
- The date when the options first may be exercised is the *vesting date;* and the date by which the option must be exercised is the *maturity date* or *expiration date*.

For example, the options Tyco granted to Kozlowski were call options (they gave him the right to buy stock). In fiscal 2001 the largest option granted Kozlowski came in October 2000, an option on 600,000 shares with a strike or exercise price of $53.05—meaning that Kozlowski had the right to buy 600,000 Tyco shares for that price. The options vested three years after being granted and had a term of ten years from the grant date, giving him the right to buy stock by "exercising" his options beginning in October 2004 and ending in October 2011.

The payoff of a stock option depends on the market price of the company's shares when the option holder exercises the options. Suppose that on the expiration date in 2011, Tyco's shares had fallen to only $30. Roughly what would one of Kozlowski's options (on one Tyco share) be worth then? In general, if the stock price is less than the exercise price of the option, the option is said to be *out of the money* or *under water*.

Now, suppose the Tyco shares are worth $100 in 2011? Roughly what would an option on one Tyco share be worth? In general, if the price of the stock is greater than the exercise price, the option is said to be *in the money.* (If the price of the stock equals the exercise price, the option is said to be *at the money.*) An option in the money creates an opportunity for immediate profit—that is, the executive can exercise the option and buy the stock below market, and then resell it at market.

How much do *out of the money* options cost the company? In theory, they might be seen as "free" when granted—since there is no assurance the company's stock price will rise above the exercise price during the exercise period. For this reason many companies in the 1990s did not treat option grants as an "expense" to be subtracted from revenues in computing net income. Instead, option grants appeared as a footnote in the company's financial statements, indicating the possibility that the option holders might in the future buy company stock at a below-market price, thus diluting existing shareholders.

Under this approach, if Tyco's stock price rose in 2011 to $100 and Kozlowski exercised his option to buy 600,000 shares, he would be acquiring each share at a $46.95 discount—and Tyco shareholders (whose holdings would be diluted by Kozlowski) would lose $28,170,000 in value. Assuming the options had not been "expensed," this dilution would appear in Tyco's financial statements only in 2011 when the options were exercised.

Whether stock options should be "expensed" has been controversial. In December 2004 the Financial Accounting Standards Board issued a statement that requires public companies, beginning in June 2005, to expense the fair value of the cost of any share-based compensation, in particular stock options. Although the SEC delayed the FASB mandate for a year, the true cost of stock options (and other share-based compensation, such as restricted stock grants and performance-based awards) will be more transparent by reducing reported earnings—and thus the all-important earnings per share—in the year that options are granted.

How are the contingent rights inherent in a stock option valued? The FASB does not specify a valuation method. Instead, there a number of sophisticated methods that take into account the company's current stock price, the exercise price and period (the longer, the more likely the option will be in the money), the volatility of the company's stock price (the more volatile, also the better), the company's dividend policy (the higher the dividends, the less likely the option will be in the money), and general interest rates. The most common valuation model, the Black–Scholes model,* does not work well on long-maturity stock options—precisely the kind typically granted corporate executives—since volatility can fluctuate over time. By some estimates, typical executive stock options may have only half the value estimated by Black-Scholes.

---

* The model is named after economists Fischer Black and Myron Scholes, who in 1973 described the mathematics of valuing call options on publicly-traded stock, work that later won a Nobel Prize in Economics. The use of the Black–Scholes formula is pervasive in financial markets, so much so that it is common practice for companies to disclose the implied volatility of their stock. This known, it's a simple matter to plug the other readily-ascertainable variables into the formula to determine the option price.

An alternative to Black–Scholes is the binomial option pricing model, which evaluates options using a decision tree format. Such models are widely used in practice and can be more accurate and flexible than Black–Scholes, but most companies disclose option valuations based on Black–Scholes, which can be simpler to use and understand. Regulators also appear to be more comfortable with this model. To solve this valuation conundrum, a recent proposal would permit some long-term employee stock options to be traded, to set a market price!

Questions:

1. What was Kozlowski's total pay package in 2001? How much of it was based on actual performance? How much was meant as inducement for future performance?

2. What is the difference between paying a CEO with stock grants, compared to stock options? How is each accounted for in the company's financial statements? What does it mean that stock options, if exercised, can "dilute" other shareholders?

3. Remember that stock options represent the *right* (but not the *obligation*) to buy stock. What are the differences in executive incentives between being paid with stock compared to stock options?

---

2. PROCESS FOR SETTING EXECUTIVE COMPENSATION

In public corporations, executive compensation is usually determined by a compensation committee of the board of directors. Codifying a "best practice" adopted by many public companies over the last two decades, the NYSE and NASDAQ listing standards (as of 2003) generally require that the compensation committee of listed companies be composed *solely* of three or more "independent directors" (as defined in the listing standards).

A leading pay consultant, writing in the early 1990s, described the process for setting executive compensation:

> Imagine yourself as the CEO of a large company. Being a red-blooded American who has fought his way to the top of the organization, you're always ready to earn more money. [After talking to your CEO buddies and getting a pay consultant,] you have to decide on the line of attack you will be pursuing with your board. If yours is a great-performing company, then, you only have to mention your performance, followed by the mantra "We want to pay for performance," and your compensation consultant will be on his way.
>
> If yours is a poor-performing company, you have a bit more of an uphill struggle to get a raise. But nothing is impossible if you have the right attitude and the right consultant. First, you should admit the company is having some hard times, and you promptly and predictably blame the hard times on external events. If you are

the head of a major automobile company, for example, you point to the fact that every one of the Big Three automakers is in trouble, not just your company, and you excoriate the Japanese for not playing the international trade game fairly. Once you finish laying the blame off onto others, you note that you are starting to lose key people. Performance has been so bad that you haven't been able to pay bonuses, and even salary increases have slowed to a crawl. What's more, all those options that were awarded to you three years ago are underwater that is, the strike prices of the options-what you have to pay to exercise them-are now a lot higher than the current market price.

That wasn't the way things were supposed to work out. The market price was supposed to rise above the strike price so as to give you a good profit. But all those external, and uncontrollable, events intervened to produce an unintended result. During this part of the discussion, you note to the consultant that an executive in your company can quit, cross the street, and go to work for a competitor whose stock has also fallen. But in so doing, he will be exchanging underwater stock options for new options where the strike price is equal to the current market price, and not higher. He'll recommend to the board that they simply erase the old strike price on each executive's option agreement and substitute a new, lower strike price.

The consultant will never stop to ponder a difficult problem of logic. If it makes sense to reward a CEO in good times, because that is only just, and if it makes sense to reward a CEO in bad times because you need to keep him with the company, and if there are only two types of times—good times and bad times—then just when, pray tell, is the CEO ever going to get his pay cut? The answer, distressingly, is never.

No matter how the consulting assignment starts, it will almost always end in the meeting room of the compensation committee of the board. It is here that the consultant will make his recommendations. [The CEO, with his company-paid consultant, will have the advantage. The CEO is an informed seller of his talents, and the compensation committee is an uninformed buyer.] It meets only a few times a year, and then only for an hour or so each time. Its members are not pay experts, and they are not given any independent counsel of their own. So they must of necessity rely heavily on what the company's compensation consultant is telling them.

While you're pondering this process, think also about the fact that many of the compensation committee members may be the personal friends of the CEO. And think about the fact that it is the CEO who suggests to the board members how much they should pay themselves. In saying this, I don't mean to suggest that compensation committee members and board members are dishonest people who are willing to sell themselves for a few bucks. Rather, I am only observing that there is a climate of friendship and trust operating here, rather than the more cautious attitude that one usually presents toward someone who is trying to sell you something that will cost you quite a bit of money.

So that's how they do it. A lot of rationalization goes on, and a lot of high-priced talent is retained to prove a conclusion that the CEO has already made. And everybody wins. The CEO gets a raise, the compensation consultant gets his bills paid, and the compensation committee goes home feeling good that it is paying for performance or keeping good people or both. Or almost everybody wins. Everybody but the shareholders.

GRAEF S. CRYSTAL, IN SEARCH OF EXCESS: THE OVERCOMPENSATION OF AMERICAN EXECUTIVES 42–50 (1991).

In 1992, the SEC amended its rules on disclosure of executive compensation. Besides requiring tabular presentation of the pay of the company's CEO and for other highest paid executives, the SEC rules also require disclosure of the process by which compensation is set in the company. Here is the report of the Tyco board's compensation committee on how it set executive compensation in 2001, particularly for CEO Kozlowski:

> The Compensation Committee of the Board of Directors is composed solely of independent directors, none of whom has any interlocking relationships with Tyco that are subject to disclosure under rules of the SEC relating to proxy statements. The Compensation Committee [which had seven official meetings in fiscal year 2001] approves all of the policies under which compensation is paid or awarded to Tyco's Chief Executive Officer, reviews and, as required, approves such policies for executive officers and key managers, and has oversight of the administration of executive compensation programs. The Compensation Committee reviews the compensation policies in light, among other things, of the competitive environment in which Tyco must compete for superior executive talent and the benefit to the Company and its shareholders of having a large portion of incentive compensation tied to the equity value of the Company.
>
> Executive compensation for fiscal year 2001 reflected the completion of another successful year for the Company overall. Fiscal 2001 is the eighth consecutive year in which Tyco substantially increased revenues and earnings. Revenues for fiscal 2001 increased to $36.3 billion, a 26% increase over fiscal year 2000 revenues of $28.9 billion. Income before non-recurring charges and credits, extraordinary items, and the adoption of SAB 101, rose to $2.81 per diluted share, an increase of 29% over the prior year's diluted per share earnings of $2.18 before such items. [The Committee also described the company's many business acquisitions during the year.]

The Compensation Committee believes that evaluation of the overall performance of Tyco's senior executives cannot be reduced to a fixed formula and that the prudent use of discretion in determining pay levels is in the best interests of Tyco and its shareholders.

The Compensation Committee meets at least annually to consider and make its determination regarding the total compensation of the Chief Executive Officer for the ensuing year. The Committee retains a nationally recognized consulting firm to review and analyze Tyco's executive compensation practices relative to the Company's performance, as well as the marketplace for executive talent. The Committee also observed that Tyco and Mr. Kozlowski's leadership of Tyco have received many favorable comments from the business and financial community. The Committee noted that Tyco was named the best performing company by *Business Week* in its Spring 2001 special edition featuring its choice of the 50 best performing companies and that more recently Mr. Kozlowski was named one of the top 25 managers of the year by *Business Week* in its January 14, 2002 edition.

Mr. Kozlowski has led Tyco from a $3 billion manufacturing corporation in 1993 to a $36 billion diversified service and manufacturing corporation in 2001 that has provided 910% in total cumulative shareholder return from 1993–2001.

You might wonder who were the directors on the Tyco compensation committee in 2001. They were a fairly typical group of outside directors, all executives from other major companies and investment firms. Here is their biographical information from the 2001 Tyco proxy statement:

Stephen W. Foss (age 58, Tyco director since 1997, owner of 146,694 Tyco shares). Chairman and Chief Executive Officer, Foss Manufacturing Company, Inc. (manufacturer of synthetic fibers and nonwoven fabrics) (1969–present); Director, Ameron International Corp.; Director, Former Tyco (1983–1997)

Philip M. Hampton (age 68, Tyco director since 1997, owner of 70,471 Tyco shares). Co-Managing Director, R. H. Arnold & Co. (investment bank) (April 1997–present); Chairman of the Board, Metzler Corporation (investment bank) (October 1989–March 1997); Director, Former Tyco (1985–1997)

James S. Pasman, Jr. (age 69, Tyco director since 1992, owner of 27,147 Tyco shares). Director, CSAM Income Fund, Inc., CSAM Strategic Global Income Fund, Inc. and Education Management Corp.; Trustee, Deutsche Bank VIT Funds; Director of approximately 50 funds in the Warburg Pincus Funds Complex and the Credit Suisse Institutional Funds Complex

W. Peter Slusser (age 71, Tyco director since 1992, owner of 27,439 Tyco shares). President, Slusser Associates, Inc. (investment banking firm) (1988–present); Director, Ampex Corporation and Sparton Corporation

Questions:

1. Based on your reading (perhaps between the lines) of the Tyco report, was the company's process for setting executive compensation in 2001 different from that generally described by Graef Crystal in 1991?
2. Does the Tyco compensation committee explain why Kozlowski's compensation package is so heavily weighted toward stock options? Does the report mention how much Kozlowski stood to make if shareholder returns continued apace?
3. In reviewing the profiles of the members of the Tyco compensation committee, what do you think were their motives and incentives in setting Kozlowski's pay?

3. DEBATE OVER EXECUTIVE COMPENSATION

In recent years, no area of corporate governance has provoked as much public debate, outrage and publicity as executive compensation. Starting with Plato's dictum that nobody in a community should earn more than five times that of the average worker, critics have pointed to the spiraling compensation of CEOs in large U.S. companies. While average CEO compensation was 42 times average worker pay in 1980, it has climbed to over 300 times average pay in the 2000s. As of 2004, the average compensation for CEOs of large U.S. public companies was $9.6 million, compared with average worker wages of $33,176.

For some, the question is of proportion and size. Can an employee, as opposed to the entrepreneur who creates a business, ever be worth $1 billion over his career? It is hard to believe that particular CEOs are so particularly talented or far-sighted that their managerial services could be worth so much. Critics point out that successful companies in Europe and Japan are able to hire executives for a fraction of the cost of U.S. executives, without heavy reliance on stock options or "reward for failure" termination fees.

For others, the question is one of incentives. Before the 1990s, the prevalent compensation model linked executive pay to company size, which prompted executives to focus on revenues and company size, not profits or stock price. Then, in response to academic arguments that stock-based compensation "ties managers to the mast," executive pay in the 1990s increasingly tended toward stock option grants. Compensation committees viewed stock options as essentially free, and awarded them widely. Do stock options, whose value depends on rising stock prices, actually align CEO incentives with shareholders interests?

Critics of stock options have mounted a withering attack:

Expensive. The cost to the company is generally greater than the value to the executives. Why? A rational CEO would rather have $1 million in a diversified portfolio (or in cash) than $1 million of his company's stock options—given that the CEO's reputational, salary, bonus, retirement and other compensation is tied to the company. Thus to pay a CEO $1 million of value (to the CEO), the company must grant (studies show) $2 million of options. CEOs value diversification, like anyone else.

Poor alignment. Stock options align incentives in only one direction since managers (unlike shareholders) suffer no downside losses if stock prices fall. This makes managers with options more willing to gamble. And if prices fall, managers will often seek to have their options "repriced" to a lower exercise price—as we saw in the problem in Chapter 14 (pages 468–471) where a company with a falling stock price considered repricing its *under water* options. Win either way.

Poor design. Stock options can become valuable if an executive merely stays in office during a rising market. "Outperformance" options, whose value depends on the company's stock beating a selected index, never caught on. In the 1990s, only 1 in 1000 public companies used them—perhaps because unlike fixed-price options they had to be "expensed."

Distorted incentives. Because dividends are not paid on options, CEOs who receive option grants have an incentive to have the company retain cash and reduce dividends. In fact, the dividends paid by public companies decreased dramatically during the 1 990s. Before that, dividends—not capital gains—accounted for three-fourths of the returns from stocks as companies signaled they were doing well by paying high cash dividends.

Encourages fraud. Executives with options have an incentive to increase their company's stock price—no matter how. Options become an "inducement for greed" as CEOs manipulate reported earnings to push the share price up, then sell before the price falls. And even if the CEO do not actually mislead, there is a strong incentive to "smooth earnings" across different reporting periods to create the impression of steady and increasing financial results.

In response to these criticisms, many companies have redesigned their stock-based compensation plans. Grants of stock options are down, while grants of restricted stock that vests in the future based on company performance are up significantly. In addition, rather than focus on stock price appreciation, these incentive plans increasingly are pegged to other performance measures, such as net income, cash flow, even customer satisfaction. Newer stock options are granted at a premium (above the current market price) and are not subject to adjustment, so if performance is poor executives receive no payouts.

Despite these changes, the criticism continues. Some have argued that there is a disconnect between executive pay levels and company performance, and that current pay levels for U.S. executives are best explained by greed ("managerial rent-seeking") rather than arm's-length bargaining. Even early advocates of stock options as a way of aligning manager and shareholder interests have concluded that stock options tempt managers to choose business strategies, make investments and juggle the accounting numbers so the company looks good when the stock options become exercisable.

What should be done? Some say, nothing. They point out that there is no evidence of what optimal pay levels should be, or that the compensation system is broken. In fact, there is some indication this system is self-correcting and functional. For example, in 2002–2003, while executive pay rose by 22% for the top-performing companies, it fell by 51% for the bottom-performing companies during the same period. Pay is linked to performance. Moreover, studies show that companies managed by skilled CEOs who are highly paid—where "skill" is measured by a track record of maintaining good performance and reversing bad performance—significantly outperform companies managed by skilled, but poorly-paid CEOs. High pay creates better incentives.

Others argue that the compensation system just needs find-tuning. For example, they urge more transparency on the impact of pay packages in a forward-looking "Compensation Discussion & Analysis" that would be subject to shareholder approval, as in Britain. In the process, the compensation committee would be forced to confront whether pay really is creating the right incentives and to stake their reputation on it working. Not surprisingly, compensation consultants have urged better design in pay packages. Some would de-emphasize stock options and focus on stock grants that vest upon meeting particular targets (in sales, customer satisfaction, stock price). Some would have compensation committees focus on "strategic value" created by managers, rather than short-term earnings figures. And, instead of repricing *under water* options, some have suggested that poorly-performing companies sell their executives new lower-priced options, thus creating some downside discomfort.

Others assert that the compensation system is broken. They argue that three mechanisms are absent from the system: (1) boards, acting at arm's length, that design pay packages that maximize shareholder value; (2) market and social forces that constrain executives from negotiating for non-optimal pay packages; and (3) shareholders that exercise their voting and litigation rights to block non-optimal pay arrangements. They urge that boards become more answerable to shareholders, including by permitting shareholders to nominate directors to the board.

B. STATE LAW

Compensation of employees and officers is generally a matter of business judgment. Even when the duty of loyalty is implicated—as when directors fix the compensation of the company's CEO who sits on the board—courts do not necessarily use a fairness standard. Instead, executive compensation is reviewed under the standards of waste (when the compensation seems irrationally exorbitant), care (when the process of approval is badly flawed), and fairness (when interested or dominated directors set their own or others' compensation).

Efforts by shareholders to challenge executive pay through the voting process in public companies have met with only limited success. Although shareholders frequently have the right to vote on stock option plans and shareholder opposition to such plans has grown, few plans are ever defeated. In addition, shareholders have increasingly submitted shareholder proposals using Rule 14a–8 that seek to limit executive pay, but rarely do such proposals garner majority support and even when this happens board implementation is not mandatory. Compensation committees have responded to the more popular proposals by slowing executive pay increases or shifting from stock options to other performance-based pay.

Shareholder derivative suits challenging corporate pay levels and practices, though they are brought relatively infrequently, have met with some success. Based on a recent study of 124 reported cases over the last century challenging executive pay, shareholders have experienced surprisingly high rates of success—on motions to dismiss, motions for summary judgment, trial and appeal. Randall S. Thomas & Kenneth J. Martin, *Litigating Challenges to Executive Pay: An Exercise in Futility?*, 79 Wash. U. L. Q. 569 (2001). The study found that success rates have been higher in close corporations and in courts outside of Delaware:

Plaintiff Success Rates (124 executive pay cases from 1912-2000)	Delaware	Non-Delaware	Total
Waste	29%	46%	40%
Care	27%	33%	30%
Loyalty (fairness)	28%	39%	35%
Public corporation (at least one theory)	34%	30%	32%
Close corporation (at least one theory)	50%	53%	52%

Success at any stage of the litigation changes the dynamics of settlement, and surviving a motion to dismiss often constitutes complete victory for challenging shareholders. In Delaware, where derivative plaintiffs must make a pre-suit demand on the board or show why such demand would have been futile, challenges to executive pay often turn on the issue of demand futility. To avoid demand the plaintiff must show the challenged pay practice or procedure is not protected by the business judgment rule.

As you read the following materials, consider what standard the courts employ to review executive compensation. You will notice the standard of review has not remained static. What standard do you believe is appropriate?

1. TRADITIONAL APPROACH

The American Tobacco Litigation. Litigation involving bonuses paid to officers of the American Tobacco Co. crystallized the traditional judicial approach to executive compensation. In 1912, American Tobacco's shareholders adopted a by-law providing for payment of annual bonus payments to the corporation's officers in amounts equal to a percentage of net profits in excess of a stated threshold. The soaring fortunes of American Tobacco led to a dramatic increase in those bonuses. A shareholder brought a derivative suit to recover allegedly excessive compensation paid to the company's president and five vice presidents. In *Rogers v. Hill,* 289 U.S. 582, 53 S.Ct. 731, 77 L.Ed. 1385 (1933), the Supreme Court, reversing a Second Circuit decision dismissing plaintiffs complaint, stated:

> It follows from what has been shown that when adopted the by-law was valid. But plaintiff alleges that the measure of compensation fixed by it is not now equitable or fair. And he prays that the court fix and determine the fair and reasonable compensation of the individual defendants, respectively, for each of the years in question. The only payments that plaintiff by this suit seeks to have restored to the company are the payments made to the individual defendants under the by-law.
>
> We come to consider whether these amounts are subject to examination and revision in the District Court. As the amounts payable depend upon the gains of the business, the specified percentages are not per se unreasonable. The by-law was adopted in 1912 by an almost unanimous vote of the shares represented at the annual meeting and presumably the stockholders supporting the measure acted in good faith and according to their best judgment. Plaintiff does not complain of any [payments] made prior to 1921. Regard is to be had to the enormous increase of the company's profits in recent years. The 2 1/2 per cent yielded President Hill $447,870.30 in 1929 and $842,507.72 in 1930. The 1 1/2 per cent yielded to each of the vice-presidents, Neiley and Riggio, $115,141.86 in 1929 and $409,495.25 in 1930 and for these years payments under the by-law were in addition to the cash credits and fixed salaries shown in the statement.
>
> While the amounts produced by the application of the prescribed percentages give rise to no inference of actual or constructive fraud, the payments under the by-law have by reason of increase of profits become so large as to warrant investigation in equity in the interest of the company. Much weight is to be given to the action of the stockholders, and the by-law is supported by the presumption of regularity and continuity. But the rule prescribed by it cannot, against the protest of a shareholder, be used to justify

payments of sums as salaries so large as in substance and effect to amount to spoliation or waste of corporate property. The dissenting opinion of Judge Swan indicates the applicable rule:

> "If a bonus payment has no relation to the value of services for which it is given, it is in reality a gift in part and the majority stockholders have no power to give away corporate property against the protest of the minority." 60 F.2d 109, 113. The facts alleged by plaintiff are sufficient to require that the District Court, upon a consideration of all the relevant facts brought forward by the parties, determine whether and to what extent payments to the individual defendants under the by-law constitute misuse and waste of the money of the corporation.

Id. at 590–92.

Other shareholders subsequently sued to recover American Tobacco bonus payments made in later years. In *Heller v. Boylan,* 29 N.Y.S.2d 653 (Sup.Ct.194 1), *affd mem.* 263 App.Div. 815, 32 N.Y.S.2d 131 (1st Dept.1941), the court rejected their attack, stating:

> Yes, the Court possesses the *power* to prune these payments, but openness forces the confession that the pruning would be synthetic and artificial rather than analytic or scientific. Whether or not it would be fair and just, is highly dubious. Yet, merely because the problem is perplexing is no reason for eschewing it. It is not timidity, however, which perturbs me. It is finding a rational or just gauge for revising these figures were I inclined to do so. No blueprints are furnished. The elements to be weighed are incalculable; the imponderables, manifold. To act out of whimsy or caprice or arbitrariness would be more than inexact it would be the precise antithesis of justice; it would be a farce.
>
> If comparisons are to be made, with whose compensation are they to be made—executives? Those connected with the motion picture industry? Radio artists? Justices of the Supreme Court of the United States? The President of the United States? Manifestly, the material at hand is not of adequate plasticity for fashioning into a pattern or standard. Many instances of positive underpayment will come to mind, just as instances of apparent rank overpayment abound. Haplessly, intrinsic worth is not always the criterion. A classic might perhaps produce trifling compensation for its author, whereas a popular novel might yield a titanic fortune. Merit is not always commensurately rewarded, whilst mediocrity sometimes unjustly brings incredibly lavish returns. Nothing is so divergent and contentious and inexplicable as values.
>
> Courts are ill-equipped to solve or even to grapple with these entangled economic problems. Indeed, their solution is not within the juridical province. Courts are concerned that corporations be honestly and fairly operated by its directors, with the observance of the formal requirements of the law; but what is reasonable compensation for its officers is primarily for the stockholders. This does not

mean that fiduciaries are to commit waste, or misuse or abuse trust property, with impunity. A just cause will find the Courts at guard and implemented to grant redress. But the stockholder must project a less amorphous plaint than is here presented.

On this branch of the case, I find for the defendants. Yet it does not follow that I affirmatively approve these huge payments. It means that I cannot by any reliable standard find them to be waste or spoliation; it means that I find no valid ground for disapproving what the great majority of stockholders have approved. In the circumstances, if a ceiling for these bonuses is to be erected, the stockholders who built and are responsible for the present structure must be the architects.

Id. at 679–80.

Effect of shareholder approval. In the years following the American Tobacco litigation, most publicly-held corporations sought to minimize the possibility of successful legal challenges by seeking approval of executive compensation plans from disinterested directors, disinterested shareholders, or both. By securing such approval, corporations shifted the burden to shareholders to prove that the compensation plan involved waste.

The judicial attitude is perhaps best exemplified by former Chancellor Allen's holding that a grant of immediately exercisable stock options is not corporate waste if "there is some rational basis for directors to conclude that the amount and form of compensation is appropriate." *Steiner v. Meyerson, 1995* WL 441999 (Del.Ch.1995). Chancellor Allen observed:

Absent an allegation of fraud or conflict of interest courts will not review the substance of corporate contracts; the waste theory represents a theoretical exception to the statement very rarely encountered in the world of real transactions. There surely are cases of fraud; of unfair self-dealing and, much more rarely negligence. But rarest of all—and indeed, like Nessie, possibly non-existent—would be the case of disinterested business people making non-fraudulent deals (non-negligently) that meet the legal standard of waste!

Id. at 5.

2. EVOLVING DELAWARE APPROACH

The following case describes the shifting approaches in Delaware over the years to executive compensation (particularly stock options) challenged as excessive. The court addresses both what disclosure must be made to shareholders who are asked to approve a compensation plan and what level of judicial review is appropriate for a shareholder-approved plan.

LEWIS v. VOGELSTEIN
699 A.2d 327 (Del.Ch.1997)

ALLEN, CHANCELLOR.

This shareholders' suit challenges a stock option compensation plan for the directors of Mattel, Inc., which was approved or ratified by the shareholders of the company at its 1996 Annual Meeting of Shareholders ["1996 Plan" or "Plan"].

I.

The facts as they appear in the pleading are as follows. The Plan was adopted in 1996 and ratified by the company's shareholders at the 1996 annual meeting. It contemplates two forms of stock option grants to the company's directors: a one-time grant of options on a block of stock and subsequent, smaller annual grants of further options.

With respect to the one-time grant, the Plan provides that each outside director will qualify for a grant of options on 15,000 shares of Mattel common stock at the market price on the day such options are granted (the "one-time options"). The one-time options are alleged to be exercisable immediately upon being granted although they will achieve economic value, if ever, only with the passage of time. It is alleged that if not exercised, they remain valid for ten years.

With respect to the second type of option grant, the Plan qualifies each director for a grant of options upon his or her re-election to the board each year (the "Annual Options"). The maximum number of options grantable to a director pursuant to the annual options provision depends on the number of years the director has served on the Mattel board. Those outside directors with five or fewer years of service will qualify to receive options on no more than 5,000 shares, while those with more than five years service will qualify for options to purchase up to 10,000 shares. Once granted, these options vest over a four year period, at a rate of 250% per year. When exercisable, they entitle the holder to buy stock at the market price on the day of the grant. According to the complaint, options granted pursuant to the annual options provision also expire ten years from their grant date, whether or not the holder has remained on the board.

When the shareholders were asked to ratify the adoption of the Plan, as is typically true, no estimated present value of options that were authorized to be granted under the Plan was stated in the proxy solicitation materials.

II.

As the presence of valid shareholder ratification of executive or director compensation plans importantly affects the form of judicial review of such grants, it is logical to begin an analysis of the legal sufficiency of the complaint by analyzing the sufficiency of the attack on the disclosures made in connection with the ratification vote.

A. DISCLOSURE OBLIGATION:

The defect alleged is that *the shareholders were not told the present value of the compensation to the outside directors that the Plan contemplated i.e.,* the present value of the options authorized. According to plaintiff, the shareholders needed to have specific dollar valuation of the options in order to decide whether to ratify the 1996 Plan. Such a valuation could, plaintiff suggests, be determined by application of the [Black–Scholes model].

B. DISCLOSURE OF ESTIMATED PRESENT VALUE OF OPTIONS TO BE GRANTED.

[There are three problems associated with applying the Black–Scholes method to estimate the value of options with terms such as those granted to the directors. First, the method assumes that the options are issued and publicly traded, but these options include restrictive terms not typical of publicly traded options. Second, the model overstates the value of options that can be exercised at any time during their term, as these may be, because it does not take into account the value reducing effect of early exercise. Third, the value of publicly-traded options increases with increased volatility, but the value of the restricted options granted to the directors arguably decreases with increased volatility.]

What makes good sense—good policy—in terms of *mandated corporate disclosure* concerning prospective option grants involves not simply the moral intuition that directors should be candid with shareholders with respect to relevant facts, but inescapably involves technical judgments concerning what is feasible and helpful in varying circumstances. Judgments concerning what disclosure, if any, of estimated present values of options should be mandated are best made at this stage of the science, not by a court under a very general materiality standard, but by an agency with finance expertise. Clearly, determining whether disclosure of estimates of the present value of options ought to be mandated, and how those values ought to be calculated, is not a subject that lends itself to the blunt instrument of duty of loyalty analysis.

While generally the materiality of "facts" omitted from a proxy statement is a question of fact unsuitable for determination on a motion to dismiss, nevertheless, I conclude that the allegations of failure to disclose estimated present value calculations fails to state a claim upon which relief may be granted. Where shareholder ratification of a plan of option compensations is involved, the duty of disclosure is satisfied by the disclosure or fair summary or all of the relevant terms and conditions of the proposed plan of compensation, together with any material extrinsic fact within the board's knowledge bearing on the issue. The directors' fiduciary duty of disclosure does not mandate that the board disclose one or more estimates of present value of options that may be granted under the plan.

III.

C. RATIFICATION OF OFFICER OR DIRECTOR OPTION GRANTS

Let me turn now to the history of the Delaware law treating shareholder ratification of corporate plans that authorize the granting of stock options to corporate officers and directors. What is interesting about this law is that while it is consistent with the foregoing general treatment of shareholder ratification—i.e., it appears to hold that informed, non-coerced ratification validates any such plan or grant, unless the plan is wasteful in its earlier expressions, the waste standard used by the courts in fact was not a waste standard at all, but was a form of "reasonableness" or proportionality review.

1. *Development of Delaware law of option compensation:* The early Delaware cases on option compensation established that, even in the presence of informed ratification, in order for stock option grants to be valid a two part test had to be satisfied. First it was seen as necessary that the court conclude that the grant contemplates that the corporation will receive "sufficient consideration." *E.g., Kerbs [v. California Eastern Airways, Inc.,* Del. Supr.], 90 A.2d 652, 656 (1952). "Sufficient consideration" as employed in the early cases does not seem like a waste standard: "Sufficient consideration to the corporation may be, inter alia, the retention of the services of an employee, or the gaining of the services of a new employee, provided there is a reasonable relationship between the value of the services . . . and the value of the options. . . .

Secondly it was held early on that, in addition, the plan or the circumstances of the grant must include "conditions or the existence of circumstances which may be expected to insure that the contemplated consideration will in fact pass to the corporation." *Kerbs* at 656 (emphasis added).

This (1) weighing of the reasonableness of the relationship between the value of the consideration flowing both ways and (2) evaluating the sufficiency of the circumstances to insure receipt of the benefit sought, seem rather distant from the substance of a waste standard of judicial review. Indeed these tests seem to be a form of heightened scrutiny that is now sometimes referred to as an intermediate or proportionality review. *Cf Unocal Corp. v. Mesa Petroleum, Co.,* [(Chapter 22)]: *Paramount Communications v. QVC Network,* [(Chapter 22)].

In *Beard v. Elster,* Del.Supr., 160 A.2d 731 (1960), the Delaware Supreme Court relaxed slightly the general formulation of *Kerbs,* et al., and rejected the reading of *Kerbs* to the effect that the corporation had to have (or insure receipt of) *legally cognizable* consideration in order to make an option grant valid. The court also emphasized the effect that approval by an independent board or committee might have. It held that what was necessary to validate an officer or director stock option grant was a finding that a reasonable board could conclude from the circumstances that the corporation may reasonably expect to receive a proportionate benefit. A good faith determination by a disinterested board or committee to that effect, at least when ratified by a disinterested shareholder vote, entitled such a grant to business judgment protection (i.e., classic waste standard). After *Beard,* judicial review of officer and director option grants sensibly focused in practice less on attempting independently to assess whether the corporation in fact would receive proportionate value, and more on the procedures used to authorize and ratify such grants. But *Beard* addressed only a situation in which an independent committee of the board functioned on the question.

2. *Current law on ratification effect on option grants:* A substantive question that remains however is whether in practice the waste standard that is utilized where informed shareholders ratify a grant of options adopted and recommended by a self-interested board is the classical waste test (i.e., no consideration; gift; no person of ordinary prudence could possibly agree, etc.) or whether, in fact, it *is a species of intermediate review* in which the court assesses reasonableness in relationship to perceived benefits.

The Supreme Court has not expressly deviated from the "proportionality" approach to waste of its earlier decision, although in recent decades it has had few occasions to address the subject. In *Michelson v. Duncan,* Del.Supr., 407 A.2d 211(1979), a stock option case in which ratification had occurred, however, the court repeatedly referred to the relevant test where ratification had occurred as that of "gift or waste" and plainly meant by waste, the absence of *any consideration* ("... when there are issues of fact as to the *existence of consideration,* a full hearing is required regardless of shareholder ratification." 407 A.2d at 223). Issues of "sufficiency" of consideration or adequacy of assurance that a benefit or proportionate benefit would be achieved were not referenced.

The Court of Chancery has interpreted the waste standard in the ratified option context as invoking not a proportionality or reasonableness test a la *Kerbs* but the traditional waste standard referred to in *Michelson. See, e.g., Steiner v. Meyerson,* Del.Ch., C.A. No. 13139, 1995 WL 441999, Allen, C. (July 18, 1995); *Zupnick v. Goizueta,* Del.Ch., 698 A.2d 384, Jacobs, V.C. (1997) (both granting motions to dismiss shareholder claims that options grants constituted actionable waste).

In according substantial effect to shareholder ratification these more recent cases are not unmindful of the collective action problem faced by shareholders in public corporations. These problems do render the assent that ratification can afford very different in character from the assent that a single individual may give. In this age in which institutional shareholders have grown strong and can more easily communicate, however, that assent, is, I think, a more rational means to monitor compensation than judicial determinations of the "fairness," or sufficiency of consideration, which seems a useful technique principally, I suppose, to those unfamiliar with the limitations of courts and their litigation processes. In all events, the classic waste standard does afford some protection against egregious cases or "constructive fraud."

Before ruling on the pending motion to dismiss the substantive claim of breach of fiduciary duty, under a waste standard, I should make one other observation. The standard for determination of motions to dismiss is of course well established and understood. Where under any state of facts consistent with the factual allegations of the complaint the plaintiff would be entitled to a judgment, the complaint may not be dismissed as legally defective. It is also the case that in some instances "mere conclusions" may be held to be insufficient to withstand an otherwise well made motion. Since what is a "well pleaded" fact and what is a "mere conclusion" is not always clear, there is often and inevitably some small room for the exercise of informed judgment by courts in determining motions to dismiss under the appropriate test. Consider for example allegations that an arm's-length corporate transaction constitutes a waste of assets. Such an allegation is inherently factual and not easily amenable to determination on a motion to dismiss and indeed often not on a motion for summary judgment. Yet it cannot be the case that allegations of the facts of any (or every) transaction coupled with a statement that the transaction constitutes a waste of assets, necessarily states a claim upon which discovery may be had; such a rule would, in this area, constitute an undue encouragement to strike suits. Certainly some set of facts, if true, may be said as a matter of law not to constitute waste. For example, a claim that the grant of options on stock with a market price of say $5,000 to a corporate director, exercisable at a future time, if the optionee is still an officer or director of the issuer, constitutes a corporate waste, would in my opinion be subject to dismissal on motion, despite the contextual nature of judgments concerning waste. *See Steiner v. Meyerson, supra; Zupnick v. Goizueta, supra.* In some instances the facts alleged, if true, will be so far from satisfying the waste standard that dismissal is appropriate.

This is not such a case in my opinion. Giving the pleader the presumptions to which he is entitled on this motion, I cannot conclude that no set of facts could be shown that would permit the court to conclude that the grant of these options, particularly focusing upon the one-time options, constituted an exchange to which no reasonable person not acting under compulsion and in good faith could agree. In so concluding, I do not mean to suggest a view that these grants are suspect, only that one time option grants to directors of this size seem at this point sufficiently unusual to require the court to refer to evidence before making an adjudication of their validity and consistency with fiduciary duty. Thus, for that reason the motion to dismiss will be denied. It is so Ordered.

Questions:

1. To whom were the stock options granted in this case? Were the options approved by shareholders? Why does Chancellor Allen believe the court should be reviewing the options at all?

2. What standard of review does Chancellor Allen use in the case? Is this standard different from that articulated by the Supreme Court in *Rogers v. Hill* or applied by the court in *Heller v. Boylan?*

3. Would the standard of review be different if the stock option plan had *not been approved* by shareholders? or had *not been properly disclosed* to shareholders when the company sought approval of the plan?

Perhaps the most celebrated recent case involving executive compensation arose from a $140 million severance package of cash and stock options paid by the Walt Disney Company to Michael Ovitz, who had been hired as the number-two executive even though he lacked any managerial experience in a public corporation. Although terminated less 13 months after being hired, Ovitz ended up receiving *daily* compensation of nearly $350,000 even though his tenure at Disney was seen as a failure.

The Delaware courts' response to the case reveals an evolving judicial attitude toward what constitutes adequate board attention to executive compensation. When originally filed in 1998, the case got short shrift by Chancellor Chandler. Finding that Ovitz's employment agreement was not "sufficiently unusual" to warrant an evidentiary hearing on whether it constituted waste, Chandler dismissed the complaint and clearly signaled his lack of sympathy with the plaintiffs' claims:

> This case arises from a corporate board's decision to approve a large severance package for its president. Certain shareholders of the corporation seek relief from the Court of Chancery because that board actually honored the corporation's employment contract when the president left the company. The sheer magnitude of the severance package undoubtedly sparked this litigation, as well as the intense media coverage of the ensuing controversy over the board's decision. Nevertheless, the issues presented by this litigation, while larger in scale, are not unfamiliar to this Court.
>
> Just as the 85,000-ton cruise ships Disney Magic and Disney Wonder are forced by science to obey the same laws of buoyancy as Disneyland's significantly smaller Jungle Cruise ships, so is a corporate board's extraordinary decision to award a $140 million severance package governed by the same corporate law principles as its everyday decision to authorize a loan. Legal rules that govern corporate boards, as well as the managers of day-to-day operations, are resilient, irrespective of context. When the laws of buoyancy are followed, the Disney Magic can stay afloat as well as the Jungle Cruise vessels. When the Delaware General Corporation Law is followed, a large severance package is just as valid as an authorization to borrow. Nature does not sink a ship merely because of its size, and neither do courts overrule a board's decision to approve and later honor a severance package, merely because of its size.

In re The Walt Disney Company Derivative Litigation ("Disney I"), 731 A.2d 342, 351 (Del. Ch. 1998).

The Delaware Supreme Court expressed a bit more concern about the size of the severance package for Ovitz, but affirmed the dismissal *with leave to amend:*

> This is potentially a very troubling case on the merits. [I]t appears from the Complaint that: (a) the compensation and termination payout for Ovitz were exceedingly lucrative, if not luxurious, compared to Ovitz' value to the Company; and (b) the processes of the boards of directors in dealing with the approval and termination of the Ovitz Employment Agreement were casual, if not sloppy and perfunctory. From what we can ferret out of [the] deficient pleading, the processes of the Old Board [which had approved the hiring and pay agreement] and the New Board [which acquiesced in the non-fault termination] were hardly paradigms of good corporate governance practices. Moreover, the sheer size of the payout to Ovitz, as alleged, pushes the envelope of judicial respect for the business judgment of directors in making compensation decisions. Therefore, both as to the processes of the two Boards and the waste test, this is a close case.
>
> But our concerns about lavish executive compensation and our institutional aspirations that boards of directors of Delaware corporations live up to the highest standards of good corporate practices do not translate into a holding that these plaintiffs have set forth particularized facts excusing a pre-suit demand under our law and our pleading requirements.

Brehm v. *Eisner,* 746 A.2d 244, 249 (Del. 2000).

Then things got interesting. On remand, buttressed by new information gathered through a statutory request to inspect the company's internal documents surrounding Ovitz's ill-fated employment, the plaintiffs repled a quite different case—one of virtual abdication by the directors of their decision-making responsibilities. Chandler faced a trilemma. First, the Supreme Court had said Ovitz's pay package (though exorbitant) was not wasteful, and the new complaint did not change this. Second, even if the Disney compensation committee and board had been clueless, the company's exculpation provision pursuant to DCCL § 102(b)(7) insulated the directors from personal liability for breaching their duty of care. Third, despite the evidence of Eisner's close (and accommodating) friendship with Ovitz, it did not necessarily implicate a loyalty breach, since Eisner did not stand to gain personally from the corporation's generosity to Ovitz.

What was Chandler to do? Soon after the Supreme Court's decision, Chief Justice Veasey had given a speech signaling a new approach for dealing with excessive pay. Reviving a concept interspersed in Delaware corporate law, but never before given precise content, Veasey had suggested that a duty of "good faith" could be used to evaluate board decisions where something smelled bad:

> [If directors say] they base compensation decisions on some performance measure and don't do so—or if they are disingenuous

or dishonest about it—it seems to me that the courts in some circumstances could treat their behavior as a breach of good faith.

I would urge boards of directors to demonstrate their independence, not only as a guard against the intrusion of the federal government but as a guard against anything that might happen to them in court from a properly presented complaint. We didn't fall off of the turnip truck, you know. We can tell whether somebody is acting independently or not. Directors who are supposed to be independent should have the guts to be a pain in the neck and act independently.

On remand, Chandler took a new approach to judicial review of executive compensation. The issue remained whether the plaintiffs had demonstrated that demand on the board should be excused since the board's decision was not a valid exercise of business judgment.

IN RE THE WALT DISNEY COMPANY DERIVATIVE LITIGATION ("DISNEY II")

825 A.2d 275 (Del. Ch. 2003).

[The amended complaint alleged that when the Disney compensation committee first met to discuss Michael Ovitz's compensation, on September 26, 1995, the committee members received only a rough summary of a draft employment agreement. The summary indicated that Ovitz was to receive options to purchase five million shares of stock. The summary did not specify the exercise price or other terms of the options. At this meeting, which lasted for just under an hour, the committee was informed that specific terms of the stock option grant would be determined at a later date.

With the price of Disney stock in the range of $50 to $60 per share, the value of one option would have been in the range of $16 to $20 per share (based on a rough rule-of-thumb that a 10–year at-the-money stock option of a typical company is worth approximately one-third of its exercise price). Accordingly, based on a very rough calculation, the value of five million options would have been approximately $80–100 million. However, it does not appear that the compensation committee attempted to make any such calculation.

Immediately after the compensation committee adjourned, the Disney board met. Minutes from the board meeting indicate that no one asked questions about the details of the options. Based on the committee's recommendation, the Disney board approved the contract, and left it to Michael Eisner, who the board knew viewed Ovitz to be a personal friend, to negotiate specific terms, including the terms of the options.

At a meeting on October 16, 1995, the compensation committee set the exercise price of Ovitz's options at $56.875 per share, the price of Disney stock on that date. However, the parties did not sign the stock option agreement immediately. Instead, Disney executed the agreement on December 12, 1995, after the stock had risen to $61.50 per share. Disney granted the options to Ovitz on that date.]

It is rare when a court imposes liability on directors of a corporation for breach of the duty of care, and this Court is hesitant to second-guess the business judgment of a disinterested and independent board of directors. But the facts alleged in the new complaint do not implicate merely negligent or grossly negligent decision making by corporate directors. Quite the contrary; plaintiffs' new complaint suggests that the Disney directors failed to exercise any business judgment and failed to make any good faith attempt to fulfill their fiduciary duties to Disney and its stockholders. Allegations that Disney's directors abdicated all responsibility to consider appropriately an action of material importance to the corporation puts directly in question whether the board's decision-making processes were employed in a good faith effort to advance corporate interests. In short, the new complaint alleges facts implying that the Disney directors failed to "act in good faith and meet minimal proceduralist standards of attention."

Should a non-fault termination occur, however, the terms of the final version of the employment agreement appeared to be even more generous. Under a non-fault termination, Ovitz was to receive his salary for the remainder of the contract, discounted at a risk-free rate keyed to Disney's borrowing costs. He was also to receive a $7.5 million bonus for each year remaining on his contract, discounted at the same risk-free rate, even though no set bonus amount was guaranteed in the contract. Additionally, all of his "A" stock options were to vest immediately, instead of waiting for the final three years of his contract for them to vest. The final benefit of the non-fault termination was a lump sum "termination payment" of $10 million. The termination payment was equal to the payment Ovitz would receive should he complete his full five-year term with Disney, but not receive an offer for a new contract. Graef Crystal [the pay consultant whose book excerpt in Section A. 1 described the process by which compensation is set in public companies] opined in the January 13, 1997, edition of California Law Business that "the contract was most valuable to Ovitz the sooner he left Disney."

Defendants assert that even if the complaint states a breach of the directors' duty of care, Disney's charter provision, based on 8 Del. C. § 102(b)(7), would apply and the individual directors would be protected from personal damages liability for any breach of their duty of care. A fair reading of the new complaint, in my opinion, gives rise to a reason to doubt whether the board's actions were taken honestly and in good faith. Since acts or omissions not undertaken honestly and in good faith, or which involve intentional misconduct, do not fall within the protective ambit of § 102(b)(7), I cannot dismiss the complaint based on the exculpatory Disney charter provision.

On December 27, 1996, when Eisner and Litvack accelerated Ovitz's non-fault termination by over a month, the board again failed to do anything. Instead, it appears from the new complaint that the New

Board played no role in Eisner's agreement to award Ovitz more than $38 million in cash and the three million "A" stock options, all for leaving a job that Ovitz had allegedly proven incapable of performing. [T]he New Board directors refused to explore any alternatives, and refused to even attempt to evaluate the implications of the non-fault termination—blindly allowing Eisner to hand over to his personal friend, Ovitz, more than $38 million in cash and the three million "A" stock options [which the plaintiff alleged together had a total present value of $140 million].

These facts, if true, do more than portray directors who, in a negligent or grossly negligent manner, merely failed to inform themselves or to deliberate adequately about an issue of material importance to their corporation. Instead, the facts alleged in the new complaint suggest that the defendant directors *consciously and intentionally disregarded their responsibilities,* adopting a "we don't care about the risks" attitude concerning a material corporate decision. Knowing or deliberate indifference by a director to his or her duty to act faithfully and with appropriate care is conduct, in my opinion, that may not have been taken honestly and in good faith to advance the best interests of the company. Put differently, all of the alleged facts, if true, imply that the defendant directors *knew* that they were making material decisions without adequate information and without adequate deliberation, and that they simply did not care if the decisions caused the corporation and its stockholders to suffer injury or loss. Viewed in this light, plaintiffs' new complaint sufficiently alleges a breach of the directors' obligation to act honestly and in good faith in the corporation's best interests for a Court to conclude, if the facts are true, that the defendant directors' conduct fell outside the protection of the business judgment rule.

Questions:

1. Assuming Ovitz had been as ineffective as portrayed in the amended complaint, would his large termination package have survived judicial scrutiny if the Disney directors had been more attentive and assertive? Consider Chandler's comment: "If the board had taken the time or effort to review these or other options, perhaps with the assistance of expert legal advisors, the business judgment rule might well protect its decision." 825 A.2d at 291.

2. What questions should the compensation committee have asked about Ovitz's options package? Would it have been necessary for the committee to have sought an expert valuation of the Ovitz options?

3. Because the options were *in the money* when granted on December 12, 1995, they were then even more valuable than when authorized two months earlier. In very rough terms, the stock price had risen by $3 per share and the value of the options also had risen by $3 per option. In other words, the five million options were worth approximately $15 million more when Disney executed Ovitz's agreement than when the compensation committee set the exercise price. How

should the board have handled the change in circumstance that the options went from being *at the money* to being *in the money*?

THE GOOD FAITH THAUMATROPE: A MODEL OF RHETORIC IN CORPORATE LAW JURISPRUDENCE

Sean J. Griffith
SSRN Paper 571121 (Dec. 2004)

In the context of corporate law, it is difficult to give good faith any content that does not merely restate either the duty of care or the duty of loyalty. If we think of good faith as doing the job right or adequately fulfilling one's fiduciary obligations, then it drifts towards the sort of prudential issues ordinarily addressed under the duty of care. Likewise, if we think of good faith as acting faithfully or selflessly in the corporation's interest, then it slides towards issues typically analyzed under the duty of loyalty.

What, then, does the *Disney* opinion teach about good faith? At the very least by sustaining the claim on the basis of good faith when neither care nor loyalty was available, *Disney* shows that good faith has a doctrinal effect that is independent of either traditional fiduciary duty. The mode of analysis that *Disney* supplies for good faith claims, however, is closely tied to the traditional fiduciary duties. This mode of analysis can be summarized (somewhat glibly) as follows: First, recite facts drawing both the duty of care and the duty of loyalty into question. But, rather than pursuing either traditional analysis through to a conclusion, alternate between the two and, in so doing, blend the issues together. Have thus formed a composite picture of the board's conduct, conclude that the analysis raises doubts concerning the good faith of the defendant directors. In seeking to answer the basic corporate law question, courts applying the good faith standard confine themselves to the analytics of neither traditional fiduciary duty. Instead, good faith is used as a loose rhetorical device that courts can wield to find liability or enjoin actions that do not quite fit within established doctrinal categories.

In the *Disney* opinion Chancellor Chandler analyzed the board's good faith by emphasizing elements both of loyalty and care, describing the stages of the board's decision-making process, but continually returning to remark on the relationship between "Ovitz and his good friend, Eisner." Process review is, of course, duty of care review, while conflict issues raise loyalty concerns. In its good faith analysis, the Chancery Court oscillated between the two modes of analysis, repeatedly raising both care and loyalty concerns without pursuing either to a conclusion, but rather switching between both in order to raise doubts concerning the good faith of the board.

The *Disney* opinion clearly resembles a thaumatrope [an optical toy in which two images on opposite sides of a circular card appear to converge and become one as the card spins on its axis]. On one side of the card, Chancellor Chandler emphasized facts raising issues under the duty of loyalty and, on the other, facts raising issues under the duty of care. When he spun the card, the thaumatrope produced an image of a very bad board of directors, which the Chancellor found may well have violated their duty of good faith. The image of good faith produced by [this case] is not a new and distinct doctrinal pillar. It is, instead, the middle-space between the twin doctrine of care and loyalty. Thaumatrope analytics, however, only appear unprincipled if the two doctrinal categories between which the analysis oscillates are viewed as rigidly formalistic and hermetically sealed. But care and loyalty, in fact, are not mutually exclusive. To put it another way, the fundamental question underlying both duties really is good faith. Are the directors doing their best in acting for someone else? Arguably, that is the only question in all of corporate law. It is simply asked in different ways in different contexts.

Questions:

1. From your reading of Chancellor Chandler's decision in *Disney II*, does "good faith" apply to contexts besides executive compensation? If so, does *Disney II* change the analytical framework for the law of corporate fiduciary duty? Is it useful to blend the notions of care and loyalty—thus to allow claims that would survive neither care nor loyalty analysis? Or is this approach too unprincipled, a kind of judicial *carte blanche?*

2. Some who have looked at the "duty of good faith" have concluded its real focus is on intent—that is, directors fail to act in good faith "when they abdicate, subvert, or ignore responsibilities, or act with deliberate indifference toward them." Does defining "good faith" in terms of recklessness or intent solve the problem of distinguishing it from the duty of care?

3. Or should "good faith" be understood as Delaware's rhetorical response to the outcry against recent corporate scandals and the post-Enron federal intervention? Once the current popular and political attention on corporate governance dies down, will "good faith" also go away?

C. FEDERAL LAW

The run-up in executive compensation in U.S. public companies has caught the attention of federal regulators. Although no federal law directly regulates pay levels, tax and disclosure rules in the early 1990s have played a role in the setting of executive compensation. Sarbanes–Oxley also turned its regulatory attention to the subject.

1. DISCLOSURE

In 1992, responding to the public outcry against overpaid executives, the SEC significantly revised its rules on disclosure of executive compensation in public companies. As illustrated in the Tyco disclosures at the beginning of this chapter, the SEC rules require the company's annual proxy statement to disclose the compensation of the CEO and the four highest-paid executives. Such information as salary, bonus, restricted stock awards, stock appreciation rights, incentive plan payments, and perquisites must all be disclosed in tabular form, sometimes with detailed footnotes. In addition, information about stock options (the number granted, exercise price, expiration date, potential value, present value) must also be presented in tabular form. To give shareholders a sense of whether their executives are worth it, the company must present a line graph comparing the company's cumulative stock returns over the last five years compared to the market as a whole (such as the "S & P 500") or the company's industry peers (such as the "Dow Jones Transportation Average").

These SEC disclosures are carefully followed by the business press, which uses them to report annually on the highest paid executives and "grade" their relative value. Although there was some hope that disclosure would shame board compensation committees into reining in compensation excesses, the greater information fueled an upward spiral as companies sought to out-compensate each other. During the 1990s institutional shareholders seemed indifferent.

2. DEDUCTIBILITY OF EXECUTIVE COMPENSATION

In 1993 Congress also responded by revising the tax laws to disallow corporate deductions for executive compensation to the CEO and four highest-paid executives in excess of $1 million per year. An exception is made for compensation based on performance goals (1) determined by a compensation committee composed solely of outside directors, (2) approved by shareholders after disclosure of material terms, and (3) certified by the compensation committee to have been met. See I.R.C. § 162(m).

The effect of the tax provisions has been to compel the composition of board compensation committees and to force companies to submit compensation plans for senior executives for shareholder approval. The effect of the 1993 tax change, however, was to set $1 million as the floor for CEO salaries and to induce companies to increase incentive compensation (particularly stock options) linked to the companies' stock prices.

3. SARBANES–OXLEY ACT

As we saw in Chapter 17 (pages 633–635), Congress passed the Sarbanes–Oxley Act in 2002 in response to a spate of corporate and accounting scandals. The Act, among other things, takes aim at executive compensation at a number of levels.

Prohibition of loans to insiders. In response to stories of profligate (often undisclosed) lending by public companies to corporate insiders, Congress prohibited public companies from giving "personal loans" to directors and executive officers. Securities Exchange Act § 13(k), Sarbanes–Oxley § 402. The provision contains a limited exception for loans to insiders made in the normal course of the company's business, such as credit card offered by a bank corporation to its executives on the same terms as offered to other customers.

The federal prohibition, which displaces state law, changes "business as usual." Companies have had to reassess whether they can give executives such perks as travel advances, personal use of a company credit card (subject to reimbursement), retention bonuses (again subject to reimbursement), indemnification advances by the company (where executive must reimburse the company if ultimately not entitled to indemnification), loans from 40 1(k) plans, and cashless exercise of stock options (where the company or a broker gives the executive a short-term loan so the executive can exercise the options and then repay the loan once he sells the underlying shares).

Escrow of "extraordinary payments" during SEC proceedings. As a complement to the SEC's authority to ensure compliance with the securities laws, Sarbanes–Oxley authorizes the SEC to seek a judicial order for the escrow of "extraordinary payments" made to corporate executives pending the outcome of an investigation and any charges against them. Securities Exchange Act § 21C(c)(3); Sarbanes–Oxley § 1103.

What are "extraordinary payments"? In a recent case, the Ninth Circuit (in an en banc decision) decided that a company that had overstated revenues could be ordered to withhold "restructuring payments" of $37.6 million made to the company's CEO and CFO, along with stock grants and stock options on 6.7 million shares. The payments were made pursuant to an agreement in which the corporate officers resigned their corporate offices to become "employees" of the company. *SEC v. Gemstar-TV Guide Int'l Inc.*, 401 F.3d 1031 (9th Cir. 2005). The court determined the termination payments were "extraordinary" given both the unusual circumstances in which they were approved and their relative size, which was 5–6 times larger than the executives' base salary in the previous year. The court noted that the payments had been justified as a bonus based on the "fruit of the alleged fraudulent financial results."

The Ninth Circuit also offered an insight into a perhaps evolving judicial attitude after Sarbanes–Oxley on the question of "extraordinary compensation." The court rejected the argument that to establish what is "extraordinary" the SEC had to show what constitute "usual or ordinary payments" to a executives in similar circumstances:

> The idea that a court needs somehow to have evidence of a "norm for corporate decision-making *of this type*," i.e., rampant fraud and a world of trouble, is off the mark. Odd it would be indeed to shield payments from escrow simply because an ousted insider at some other corporation has been similarly enriched. In some cases, it might be probative to look to a broader norm, but not here. Legal "probable cause" statements, of which this is a variant, do not need

information about how normal people act to create a reasonable suspicion with respect to the targeted suspects.

These insiders appear, from the record submitted to the district court, to be part of an enterprise engaged in cookie jar mismanagement. The Commission subsequently sued them for multiple securities fraud violations, seeking anti-fraud injunctions, civil money penalties, and disgorgement of ill-gotten gains, including salaries, bonuses, and proceeds from the sale of stock—each one of which is at the epicenter of the payments at issue. The Commission's complaint alleges that because their compensation was linked to Gemstar's reported financial results, Yuen and Leung reaped millions of dollars in financial gains—in excess salary, bonuses, and options—from their fraudulent manipulations of Gemstar's revenues, to the tune of an overstatement of those revenues by at least $223 million.

Congress designed Section 1103 to add necessary teeth to the Commission's ability to perform its mission. It ensures that recovery by way of disgorgement, etc., is effective rather than empty.

401 F.3d at 1047.

Disgorgement of incentive pay made while financials misstated. Sarbanes–Oxley seeks to prevent corporate executives from profiting from misstated financial information. If a public company is required to restate its financial statements as a result of "misconduct," the company's CEO and CFO must reimburse the company for any incentive pay (such as bonuses or equity-based compensation) received from the company during the 12–month period after the misstated financials were issued or filed. Sarbanes–Oxley § 304, 15 U.S.C. § 7243.

The provision, as yet untested in court, raises a variety of uncertainties—not the least of which is whether the reimbursement action may be brought only directly by the company, or indirectly in a derivative suit, or even through an enforcement action by the SEC. Also unclear is what constitutes misconduct and whether the CEO or CFO subject to reimbursement must have actually engaged in misconduct. Given the frequency and prevalence of financial restatements by public companies, the liability provision of § 304 could have significant ramifications on the certainty of executive compensation.

Chapter 19

DUTY OF CONTROLLING SHAREHOLDERS

B. CASH OUT MERGERS

Add at page 245 (before C. SALE OF A CONTROLLING INTEREST):

Does the liability of outside directors vary according to their level of expertise? For example, does a lawyer who sits on a corporate board have additional duties to counsel fellow directors and ask questions about the legal matters? Or does a director with financial expertise have special responsibilities when a controlling shareholder proposes to buy out the public shareholders and take the company private?

In July 2004, Vice Chancellor Jack Jacobs surprised many lawyers and corporate directors by holding that an outside director with expertise in a particular industry was subject to a higher standard than other less knowledgeable outside directors. Jacobs found that this director, Salvatore Muoio, was liable, because he possessed specialized financial expertise and therefore had a unique ability to understand that the price of shares sold to a controlling shareholder was too low to be fair. Muoio had been a general partner in an investment banking firm and had significant experience in finance and the telecommunications sector.

As you read this decision, keep in mind the differences in the backgrounds of the various directors, and try to discern which factors were most important to Jacobs in deciding which directors would be liable. How important are a director's background and expertise, relative to the director's degree of diligence or conflicts of interest? Put another way, which is most likely to generate liability: negligence and self-dealing? Or expertise?

IN RE EMERGING COMMUNICATIONS, INC. SHAREHOLDERS LITIGATION
2004 WL 1305745 70 (Del.Ch.).

JACOBS, J.

These actions all arise out of the two-step "going private" acquisition of the publicly owned shares of Emerging Communications, Inc.

("ECM"), by Innovative Communications Corporation, L.L.C. ("Innovative"), ECM's majority stockholder. The first step tender offer was commenced on August 18, 1998 by Innovative for 29% of ECM's outstanding shares at a price of $10.25 per share. The balance of ECM's publicly held shares were acquired in a second-step cash-out merger of ECM into an Innovative subsidiary, at the same price, on October 19, 1998.

At the time of this two-step transaction (the "Privatization"), 52% of the outstanding shares of ECM, and 100% of the outstanding shares of Innovative, were owned by Innovative Communication Company, LLC ("ICC"). ICC, in turn, was wholly owned by ECM's Chairman and Chief Executive Officer, Jeffrey J. Prosser ("Prosser"). Thus, Prosser had voting control of both of the parties to the Privatization transaction.

[In June 1998, shortly after the Privatization proposal was announced, a fiduciary duty class action was brought on behalf of the former public shareholders of ECM by Brickell Partners, an ECM shareholder. On February 10, 1999, four months after the Privatization was consummated, an appraisal action was filed by Greenlight Capital, L.P., which included three investment funds that lost money on hundreds of thousands of ECM shares.

There are two groups of defendants: (1) the "ECM defendants," which consist of ECM, ICC, and Innovative; and (2) the "Board defendants," who were ECM's directors at the time of the Privatization. In addition to Jeffrey Prosser, who was also ECM's Chairman and Chief Executive Officer, ECM's directors were Richard Goodwin; John Raynor; Sir Shridath Ramphal; Salvatore Muoio; John Vondras; and Terrence Todman. Each of the board defendants served as an ECM director at Prosser's request.]

Richard Goodwin, a member of the Massachusetts Bar, is a noted author of books on American history, government, and politics. In 1959, Mr. Goodwin served as a law clerk to United States Supreme Court Justice Felix Frankfurter, and during the 1960's, he served as Assistant Special Counsel to President John F. Kennedy. After President Kennedy's assassination, Goodwin served as Deputy Assistant Secretary of State for Inter–American Affairs and as Special Assistant to President Lyndon B. Johnson. In the late 1960's Mr. Goodwin served as campaign advisor to Senator Robert F. Kennedy. During the 1980's and part of the 1990's, Mr. Goodwin also served as a consultant to the government of the USVI.

Sir Shridath S. Ramphal ("Ramphal"), a native of Guyana, is a Barrister at. Law who has held numerous prestigious government and academic positions. Between 1965 and 1993, Ramphal served successively (from 1965 to 1975) as Solicitor General of British Guyana, Assistant Attorney General of the West Indies, Attorney General of Guyana, and Guyana's Minister of Foreign Affairs of Justice. From 1975 to 1990, Ramphal served as Secretary General of the British Commonwealth, a group of 58 nations headquartered in London, England. Ramphal also served as Vice President of the United Nations General Assembly (from 1968 to 1973), Chairman of the United Nations Committee on Development Planning (from 1984 to 1987), Special Advisor to the United Nations Conference on Environment and Development (1992), Chairman of the West Indian Commission (1990 to 1992), and as President of the World Conservation Union (from 1990 to 1993). Finally, Ramphal served as chancellor of the University of Guyana from 1988 to 1992, and as chancellor of the University of Warwick in the United Kingdom and chancellor of the University of the West Indies, since 1989. Apart from these positions, Ramphal served as a director of, and a paid consultant to, ATN (ECM's corporate predecessor) in 1992, 1993, 1994, and 1995, during which years he was paid (respectively), $20,000, $140,000, $140,000, and $120,000.

John G. Vondras ("Vondras") is a professional engineer, with over 25 years of independent experience in the telecommunications industry. Vondras has served and continues to serve as a director (and as President Director) of PT ARIAWEST International, a joint venture company that operates a partnership with PT TELKOM, which provides wireless and land based telephone services in Indonesia. In 1986, Vondras spent two weeks in the USVI assisting Prosser on technical due diligence in Prosser's purchase of Vitelco. Vondras also served as a director of ATN.

Salvatore Muoio ("Muoio") is a principal and general partner of S. Muoio and Co., LLC, an investment advising firm, with significant experience in finance and the telecommunications sector. Mr. Muoio's background includes employment as a securities analyst and vice president at Lazard Freres & Co., from 1995 to 1996 in the telecommunications and media sector, and then for Gabelli & Co., Inc., from 1985 to 1995, serving both as a generalist and in the communications sector. During his career, Mr. Muoio has been quoted in many well-regarded financial newspapers and periodicals.

Terrence Todman, ("Todman"), a USVI native, is a former United States ambassador to Argentina, Denmark, Spain, Costa Rica, Guinea, and Chad, and has served as special advisor to the Governor of the USVI. Todman, who is now retired, serves on the boards of directors of several other companies, including Areolineas Argentinas and the Exxel Group.

John P. Raynor, ("Raynor"), a practicing attorney, was a partner of an Omaha, Nebraska law firm, and served as Prosser's personal attorney as well as ECM's counsel. Raynor was also a business associate of Mr. Prosser, had been a director of ATN, and acted as Prosser's advisor in formulating the terms of the Privatization transaction.

On December 31, 1997, ECM began trading as a public company on the American Stock Exchange. Shortly after Prosser obtained control of ECM, he appointed his long-time ATN directors, Raynor and Ramphal, to the ECM board. Prosser also appointed Messrs. Goodwin, Muoio and Vondras to the ECM board.

On May 21, 1998, Prosser, together with Raynor, met with representatives of Prudential [a securities firm] and Cahill Gordon [a law firm] to discuss the feasibility of Innovative acquiring all of the outstanding stock of ECM. Between May 22 and May 28, Prosser, Prudential and Cahill formulated the terms of a Privatization proposal to be presented to ECM's board. The next day, Prosser delivered to the ECM board a letter proposing instead that Innovative acquire all the ECM shares it did not already own. The proposed Privatization was structured as a first-step cash tender offer for ECM's publicly traded shares at $9.125 per share, to be followed by a second-step cash-out merger at the same price.

At the May 29 ECM directors' meeting, the board formed a special committee (the "Second Special Committee") to review the fairness of the proposed Privatization. The directors selected to serve as members of this Second Special Committee were Messrs. Richard Goodwin, John Vondras, and Shridath Ramphal.

There were several obstacles to the ability of these three directors to operate as a fully functioning Special Committee. Located on different continents and separated by a time difference of 14 hours, the three Committee members were never able to meet in person. Instead, they had to conduct their business by telephone and fax. Even teleconferences were difficult to arrange and as a result, the Second Special Committee never met collectively—even by telephone—to consider the $10.25 final negotiated offer whose approval it ultimately recommended.

Because one of the Second Special Committee members lived in Indonesia and the other lived in England, practicality dictated that Goodwin would be the Committee chair. In that capacity, Goodwin was designated to—and did—take the lead role in negotiating with Prosser and in selecting the Committee's legal and financial advisors. Mr. Goodwin interviewed William Schwitter of Paul, Hastings, Janofsky & Walker LLP ("Paul Hastings"), as a potential legal advisor to the Second Special Committee, and on June 5, 1998, the Committee retained the Paul Hastings firm as its legal counsel. Later, after meeting with representatives of J.P. Morgan and Houlihan Lokey Howard & Zukin ("Houlihan") at his home in Massachusetts, Goodwin recommended that the Committee retain Houlihan as its financial advisor, and in mid-July, 1998, the Second Special Committee retained Houlihan in that capacity.

As part of its pre-financial analysis investigation of ECM, Houlihan conducted (among other things) a review of ECM's financial information. That information included financial projections for ECM, dated March 25, 1998 (the "March projections"), that had been prepared by James Heying, ECM's then-Chief Financial Officer and Executive Vice President of Acquisitions. What Houlihan was *not* provided, however, were financial projections dated June 22, 1998 (the "June projections") that Prosser had caused Heying to prepare as part of Prosser's and ICC's application to the Rural Telephone Finance Cooperative ("RTFC") to finance the acquisition of ECM's minority shares.

The June projections forecasted substantially higher growth than did the March projections. Based on the June projections, as modified by the RTFC, the RTFC concluded in July 1998 that ECM was worth (for loan approval purposes) approximately $28 per share. Recognizing that the Privatization gave Prosser "the opportunity to retain control at a price below the true market value of the company," the RTFC approved financing that would enable Prosser to offer up to $11.40 per share. That suggests, and Prosser later confirmed, that he always planned (and gave himself sufficient elbow room) to increase his initial offer by some amount. Moreover, the $60 million RTFC loan represented the amount Prosser had asked for, not the limit of what the RTFC would have allowed him to borrow.

Although Prosser made the June projections available to his legal advisor (Cahill), his financial advisor (Prudential), and his lender (the RTFC), the June projections were never provided to the Second Special Committee, Houlihan, or the ECM board. Instead, Prosser directed Heying to send Houlihan the March projections, even though the June projections were available by that point. As a result, the Committee and its advisors believed—mistakenly—that the March projections were the most recent projections available.

On August 4, 1998, the Committee met with Houlihan to discuss Houlihan's preliminary analysis, which had been furnished to the Committee members in the form of a draft presentation booklet. After explaining in detail his firm's assumptions and methodologies, Houlihan's representative informed the Committee that it was not prepared to opine that $9.125 was a price that was fair to the minority stockholders. After further discussion, the Second Special Committee agreed that $9.125 would not provide adequate compensation to the ECM minority.

Between August 5 and August 10, 1998, in a series of telephone conversations, Messrs. Goodwin and Prosser negotiated the buyout price for ECM's publicly held shares. Eventually, Prosser told Goodwin that he would consider the matter and call Goodwin back. Shortly thereafter, Prosser raised his offer by one eighth of a point, to $9.25 per share. Goodwin reported that offer to the Second Special Committee, which rejected it as inadequate. Goodwin then called Prosser and told Prosser that he would have to improve his offer. In a later negotiation, Prosser raised his offer to $10 per share. Again, Goodwin reported that offer to his fellow Committee members and to Houlihan. The Committee rejected that revised offer, and thereafter, Prosser raised his offer to $10.125 per share. The Second Special Committee rejected that offer as well.

In response, Prosser raised his offer to $10.25 per share, but told Goodwin that $10.25 was his final offer. Because the price had been going up in roughly quarter point increments, Goodwin countered by asking for $10.50 per share. Prosser rejected that request, pointing out that $10.25 was already "straining the limits of [his] financing" for the transaction. At that point, Goodwin made a judgment that the Committee "had reached the limits of how far we could push ... ," and informed the other Committee members—Ramphal and Vondras—of his conclusion. Ramphal and Vondras agreed to stop the negotiations at that point.

Thereafter, Goodwin asked Houlihan if it could furnish a fairness opinion at $10.25 per share. Houlihan responded that it could, because that price was within the valuation ranges resulting from its market multiple analysis and its discounted cash flow (DCF) analysis.

The Committee having obtained what they believed was the highest available price, the question then became whether that price was fair. On August 12, 1998, Goodwin and Vondras had a telephonic meeting with Houlihan and Paul Hastings to review Prosser's $10.25 offer. Having updated its financial analysis, Houlihan concluded that the revised offer price of $10.25 was fair to ECM's public shareholders from a financial point of view. Goodwin and Vondras thereafter voted to recommend that the full ECM board approve the Privatization.[28]

A telephonic meeting of the ECM board to consider Prosser's revised offer to buy all of ECM's publicly held stock for $10.25 per share, was held on August 13, 1998, the following day. Present at that meeting were Mr. Schwitter and Houlihan representatives. Not attending were Messrs. Prosser (at the request of the Board) and Todman (due to a scheduling conflict). The Board members who had not served on the Special Committee had received copies of Houlihan's fairness analysis before the meeting.[29]

At the meeting, the Special Committee members described the process they had employed. Houlihan then explained its financial analysis and confirmed that in its opinion, the $10.25 per share price was fair to the minority stockholders from a financial point of view. After discussion, the board determined to approve the Privatization, but only if a majority of the shares held by the minority stockholders were tendered in the first-step tender offer. The meeting was then adjourned to August 17, 1998, at which time the board was told that Prosser would agree to this non-waivable minimum tender condition. The full board, acting upon the unanimous recommendation of the Second Special Committee, then voted to approve the Privatization.

On August 18, 1998, ECM publicly announced the execution of a definitive merger agreement that provided for the Tender Offer and Merger at $10.25 per share. The Merger was consummated that same day.

These appraisal and fiduciary duty class actions followed.

---

28. Ramphal did not attend the Committee's August 12 meeting, even by telephone. Shortly after the meeting, Goodwin contacted Ramphal and gave him a detailed account of what had occurred.

29. Because the copies were sent after the Committee had acted on August 12, the non-Committee member directors had less than a day to review the Houlihan materials.

IV. WAS THE TRANSACTION THE PRODUCT OF FAIR DEALING?

An entire fairness analysis normally requires the Court to decide, in addition to whether the price paid in an interested merger was "fair," whether the merger was the product of "fair dealing." A fair dealing analysis requires the Court to address "issues of when the transaction was timed, how it was initiated, structured, negotiated, and disclosed to the board, and how director and shareholder approval was obtained."

2. The Adequacy of the Minority Shareholders' Representation

(a) *The Independence Of The Board And Of The Special Committee*

A critical aspect of any fair dealing analysis is the adequacy of the representation of the minority stockholders' interests. In this case, that issue is particularly critical, because a majority of the ECM board members were not independent of Prosser, making it necessary to appoint a Special Committee to negotiate on the minority stockholders' behalf. Unfortunately, a majority of the Special Committee members also lacked independence, and the one Committee member who arguably was independent did not function effectively as a champion of the minority's interests.

Besides Prosser, the ECM board had six members, all of whom Prosser had directly appointed: Raynor, Ramphal, Muoio, Goodwin, Vondras, and Todman. It is undisputed that Prosser, whose wholly-owned entity was the acquirer of ECM's minority interest, was conflicted. But, most of the remaining directors also had disabling conflicts because they were economically beholden to Prosser. Directors who "through personal or other relationships are beholden to the controlling person[]" lack independence from that person.

Raynor, who was Prosser's long time lawyer, was clearly conflicted. In 1996, 1997, and 1998, virtually one hundred percent of the legal fees that Raynor generated for his law firm were attributable to work he performed for Prosser and Prosser-owned entities. Before 1996, the percentage of total fees represented by work Raynor performed for Prosser was always greater than fifty percent. From 1987 through 1998, ATNI and its affiliates, and thereafter ECM and its affiliates, were the largest single client of Raynor's firm. In 1998, the year of the Privatization, Raynor became "of counsel" at his firm and was put on a retainer arrangement wherein ATNCo paid compensation of $25,000 per month to Raynor, and $5,000 per month to his firm, to cover Raynor's office rental cost. That amount represented all of Raynor's compensation for 1998. Raynor also served as a Prosser nominee to the ATNI board, and as a director of Innovative, ECM, ATNCo and Vitelco. As a highly paid consultant to, and later full-time employee of, Prosser and his companies, Raynor was clearly beholden to Prosser and, thus, not independent.

If further evidence of non-independence were needed, in July 1998-during ECM's consideration of the Privatization proposal—Prosser agreed to pay Raynor $2.4 million over a five year period as compensation for his past services. There was no negotiation over that fee—

Raynor requested $2.4 million and Prosser agreed to it. Nor was the $2.4 million compensation arrangement ever disclosed to the ECM board, Compensation Committee or the Special Committee, yet Raynor voted as an ECM director to approve the Privatization. That disclosure omission was highly material. Goodwin testified that the $2.4 million payment arrangement should have been disclosed to the board. For Raynor to have participated in the board's Privatization deliberations and vote as an ECM director without disclosing this contemporaneously negotiated compensation arrangement, was misleading to Raynor's fellow directors and a breach of his fiduciary duty owed to them and to ECM.

Ramphal was similarly beholden to Prosser. Ramphal was originally introduced to Prosser by his son-in-law, Sir Ronald Sanders, who had a consulting arrangement with Prosser at that time. Like Sanders, Ramphal also fell into a lucrative consultancy with Prosser. In 1993 and 1994, Ramphal was paid consulting fees of $140,000 in both years, and in 1995 he was paid $120,000. On average, those amounts represented 22.5% of Ramphal's total income for that period. Those amounts were in addition to the $30,000 directors' fee that Ramphal received annually. Moreover, in 1998, Ramphal received $115,000 for his service on the ECM Board and special committees.

Given these undisputed facts, the defendants have not shown that Ramphal was independent of, *i.e.,* not beholden to, Prosser, and the Court affirmatively finds that he was not. That finding is strengthened by the fact that the consulting arrangement of Ramphal's son-in-law, Sanders, with Prosser would be put at risk if Ramphal, as a Special Committee member, took a position overly adversarial to Prosser. Finally, both Sanders and Ramphal were appointed as directors of Innovative after the Privatization had been completed.

Muoio was also a consultant to a Prosser entity and beholden to Prosser. As of mid–1997, Muoio was on an annual $200,000 retainer for providing banking/financial advisory services, and he viewed Prosser as a source of additional future lucrative consulting fees. In March 1998, Muoio sought up to an additional $2 million for serving as financial adviser on a potential acquisition by ECM of CoreComm Inc. That effort was unsuccessful only because the acquisition ultimately never took place.

Lastly, Goodwin, Vondras and Todman received annual directors' fees of $100,000, a generous amount given that ECM's board met only three or four times in 1998. Goodwin and Vondras each also received $50,000 and $15,000 for their service on the Special Committee. The $115,000 Vondras received in 1998 for serving on ECM's board and Special Committee represented approximately 10% of his income for that year.

Although the directors' fees received by Goodwin, Vondras and Todman would not, without more, necessarily constitute a disabling financial interest, the record shows that all three of these directors—indeed, all the board defendants—expected to continue as directors of

Prosser entities and benefit from the substantial compensation which accompanied that status. In fact, all of ECM's directors except Muoio were appointed to the Innovative board after the Privatization. That expectation, coupled with the fact that his director and committee fees represented a sizeable portion of his income, was sufficient to vitiate Vondras' independence for purposes of considering objectively whether the Privatization was fair to the minority stockholders.

The director defendants claim that they did not know they would be invited to join the Innovative board after the Privatization closed in October 1998. The evidence shows otherwise. During the negotiations over the Privatization, the ECM directors were told that they would continue on with the company "in its new incarnation." The Merger Agreement generated by the board's counsel in connection with the Privatization disclosed that the board defendants would remain directors of the surviving corporation. The Special Committee, through its counsel, received drafts of that Merger Agreement as early as July 17, 1998, before they voted to approve the transaction.

In summary, the Court finds that a majority of the full board of ECM (Prosser, Raynor, Ramphal, Vondras, and Muoio) were beholden to Prosser and, thus, were not independent of him. The Court further finds that a majority of the Special Committee (Ramphal and Vondras) were beholden to, and therefore not independent of, Prosser, leaving Goodwin as the only arguably independent Committee member and Todman as the only arguably independent non-Committee director. As previously found, Goodwin, as Committee chair, did almost all of the Committee's work himself. Unfortunately, the work that Goodwin performed in that role, including his negotiations with Prosser, were fatally compromised and, consequently, inadequate to represent the interests of ECM's minority shareholders effectively.

(b) *The Committee's Ineffectiveness As The Minority's Representative*

There are several reasons why Mr. Goodwin's efforts as the Special Committee's chairman, and as its sole functioning member, were doomed to failure.

The first is that Prosser withheld the June projections, and knowledge of their existence, from the Committee and its advisors, Houlihan and Paul Hastings. As a consequence, Goodwin and Houlihan were deprived of information that was essential to an informed assessment of the fair value of ECM and of the gross inadequacy of merger price Prosser was offering. Thus disabled, Goodwin was not in a position to negotiate vigorously for a substantial increase in Prosser's opening offer ($9.125 per share) or, alternatively, to make a considered judgment to shut down the negotiations, thereby preventing the Privatization from going forward at all. That nondisclosure, without more, was enough to render the Special Committee ineffective as a bargaining agent for the minority stockholders.

Second, Prosser misled Goodwin by falsely representing that $10.25 per share was already straining the limits of the financing available to him. In fact, Prosser's financing would have enabled him to increase his offer to $11.40 per share, and the record evidence indicates that the RTFC was willing to lend him more, based on its implied valuation of ECM as conservatively worth about $28 per share. There is no evidence that Goodwin knew of Prosser's financing arrangements or the RTFC's valuation (for merger financing purposes) of ECM.

Third, and finally, Goodwin was careless, if not reckless, by routing all of his communications with the other Special Committee members through Eling Joseph, Prosser's secretary. The result was to give Prosser access to the Committee's confidential deliberations and strategy. That inexplicable method of channeling communications to Goodwin's fellow Committee members further confirms the severe information imbalance that existed between the two "bargaining" sides. In fact, there was no effective bargaining, because Prosser held all the cards and misled Goodwin into believing that he (Goodwin) and the Committee's financial advisor (Houlihan), possessed all the information that was material to negotiating a fair price. Nothing could have been further from the truth.

The fourth and final aspect of fair dealing concerns the adequacy of the board and shareholder approvals of the challenged transaction. In this case, those approvals were uninformed and, accordingly, of no legal consequence.

It is undisputed that the Privatization was approved by a unanimous vote of all ECM directors, with Prosser abstaining, at a board of directors' meeting held on August 17, 1998. The board's approval was not informed, however, because the voting board members were ignorant of the existence of the June Projections and of the inadequacy of the Houlihan valuation that was based upon the March projections.

Moreover, Raynor, who was conflicted, voted in favor of the Privatization but did not disclose to the other voting board members, the $2.4 million compensation payout arrangement that he had recently negotiated with Prosser. As previously found, that nondisclosure was material.

By not disclosing these facts, Prosser and Raynor violated the fiduciary duty of disclosure they owed to their fellow directors of ECM.

For all these reasons, the Court finds that the Privatization transaction, and the $10.25 per share merger price that has been adjudicated as unfair, were the product of unfair dealing. Accordingly, the Court concludes that the Privatization was not entirely fair to the minority stockholders of ECM. Having so found, the Court must now assess the liability consequences of that determination.

V. THE DEFENDANTS' FIDUCIARY DUTY BREACHES AND LIABILITY THEREFOR

Having concluded that the Privatization was not entirely fair, the Court must next determine the nature of the fiduciary duty violation—whether of care, loyalty, or good faith—that resulted in the unfair transaction. Under *Emerald Partners v. Berlin, 787 A.2d 85 (Del. 2001),* that is necessary to enable the Court to adjudicate which (if any) of the director defendants is liable for money damages, because ECM's § 102(b)(7) charter provision exculpates those directors found to have violated *solely* their duty of care from liability for money damages. Article Seventh of ECM's Certificate of Incorporation provides:

> A director of the Corporation shall not be personally liable to the Corporation or its stockholders for monetary damages for breach of fiduciary duty as a director, except for liability (i) for any breach of the director's duty of loyalty, (ii) for acts or omissions not in good faith or which involve intentional misconduct or a knowing violation of the law, (iii) under Section 174 of the General Corporation Law of the State of Delaware, or (iv) for any transaction from which the director derived an improper personal benefit.

The liability of the directors must be determined on an individual basis because the nature of their breach of duty (if any), and whether they are exculpated from liability for that breach, can vary for each director.

Prosser is liable in his capacity as a director for breach of his duty of loyalty, conduct that is not exculpated under Article Seventh. Prosser is also liable on the basis that he "derived an improper personal benefit" from the Privatization transaction—which is another exception to the exculpatory coverage of Article Seventh.

Raynor also is liable for breaching his fiduciary duty of loyalty—conduct that is excluded from the exculpatory shield of Article Seventh. Raynor did not personally and directly benefit from the unfair transaction (as did Prosser), but Raynor actively assisted Prosser in carrying out the Privatization, and he acted to further Prosser's interests in that transaction, which were antithetical to the interests of ECM's minority stockholders.

Although Raynor did not benefit directly from the transactions, his loyalties ran solely to Prosser because Raynor's economic interests were tied solely to Prosser and he acted to further those economic interests. Accordingly, Raynor is liable to Greenlight and the shareholder class for breaching his fiduciary duty of loyalty and/or good faith.[184]

The Court also concludes, albeit with reluctance, that Muoio is similarly liable, even though Muoio's conduct was less egregious than

---

184. The Court employs the "and/or" phraseology because the Delaware Supreme Court has yet to articulate the precise differentiation between the duties of loyalty and of good faith. If a loyalty breach requires that the fiduciary have a self-dealing conflict of interest in the transaction itself, as at least one commentator has suggested, then only Prosser is liable on that basis. Raynor would be liable for violating his duty of good faith for consciously disregarding his duty to the minority stockholders. *See* Hillary A. Sale, *Delaware's Good Faith*, 89 Cornell L. Rev. 456 (2004). On the other hand, if a loyalty breach, does not require a self-dealing conflict of interest or receipt of an improper benefit, then Raynor would be liable for breaching his duties of loyalty *and* good faith. *See Strassburger v. Earley*, 752 A.2d 557 (Del. Ch. 2000) (director whose conduct in a transaction evidences loyalty solely to employer whose interests were adverse to the corporation held to have violated his duty of loyalty). The Court need not decide that definitional issue, because under either definition, Raynor's conduct amounted to a non-exculpated breach of fiduciary duty.

that of Prosser and Raynor. Unlike Raynor, Muoio did nothing affirmatively to assist Prosser in breaching his fiduciary duties of loyalty and good faith. Like his fellow directors, Muoio was also not independent of Prosser.

Muoio is culpable because he voted to approve the transaction even though he knew, or at the very least had strong reasons to believe, that the $10.25 per share merger price was unfair. Muoio was in a unique position to know that. He was a principal and general partner of an investment advising firm, with significant experience in finance and the telecommunications sector. From 1995 to 1996, Muoio had been a securities analyst for, and a vice president of, Lazard Freres & Co. in the telecommunications and media sector. From 1985 to 1995, he was a securities analyst for Gabelli & Co., Inc., in the communications sector, and from 1993 to 1995, he was a portfolio manager for Gabelli Global Communications Fund, Inc.

Hence, Muoio possessed a specialized financial expertise, and an ability to understand ECM's intrinsic value, that was unique to the ECM board members (other than, perhaps, Prosser). Informed by his specialized expertise and knowledge, Muoio conceded that the $10.25 price was 'at the low end of any kind of fair value you would put," and expressed to Goodwin his view that the Special Committee might be able to get up to $20 per share from Prosser. In these circumstances, it was incumbent upon Muoio, as a fiduciary, to advocate that the board reject the $10.25 price that the Special Committee was recommending. As a fiduciary knowledgeable of ECM's intrinsic value, Muoio should also have gone on record as voting against the proposed transaction at the $10.25 per share merger price. Muoio did neither. Instead he joined the other directors in voting, without objection, to approve the transaction.

ECM's directors other than Prosser and Raynor could plausibly argue that they voted for the transaction in reliance on Houlihan's opinion that the merger term price was fair. In Muoio's case, however, that argument would be implausible. Muoio's expertise in this industry was equivalent, if not superior, to that of Houlihan, the Special Committee's financial advisor. That expertise gave Muoio far less reason to defer to Houlihan's valuation. Knowing (or at least having very strong reasons to suspect) that the price was unfair, why, then, would Muoio vote to approve this deal? The only explanation that makes sense is that Muoio, who was seeking future business opportunities from Prosser, decided that it would disserve his interests to oppose Prosser and become the minority's advocate.

Admittedly, divining the operations of a person's mind is an inherently elusive endeavor. Concededly, the possibility exists that Muoio's decision was driven not by his overriding loyalty to Prosser, but by a sincere belief that the $10.25 price was minimally fair, even if not the fairest or highest price attainable. But in this case that possibility is not sufficient to carry the day, because to establish a director's exculpation from liability under *8 Del. C. § 102(b)(7),* the burden falls upon the director to show that "[his] failure to withstand an entire fairness analysis is *exclusively* attributable to a violation of the duty of care." *Emerald Partners v. Berlin*, 787 A.2d at 98 (italics added). Muoio has not carried that burden.

The credible evidence persuades the Court that Muoio's conduct is explainable in terms of only one of two possible mindsets. The first is that Muoio made a deliberate judgment that to further his personal business interests, it was of paramount importance for him to exhibit his primary loyalty to Prosser. The second was that Muoio, for whatever reason, "consciously and intentionally disregarded" his responsibility to safeguard the minority stockholders from the risk, of which he had unique knowledge, that the transaction was unfair. *See In re Walt Disney Co. Derivative Litig.*, 825 A.2d 275, 289 (Del. Ch. 2003). If motivated by either of those mindsets, Muoio's conduct would have amounted to a violation of his duty of loyalty and/or good faith. Because Muoio has not established to the satisfaction of the Court, after careful scrutiny of the record, that his motivation was of a benign character, he is not exculpated from liability to Greenlight and the shareholder class.

VI. Conclusion

For the reasons set forth above:

(1) In the appraisal action, Innovative, as the surviving corporation, is liable to Greenlight in the amount of $38.05 per share for each of the 750,300 shares that are subject to the appraisal, plus interest at the rate of 6.27%, compounded monthly, from the date of the merger to the date of the judgment.

(2) In the fiduciary duty action, defendants Innovative, ICC, Prosser, Raynor and Muoio are jointly and severally liable to the plaintiff class and to Greenlight (in its capacity as holder of litigation rights assigned by former ECM shareholders) in an amount equal to $27.80 per share.[193]

A wave of publicity followed the decision in *Emerging Communications*, with many commentators concluding that the case stands for the proposition that Delaware courts will hold outside directors with industry expertise to higher standards than their less expert colleagues. Does the case stand for such a proposition? If so, what are the benefits and risks associated with labeling certain directors as experts?

This case also raises questions about the independence of directors. Vice Chancellor Jacobs characterized the annual director's fees earned by the ECM directors as "generous." Do "generous" director's fees, by themselves, call into question a director's independence? Jacobs viewed directors Goodwin and Todman as "arguably independent," even though

---

193. $27.80 per share is equal to the difference between the fair value of ECM on the merger date ($38.05 per share) and the merger price paid to the ECM minority shareholders ($10.25 per share).

they received the same director's fees as Vondras, who Jacobs determined to be not independent. Why this different treatment?

Similarly, did Jacobs find that director Muoio was personally liable because of his personal economic interests in the going-private transaction (a breach of the duty of loyalty), or because of his conscious disregard for the minority shareholders (a breach of the duty of good faith)? If the latter, why wasn't director Vondras also held liable for the same reason? Overall, does this decision mean that the ideal director (from the standpoint of avoiding liability) is one with significant personal wealth, but little expertise?

In thinking about your answers to these questions, consider the following comments about *Emerging Communications*, from an October 2004 speech by former Delaware Supreme Court Chief Justice E. Norman Veasey.

> Directors and their counselors should, of course, take heed of this case. But this is not a Delaware Supreme Court decision of far-reaching precedential importance. Although we will not know with certainty how the Supreme Court may decide this issue if it is ever presented to the Court, I am personally inclined to think that the case should probably be read more narrowly as a factual decision in the context of this particular trial record. The beauty of Delaware's common law process is that, though 'indeterminate' at times, it is contextual and each case must be viewed on its own unique facts and procedural setting. Out of this quintessential common law process, lasting principles sometimes emerge, but that is not always true. It is too early to tell if any new principle of special liability for expert directors will emerge from this or any later cases. So, the lesson in counseling is to take heed, but not to overreact to this particular decision.

Hon. E. Norman Veasey, Juxtaposing Best Practices and Delaware Corporate Jurisprudence, Insights, December 2004, at 5.

Vice Chancellor Jacobs noted in the decision that Muoio received a $200,000 annual retainer from ECM chairman and CEO Jeffrey Prosser, who also controlled ICC and initiated the buyout. Why do you think Jacobs stressed Muoio's industry expertise instead of the potential conflicts related to this retainer? How did Muoio's conflicts compare with those of other directors, who were not found liable?

On November 16, 2004, the parties to the *Emerging Communications* litigation settled the dispute. Pursuant to this settlement, ICC, the purchaser of shares, agreed to pay the plaintiff shareholders $86 million. Muoio did not pay anything in the settlement. See David Marcus, Emerging Communications Settles, Corporate Control Alert, April 11, 2005. What does this settlement suggest about the initial reaction of lawyers and directors to Jacobs's rule in the case? Even after the settlement, some board members and commentators have suggested that directors with financial expertise will be held to a higher standard than other outside directors.

For example, former SEC Chairman Harvey Pitt stated that "One implication of this holding, especially given [the Sarbanes–Oxley Act's] requirement that public companies disclose whether or not their audit committees contain at least one outside director with financial expertise, is that those with special expertise need to take extra care if they wish their utilization of and reliance on outside experts to exculpate them from liability in shareholder litigation. Another significant implication is that those directors who lack 'specialized financial expertise' may be entitled to rely upon the judgments and opinions of those who in fact do possess specialized financial expertise." Harvey L. Pitt, The Changing Standards by Which Directors Will Be Judged, 79 St. John's L. Rev. 1 (2005).

Chapter 20

SHAREHOLDER LITIGATION

Substitute at pages 912–916 (entire section "B"):

B. DIRECT AND DERIVATIVE ACTIONS

A derivative action typically is brought by a shareholder *on behalf of the corporation* in which she holds stock. The shareholder asserts rights belonging to the corporation because the board of directors has failed to do so. The corporation is named as a nominal defendant. Any amounts recovered belong to the corporation, not the shareholder-plaintiff.

In theory, a shareholder can bring a derivative action against any party who has harmed the corporation, whether an insider or outsider. In practice, virtually all derivative actions are brought against directors or controlling shareholders who have breached duties to the corporation. Suing an outside party—for example, claiming breach of a contract with the corporation—is seen as a business judgment reserved for the board of directors.

The shareholder-plaintiff who brings a derivative action represents the corporation to vindicate the interests of all shareholders. Procedural rules require that the plaintiff "fairly and adequately represent the interests of the shareholders similarly situated in enforcing the rights of the corporation." F.R.C.P. 23.1 (applicable to derivative actions in federal court). The shareholder-plaintiff "is a self-chosen representative and a volunteer champion"—and thus assumes fiduciary responsibilities. *Cohen v. Beneficial Industrial Loan Corp.*, 337 U.S. 541, 549, 69 S.Ct. 1221, 93 L.Ed. 1528 (1949). For example, a plaintiff cannot later abandon a derivative action for personal gain. *Cf. Young v. Higbee Co.*, 324 U.S. 204, 213, 65 S.Ct. 594, 89 L.Ed. 890 (1945).

Shareholders can also sue directly *on their own behalf* to vindicate individual rights, rather than corporate rights. In public corporations, direct actions are often brought as class actions, in which a shareholder-representative brings the action on behalf of similarly situated shareholders. Direct actions, though they have their own procedural rules, are attractive because they avoid the procedural hurdles that apply to derivative actions—principally, the requirement of pre-suit demand on the board and the board's power to seek dismissal of the derivative suit before trial.

As you can imagine, corporate actions often affect shareholders both directly and derivatively. When is an action direct and when is it derivative? Although the case law is not a model of clarity, the following actions are generally treated as direct, thus not subject to derivative action procedures:

- **Protection of financial rights**—compel dividends or protect accrued dividend arrearages, compel dissolution, appoint a receiver, or obtain similar equitable relief

- **Protection of voting rights**—enforce the right to vote, prevent the improper dilution of voting rights, protect preemptive rights, or enjoin the improper voting of shares

- **Protection of governance rights**—enjoin an ultra vires or unauthorized act, challenge the use of corporate machinery or the issuance of stock for a wrongful purpose (such as to perpetuate management in control), require notice or holding of a shareholders' meeting

- **Protection of minority rights**—challenge the improper expulsion of shareholders through mergers, redemptions, or other means, prevent oppression of, or fraud against, minority shareholders, or hold controlling shareholders liable for their acts that depress minority share value

- **Protection of informational rights**—inspect corporate books and records

Some courts have sought to distinguish derivative actions from direct actions by looking at whether the shareholder plaintiff suffered a special injury (direct) or whether all shareholders are affected equally (derivative). This approach has created confusion. In response, ALI § 7.01 and more recently the Delaware Supreme Court have tried to simplify the task of distinguishing the two actions. How well does their approach work?

ALI PRINCIPLES § 7.01

Direct and Derivative Actions Distinguished

(a) A derivative action may be brought in the name or right of a corporation by a holder * * * to redress an injury sustained by, or enforce a duty owed to, a corporation. An action in which the holder can prevail only by showing an injury or breach of duty to the corporation should be treated as a derivative action.

(b) A direct action may be brought in the name or right of a holder to redress an injury sustained by, or enforce a duty owed to, the holder. An action in which the holder can prevail without showing an injury or breach of duty to the corporation should be treated as a direct action that may be maintained by the holder in an individual capacity.

(c) If a transaction gives rise to both direct and derivative claims, a holder may commence and maintain direct and derivative actions simultaneously, and any special restrictions or defenses pertaining to the maintenance, settlement, or dismissal of either action should not apply to the other.

Comment

d. Relevant criteria. In borderline cases, the following policy considerations deserve to be given close attention by the court:

First, a derivative action distributes the recovery more broadly and evenly than a direct action. Because the recovery in a derivative action goes to the corporation, creditors and others having a stake in the corporation benefit financially from a derivative action and not from a direct one. Similarly, although all shareholders share equally, if indirectly, in the corporate recovery that follows a successful derivative action, the injured shareholders other than the plaintiff will share in the recovery from a direct action only if the action is a class action brought on behalf of all these shareholders.

Second, once finally concluded, a derivative action will have a preclusive effect that spares the corporation and the defendants from being exposed to a multiplicity of actions.

Third, a successful plaintiff is entitled to an award of attorneys' fees in a derivative action directly from the corporation, but in a direct action the plaintiff must generally look to the fund, if any, created by the action.

Finally, characterizing the action as derivative may entitle the board to take over the action or to seek dismissal of the action Thus, in some circumstances the characterization of the action will determine the available defenses.

TOOLEY v. DONALDSON, LUFKIN, & JENRETTE, INC.

845 A.2d 1031 (Del. 2004).

VEASEY, CHIEF JUSTICE.

Plaintiff-stockholders brought a purported class action in the Court of Chancery, alleging that the members of the board of directors of their corporation breached their fiduciary duties by agreeing to a 22–day delay in closing a proposed merger. Plaintiffs contend that the delay harmed them due to the lost time-value of the cash paid for their shares. The Court of Chancery granted the defendants' motion to dismiss on the sole ground that the claims were, "at most," claims of the corporation being asserted derivatively. They were, thus, held not to be direct claims of the stockholders, individually. Thereupon, the Court held that the plaintiffs lost their standing to bring this action when they tendered their shares in connection with the merger.

Although the trial court's legal analysis of whether the complaint alleges a direct or derivative claim reflects some concepts in our prior jurisprudence, we believe those concepts are not helpful and should be regarded as erroneous. We set forth in this Opinion the law to be applied henceforth in determining whether a stockholder's claim is derivative or direct. That issue must turn *solely* on the following questions: (1) who suffered the alleged harm (the corporation or the suing stockholders, individually); and (2) who would receive the benefit of any recovery or other remedy (the corporation or the stockholders, individually)?

[Plaintiffs] are former minority stockholders of Donaldson, Lufkin & Jenrette, Inc. (DLJ). DLJ was acquired by Credit Suisse Group (Credit Suisse) in the Fall of 2000. Before that acquisition, AXA Financial, Inc.(AXA), which owned 71% of DLJ stock, controlled DLJ. Pursuant to a stockholder agreement between AXA and Credit Suisse, AXA agreed to exchange with Credit Suisse its DLJ stockholdings for a mix of stock and cash.

The tender offer price was set at $90 per share in cash. The tender offer was to expire 20 days after its commencement. The merger agreement, however, authorized two types of extensions. First, Credit Suisse could unilaterally extend the tender offer if certain conditions were not met. Alternatively, DLJ and Credit Suisse could agree to postpone acceptance by Credit Suisse of DLJ stock tendered by the minority stockholders.

Credit Suisse availed itself of both types of extensions to postpone the closing of the tender offer. Plaintiffs challenge the second extension that resulted in a 22–day delay. They contend that this delay was not properly authorized and harmed minority stockholders while improperly benefiting AXA. They claim damages representing the time-value of money lost through the delay.

The order of the Court of Chancery dismissing the complaint is based on the plaintiffs' lack of standing to bring the claims asserted therein. Thus, when plaintiffs tendered their shares they lost standing under the contemporaneous holding rule. The ruling before us on appeal is that the plaintiffs' claim is derivative, purportedly brought on behalf of DLJ. The Court of Chancery, relying upon our confusing jurisprudence on the direct/derivative dichotomy, based its dismissal on the following ground: "Because this delay affected all DLJ shareholders equally, plaintiffs' injury was not a special injury, and this action is, thus, a derivative action, at most.

In our view, the concept of "special injury" that appears in some Supreme Court and Court of Chancery cases is not helpful to a proper analytical distinction between direct and derivative actions. We now disapprove the use of the concept of "special injury" as a tool in that analysis.

The analysis must be based solely on the following questions: Who suffered the alleged harm—the corporation or the suing stockholder individually—and who would receive the benefit of the recovery or other remedy? This simple analysis is well imbedded in our jurisprudence, but some cases have complicated it by injection of the amorphous and confusing concept of "special injury."

The Chancellor, in the very recent *Agostino* [*v. Hicks,* 845 A.2d 1110 (Del.Ch. 2004)] case, correctly points this out and strongly suggests that we should disavow the concept of "special injury." In a scholarly analysis of this area of the law, he also suggests that the inquiry should be whether the stockholder has demonstrated that he or she has suffered an injury that is not dependent on an injury to the corporation. In the context of a claim for breach of fiduciary duty, the Chancellor articulated the inquiry as follows: "Looking at the body of the complaint and considering the nature of the wrong alleged and the relief requested, has the plaintiff demonstrated that he or she can prevail without showing an injury to the corporation?"[9] We believe that this approach is helpful in analyzing the first prong of the analysis: what person or entity has suffered the alleged harm? The second prong of the analysis should logically follow.

Determining whether an action is derivative or direct is sometimes difficult and has many legal consequences, some of which may have an expensive impact on the parties to the action. For example, if an action is derivative, the plaintiffs are then required to comply with the requirements of Court of Chancery Rule 23.1, that the stockholder: (a) retain ownership of the shares throughout the litigation; (b) make presuit demand on the board; and (c) obtain court approval of any settlement. Further, the recovery, if any, flows only to the corporation. The decision whether a suit is direct or derivative may be outcome-determinative. Therefore, it is necessary that a standard to distinguish such actions be clear, simple and consistently articulated and applied by our courts.

[A] court should look to the nature of the wrong and to whom the relief should go. The stockholder's claimed direct injury must be independent of any alleged injury to the corporation. The stockholder must demonstrate that the duty breached was owed to the stockholder and that he or she can prevail without showing an injury to the corporation.

In this case it cannot be concluded that the complaint alleges a derivative claim. There is no derivative claim asserting injury to the corporate entity. There is no relief that would go the corporation. Accordingly, there is no basis to hold that the complaint states a derivative claim.

But, it does not necessarily follow that the complaint states a direct, individual claim. While the complaint purports to set forth a direct

---

9. The Chancellor further explains that the focus should be on the person or entity to whom the relevant duty is owed. As noted in *Agostino,* this test is similar to that articulated by the American Law Institute (ALI), a test that we cited with approval in *Grimes v. Donald,* 673 A.2d 1207 (Del. 1996).

claim, in reality, it states no claim at all. The trial court analyzed the complaint and correctly concluded that it does not claim that the plaintiffs have any rights that have been injured. Their rights have not yet ripened. The contractual claim is nonexistent until it is ripe, and that claim will not be ripe until the terms of the merger are fulfilled, including the extensions of the closing at issue here. Therefore, there is no direct claim stated in the complaint before us.

Due to the reliance on the concept of "special injury" by the Court of Chancery, the ground set forth for the dismissal is erroneous, there being no derivative claim. That error is harmless, however, because, in our view, there is no direct claim either.

Questions

1. Are the *Tooley* and ALI approaches the same? For example, would shareholders claiming they had been denied preemptive rights (which ensure their proportional voting and financial rights) be making a direct or derivative claim–under each test?

2. Under the *Tooley* test, would the claim be direct or derivative if shareholders of a subsidiary claimed the parent corporation had caused the subsidiary to invest its resources wastefully?

3. Under the ALI test, assume a board of directors gives a CEO a guaranteed lifetime employment agreement and shareholders challenge the agreement as both wasteful and an illegal abdication of the board's authority. In a suit seeking to have the agreement declared invalid, is the claim direct or derivative?

C. WHO QUALIFIES AS A PLAINTIFF?

2. STANDING

Add at page 924 (before "3. Choosing Lead Plaintiff/Lead Counsel"):

d. *Encumbered Shares*

Shares can be economically or legally encumbered in ways that suggest that certain shareholders should not be entitled to qualify as plaintiffs. These encumbrances particularly arise from the practice of "shorting" shares. A person "sells short" when she borrows shares she does not own and then sells them in the market. She remains obligated to deliver shares to the lender in the future. If the shares decline in value, she makes money by repurchasing lower priced shares to give to the lender. If the shares increase in value, she loses money. Conceptually, selling short is the opposite of buying stock: short sellers make money when the share price declines and lose money when it rises.

Shares are economically encumbered if a person holds both shares and a countervailing short position. For example, consider a person who owns one share of a company and who also has sold short one thousand shares. Such a person is not injured by a corporate action that causes the value of shares to decline. Indeed, such a person would make money from such an action, and arguably should not qualify as a plaintiff.

Shares are legally encumbered if a person owns shares that are then loaned out to someone shorting shares. Brokerage agreements frequently provide that shareholders agree to such lending. Short sellers borrow shares from brokers, who obtain those shares from shareholders' accounts (in particular, from *margin accounts*, accounts in which shareholders are entitled to borrow to buy shares "on margin").

Whereas the shorting party can, and does, undertake to pay any dividend declared by the corporation, the shorting party cannot similarly undertake to transfer standing or other plaintiff's rights. Consequently, because there are only a finite number of shares, when a shareholder permits a share to be borrowed for shorting, she essentially creates a new shareholder. Share lending thereby creates the illusion that there are more shares owned beneficially than are actually registered. The last buyer of shares in the chain of lending and shorting is the final shareholder of record, and only that person technically should have the right to recover as a plaintiff.

In a shareholder class action, distributions (either in a settlement or judgment) are made to any shareholder who can demonstrate ownership of the stock during the class period. This includes encumbered shares. The settlement and judgment amount is based upon the number of record shares outstanding during the class period; however, due to legal encumbrances (i.e., lending and shorting), the actual number of shares is greater than this number. Moreover, economically encumbered shareholders are entitled to recover, even if they were not damaged (or even if, as a result of their net short position, they profited). Because encumbered shares are entitled to recover pro rata, unencumbered shares receive less than the compensation necessary to make them whole, and encumbered shares receive a windfall.

Chapter 21

REGULATION OF SECURITIES TRADING

C. INSIDER TRADING: RULE 10b–5

4. TIPPING LIABILITY (OR WHEN 15% IS NOT ENOUGH)

Add at page 1044 (before "5. Misappropriation Liability"):

Note: Martha Stewart

Perhaps the most famous recent case of insider trading, though prosecuted as a case of obstruction of justice and lying to investigators, involved the selling by Martha Stewart of ImClone Systems stock on an alleged indirect tip from Sam Waksal, the company's founder and CEO. According to the government's case, Stewart received information from her broker's assistant that Waksal and his family were selling their shares. (In fact, Waksal was selling in anticipation of an announcement by the FDA, not yet public, that it had rejected ImClone's application for a potentially profitable drug. Waksal would later be convicted of insider trading and sentenced to 7 years in jail.) After Stewart sold her relatively small ImClone holdings ($51,000), the SEC brought an administrative case and federal prosecutors brought a criminal case alleging that she had given false information about the reasons for her trade. Stewart was convicted on four counts.

The criminal case captured the public's imagination. What is insider trading? Did Martha Stewart do anything wrong? Did she know that Sam Waksal was dumping his stock? Did she have a pre-existing plan to sell once the stock fell below a certain price? What had the assistant, Douglas Faneuil, told her about Waksal's selling activities? Was the information she received from Faneuil material nonpublic information, which she had reason to know came from an ImClone insider who had breached his fiduciary duties?

Whether Martha Stewart engaged in insider trading has generated a lively, even heated debate. For some, her apparent attitude that she was entitled to use information from Faneuil reveals a troubling, and illegal, sense of privilege. For others, the swirling bits of information that surrounded her decision to sell suggest she did not trade (or should not be seen as trading) on material nonpublic information.

Consider two takes on the Martha Stewart case, the first by Scott Turow, a criminal defense attorney and writer of legal novels and the classic law student autobiography ("One L"), and the second by Henry Blodget, a former managing director and securities analyst of Merrill Lynch who was barred from the securities industry for knowingly issuing unduly favorable research reports on Internet companies.

First, Turow:

Ms. Stewart, along with her stockbroker, Peter Bacanovic, was convicted on March 5 of obstruction of justice and lying to investigators about her hurried sale of ImClone shares in December 2001. Prosecutors claimed that she dumped her stock after being tipped off by Mr. Bacanovic that Samuel Waksal, the company's founder, was trying to sell all his shares. (As the world learned the next day, the government had refused to approve a new ImClone drug.) The jury did not believe the defendants' story that they had long planned to sell her ImClone stock if its share price dropped below $60. * * *

[T]he jury returned what is called a "special verdict." That is, they did not merely find Ms. Stewart and Mr. Bacanovic guilty, but indicated on their verdict form exactly which lies they found the two had told. The list included Ms. Stewart's testimony that she didn't recall speaking to Mr. Bacanovic's assistant, Douglas Faneuil, on the day the stock was sold. (Mr. Faneuil testified that he had called her to warn her that the stock was about to collapse.) * * *

Since even before she was charged, [Ms. Stewart] has had a claque of lively defenders, many of them Wall Street insiders, who have suggested that even if she did what she was accused of doing, it was no big deal, and surely not a crime.

They have repeatedly noted that Ms. Stewart was charged only with lying after the fact about the stock sale, but not with securities fraud for the transaction itself. The Wall Street Journal editorial page, for example, said there "was something strange about prosecuting someone for obstructing justice over a crime that the government doesn't claim happened." And some feminists have suggested that Ms. Stewart was being penalized for being a powerful woman.

I don't buy any of it. What the jury felt Martha Stewart did—lying about having received inside information before she traded—is wrong, really wrong. And the fact that so many on Wall Street have unashamedly risen to her defense is galling—galling because what she did actually harms the market. Wall Street leaders should be expressing chagrin that a corporate tycoon—who was also a member of the New York Stock Exchange board—could feel free to fleece an unwitting buyer.

Virtually everybody who takes Ms. Stewart's side conveniently ignores the fact that there was some poor schmo (or schmoes) out there who bought her shares of ImClone. Those buyers, no matter how diligent, no matter how much market research they read, no matter how many analysts' reports they studied, could not have known what Martha Stewart did: that the Waksal family was dumping shares. In my book, that's fraud. Martha Stewart ripped her buyers off as certainly as if she'd sold them silk sheets that she knew were actually synthetic.

In addition to being fraud, her actions were also a type of theft. She didn't learn about the Waksals and ImClone by overhearing idle talk on an elevator. According to Mr. Faneuil's testimony, he (under Mr. Bacanovic's orders) gave her the confidential information that was supposed to have stayed within the walls of their firm, Merrill Lynch. She had to know she was in possession of confidential information she had no right to have, and by trading on it, she was a clear accessory to the Merrill employees' misappropriation of it.

It's true that Martha Stewart was not accused of securities fraud for selling her ImClone stock, because, the prosecutors said, historically no one else had been charged criminally with insider trading in similar circumstances. But Martha Stewart didn't make false statements to a federal agency because she thought her conduct in the sale was blameless. She did it to cover her tracks. Furthermore, the right response to those Wall Streeters who point out that she was not indicted for insider trading is to ask, why not? Why would any sane person want to buy stock if Wall Street bigwigs can palm off shares that they know, on the basis of secret information, are about to nose dive? What is wrong with our laws that such obvious misconduct can't be charged criminally? How could this have happened?

It happened, frankly, because of people like me: white-collar defense lawyers who are handsomely rewarded to represent the well-heeled and persuade the courts to interpret the law leniently. For decades the courts have been tied in knots as prosecutors and judges struggle to find an established legal duty that people violate when they trade on inside information. But when a seller has no special relationship of trust with the buyer, the courts have been willing to look the other way. As a result, the law strains to enforce basic principles of fair dealing—and, paradoxically, the Securities and Exchange Commission is sometimes draconian when it applies the laws it can enforce.

Perhaps the most troubling aspect of the whole case, to me anyway, is how the arguments in defense of Ms. Stewart show a widespread mentality that is all too comfortable with unwarranted privilege. It is yet another example of how justice is very different for the rich and poor.

Consider: While it's not insider trading for Martha Stewart to make some $50,000 using stolen information because she did not have the duty not to steal it, something very different would happen to you if you were caught with, say, a stolen watch in your hand. In that circumstance, the law virtually presumes you are guilty. For decades, American juries have been instructed that when a person is found in unexplained possession of recently stolen property, it is proper to infer that the person knows it is stolen, and thus almost certainly is guilty of receiving stolen property.

Likewise, while it's technically not insider trading for someone to sell shares of stock for more than what he knows, through inside information, to be their true market value, the converse, your buying or selling that hot watch at a steep discount, will almost inevitably get you convicted for trading in stolen property. When we're talking about these petty kinds of crimes, most often committed by the poor, the law does not bother with airy discussions of fiduciary duty. I can't take seriously those who want to believe that the starkly differing contours of the law in these roughly parallel circumstances are unrelated to the economic circumstances, and social standing, of the typical violators.

Scott Turow, *Cry No Tears for Martha Stewart,* The New York Times p.29 (May 27, 2004).

Next, Blodget's take on the case:

Around the time that Douglas Faneuil received the Waksals' sale requests (four hours before he spoke to Martha Stewart), ImClone's stock started trading down sharply on high volume (often a sign of trouble), and rumors began to fly that the company's Erbitux application was going to be rejected or delayed. By the time Stewart called that afternoon, ImClone's stock was down about $5 from its opening price, or nearly 10 percent, on about five times its usual trading volume (often a major sign of trouble). If Faneuil was even remotely competent (professionally speaking), he would have relayed this information to both Bacanovic and Stewart. If Bacanovic and Stewart were even remotely competent (cognitively speaking), they would have interpreted the information as a sign that the market might know something they didn't (that ImClone's FDA application was going to be rejected, for example).
* * *

So, assuming that Douglas Faneuil had a practice of also relaying publicly available information to clients, by 1:40 p.m. on Dec. 27, in the middle of her call with him, Martha Stewart probably possessed the following public information:

- The market was awaiting an imminent announcement that would likely make or break ImClone's stock for the foreseeable future.
- ImClone's stock had suddenly lurched downward on extreme volume.
- Rumors were swirling that the FDA would reject or delay the Erbitux application.

At the same time, Stewart also possessed the following nonpublic information:

- Two months earlier, she tried to sell all of her ImClone stock for $70 per share.
- One week earlier, Bacanovic recommended that she sell the rest for about $63 per share.
- Now, with the stock trading down sharply, on high volume, amid rumors of a negative development, the price was near $58. * * *

That afternoon, in other words, Martha Stewart probably had lots of information about ImClone's stock, some public, some private—more than enough information, certainly, to decide to sell. * * *

To this "mosaic" of information, the 27-year-old broker's assistant, Douglas Faneuil, allegedly added one more tidbit: Sam Waksal himself was trying to sell ImClone stock. * * * [I]f the Waksal information was, as the U.S. attorney contends, material nonpublic information, Faneuil's sharing it did not help Martha Stewart at all. On the contrary, it screwed her. Why? Because, in insider trading cases, material nonpublic information does not have to be the cause of a trade; the trader merely has to be "in possession of" it. Legally, in other words, if the Waksal sell orders were material nonpublic information, Faneuil made it impossible for Martha Stewart to trade.

But wait. Maybe, in context, the information was not, in fact, "material." Maybe it wasn't even "nonpublic." Were Douglas Faneuil and Martha Stewart sure that the market hadn't already received similar information? Investors had already chopped off nearly 10 percent of the stock's value in four hours—someone must have known something. Maybe the Waksals were selling stock through other brokerage firms (they were), in which case the news might have been all over the Street (it might have been). * * *

Perhaps, though, given the total mix of information—three days until the FDA deadline, rumors flying that the application would be rejected, the stock trading down sharply on high volume, Stewart's previous (alleged) agreement with Bacanovic, the phrasing with which Faneuil (allegedly) conveyed the Waksal information—Stewart instead concluded that the Waksal sell orders were just an additional data point in a mosaic of information that screamed "SELL!"—thought-provoking, yes, but misappropriated, material nonpublic information, no. And, perhaps, having concluded this, eager to get on her way to Mexico and put the ImClone headache behind her, she told Faneuil to dump her stock. * * *

Henry Blodget, *Dispatches from the Martha Stewart Trial,* Slate (Dec. 3, 2003).

5. MISAPPROPRIATION LIABILITY

Add at page 1057 (before "Constructive Insiders"):

A recent case illustrates the difficult task that insider trading regulation faces when it steps into family relationships and seeks to impose liability based on communications among family members. In *SEC v. Yun,* 327 F.3d 1263 (11th Cir. 2003), the communications were between a husband and wife during their divorce discussions about the division of marital assets. David Yun, the president of Scholastic Book Fairs, explained to his wife Donna that he was valuing his Scholastic stock options at $55 per share even though the stock was trading at $65, because he believed the stock price would drop after an upcoming earnings announcement. David told Donna not to disclose this information to anyone, though he knew she would talk to her lawyer who would be obligated to keep the information confidential. Donna agreed to keep the information secret.

The next day at the real estate agency where she worked, Donna while talking on the telephone with her lawyer about the post-nuptial division of assets was overheard by a co-worker that David expected Scholastic's stock price to fall. She then attended an awards banquet for her office that evening and apparently talked to other co-workers about the pending Scholastic news. One of them, Jerry Burch, called his broker the next day and, based on information he said he obtained at a cocktail party, purchased put options. When Scholastic announced its unexpectedly weak earnings and its share price dropped 40 percent, Burch realized a profit of $269,000.

Had Donna violated Rule 10b–5 by tipping Burch? On appeal from a jury finding that both Donna and Burch had violated Rule 10b–5 and were jointly liable for Burch's trading profits, Donna argued she did not have a fiduciary relationship with David (or Scholastic) that prevented her from passing on material nonpublic information.

On the question whether Donna had a fiduciary duty to David, the Eleventh Circuit turned to the Second Circuit's decision in *United States v. Chestman*, 947 F.2d 551 (2d Cir. 1991) (en banc). In that case, discussed in the Casebook at page 1057, the court majority had held that spousal communications do not trigger insider-trading liability absent a confidentiality agreement or a relationship of "reliance, control, and dominance" functionally equivalent to a fiduciary relationship. The Eleventh Circuit, however, rejected this approach:

> [T]he *Chestman* decision too narrowly defined the circumstances in which a duty of loyalty and confidentiality is created between husband and wife. We think that the majority, by insisting on either an express agreement of confidentiality or a strictly defined fiduciary-like relationship, ignored the many instances in which a spouse has a reasonable expectation of confidentiality. In our view, a spouse who trades in breach of a reasonable and legitimate expectation of confidentiality held by the other spouse sufficiently subjects the former to insider trading liability. If the SEC can prove that the husband and wife had a history or practice of sharing business confidences, and those confidences generally were maintained by the spouse receiving the information, then in most instances the conveying spouse would have a reasonable expectation of confidentiality such that the breach of the expectation would suffice to yield insider trading liability. Of course, a breach of an agreement to maintain business confidences would also suffice.

327 F.3d at 1272–73.

In a footnote, the Eleventh Circuit commented on the effect of SEC Rule 10b5–2, which was promulgated after the events in the case:

> Our conclusion is bolstered by statements the SEC has made since the trading in this case took place. SEC Rule 10b5–2, which became effective August 24, 2000, defines three non-exclusive circumstances "in which a person has a duty of trust or confidence for purposes of the 'misappropriation' theory of insider trading." 17 C.F.R. § 240.10b5–2 (2002) (preliminary note). * * * While the SEC's new rule goes farther than we do in finding a relationship of trust and confidence (e.g., the new rule creates a presumption of a relationship of trust and confidentiality in the case of close family members), the following language on the background of the rule supports the conclusion we reach: "[T]he *Chestman* majority's approach does not fully recognize the degree to

which parties to close family and personal relationships have reasonable and legitimate expectations of confidentiality in their communications." Proposed Rules, Securities and Exchange Commission, Selective Disclosure and Insider Trading, Dec. 28, 1999, 64 Fed. Reg. 72590-01, 72602.

327 F.3d at 1273 n.23.

Based on evidence that David had granted Donna access to confidential information "in reasonable reliance on a promise that she would safeguard the information" and that "Donna had agreed in this instance to keep the information confidential," the court concluded a jury could find that a duty of confidentiality existed between them.

Next, given that Donna was under a fiduciary duty, the question became whether she must have intended to gain a personal benefit when she tipped information to Burch. The court, rejecting the SEC's argument on appeal, concluded that the "personal benefit" requirement is the same whether the tip is from an insider (classic insider trading) or from an outsider (misappropriation). As the Supreme Court had concluded in *Dirks*, "[m]ere disclosure by itself is insufficient to constitute a breach."

The court spun a convoluted hypothetical to explain itself:

> Suppose the CEO of a public company decides, after conferring with select members of the company's management, to confide in his wife that he is an alcoholic and is entering a rehabilitation center. Suppose he has continually confided with her over the years and she has never broken his trust. Also suppose that the day after he enters rehab, his wife discovers that he was having a love affair with another woman. Angry, the wife decides to humiliate her husband by disclosing his alcohol problems to the local newspaper editor. The editor is savvy, and realizes that news of the CEO's alcoholism would likely cause the stock price to fall. Accordingly, the editor buys put options in the husband's company before printing the story. When the story hits the newsstand, and the stock price falls, the editor makes lots of money. The question is whether the wife and the editor are liable. The information regarding her husband's alcoholism is material and nonpublic, the wife breached a duty of loyalty and confidentiality with her husband, the editor was aware of the wife's breach, and the husband is harmed (emotionally, financially, and in terms of his reputation). But, the wife did not disclose the information with the intent that anyone would trade or benefit; she merely wanted to harm her husband emotionally.
>
> Under the SEC's approach [where liability arises from mere disclosure that harms the principal] the wife would be liable for the disgorgement of all of the editor's profits. The securities laws, however, are not designed to impose liability on a person who had no intent to trade or manipulate the market. Section 10(b) requires fraud "in connection with" the purchase or sale of securities.

327 F.3d at 1279 n.34.

Thus, the court concluded "an outsider who tips (rather than trades) is liable if he intends to benefit from the disclosure," but quickly added that the "showing to prove an intent to benefit is not extensive." A benefit can include a pecuniary gain (such as a kickback or the expectation of future reciprocal tips), enhanced reputation that would translate into future earnings, or a gift to a trading relative or friend. In the case, the court concluded there was enough evidence that Donna had expected to benefit from her tip to Burch by maintaining a good relationship between a friend and a frequent partner in real estate deals. (The court, however, remanded the case for a new trial since the jury instructions created the impression Donna could be found liable even if she had not tipped Burch for a personal benefit.)

Chapter 22

PROTECTING AND SELLING CONTROL

C. CASE LAW DEVELOPMENTS

1. THE DELAWARE COURTS' APPROACH

b. *The Contemporary Framework*

Add at page 1142 (before "c. Post–Unitrin Developments"):

Note: Do Takeover Defenses Help Directors Negotiate Better Deals?

The Delaware judiciary pins much of its solicitude for takeover defenses on the hope directors will be able to bargain for deals for shareholders better than if the firm lacked such defenses and were exposed to hostile bids. According to a recent study, the solicitude may be misplaced. See Guhan Subramanian, *Bargaining in the Shadow of Takeover Defenses,* 113 YALE L. J. 621 (2003):

> For decades, practitioners and academic commentators who believe that target boards should have broad discretion to resist hostile takeover attempts have put forward the "bargaining power hypothesis" to support their view. This hypothesis states that a target with strong takeover defenses will extract more in a negotiated acquisition than a target with weaker defenses, because the acquirer's no-deal alternative, to make a hostile bid, is less attractive against a strong-defense target. * * * Yet despite its venerable heritage and recent revitalization, the bargaining power hypothesis has generally been asserted by defense proponents and conceded by defense opponents, never subjected to a careful theoretical analysis or a comprehensive empirical test.
>
> This Essay attempts to fill this gap. I use negotiation-analytic tools to construct a model of bargaining in the "shadow" of takeover defenses. This model identifies the conditions that must exist in order for the bargaining power hypothesis to hold in a particular negotiated acquisition. I demonstrate that the bargaining power hypothesis only applies unambiguously to negotiations in which there is a bilateral monopoly

between buyer and seller, no incremental costs to making a hostile bid, symmetric information, and loyal sell-side agents. These conditions suggest that the bargaining power hypothesis is only true in a subset of all deals, contrary to the claim of some defense proponents that the hypothesis applies to all negotiated acquisitions.

I confirm the features of this model with evidence from practitioner interviews [with] the head or co-head of mergers and acquisitions at ten major New York City investment banks. Collectively these firms represented either the acquirer or the seller, or both, in seventy-two percent of negotiated acquisitions by number, and ninety-six percent by size, during the 1990s deal wave. * * *

I then test the bargaining power hypothesis against [1692] negotiated acquisitions of U.S. public company targets between 1990 and 2002. If the hypothesis is correct, then premiums should be higher in states that authorize the most potent pills (Georgia, Maryland, Pennsylvania, and Virginia), and lower in the state that provides the least statutory validation for pills (California), relative to Delaware, which takes a middle ground on the pill question. Consistent with the predictions of my model, however, I find no evidence that premiums are statistically different across these states, either overall or in those subsamples in which bargaining power is most likely to manifest itself.

These findings have implications for the current antimanagerial, pro-takeover trajectory of Delaware's corporate law jurisprudence in the aftermath of Enron. Proponents of the status quo warn that such doctrinal movements will weaken targets' bargaining power in negotiated acquisitions, which will in turn reduce overall returns for target shareholders. But by unpacking the "black box" of negotiated acquisitions and examining the microlevel underpinnings of the bargaining process, this Essay suggests that a return to the original promise of intermediate scrutiny articulated in *Unocal Corp. v. Mesa Petroleum Co.* is unlikely to yield significant negative wealth consequences for target shareholders. Rather, as I and others have argued, a controlled revitalization of the hostile takeover marketplace can help to improve overall corporate governance, an objective that has become only more important in the post-Enron era.

---

c. Post–Unitrin Developments

Add at page 1170 (before Note: Directors' Duties in a Sale of Control):

Note: Have Delaware Courts Re–Written the Takeover Rules for Delaware Corporations?

Viewing the corporation as a political constitution, Professors Marcel Kahan and Edward Rock assert that antitakeover measures included in the corporation's constitutive structure can be seen as a "a perfectly intelligible choice" by which shareholders opt for board entrenchment—a "Madisonian" model of representative governance. Kahan & Rock, *Corporate Constitution-*

alism: Antitakeover Charter Provisions as Pre–Commitment, 152 U. PA. L. REV. 473 (2003). For example, a staggered board gives the incumbent board assurances of longevity so the board can "employ selling strategies more effectively and thus [] increase the premium shareholders receive when the company is sold." The authors assert this pre-commitment binds shareholders ex ante to improve their collective position ex post.

Once shareholders have chosen an antitakeover structure, how should the Delaware courts respond when there are questions of incomplete or "sloppy" implementation—as in *Blasius* (at page 437 of the Casebook) and *Liquid Audio* (at page 1152 of the Casebook). In each case, the incumbent board discovered that its staggered board provisions could be circumvented and sought to more fully implement their antitakeover purpose, and in each case the Delaware courts concluded the board action lacked a sufficiently "compelling justification."

In analyzing *Blasius,* Professors Kahan and Rock view the case as one "in which the board's defensive actions conformed precisely to the degree of entrenchment opted for in the charter (albeit a bit tardy) [and] the courts should respect that choice...." That is, board packing that gives effect to a provision approved by shareholders warrants judicial deference, not the intrusive review articulated by Chancellor Allen.

With respect to *Liquid Audio,* however, the authors point out that the corporation's staggered board was established in the bylaws not the charter, which thus permitted shareholders to declassify the board through a bylaw amendment approved by a supermajority two-thirds vote. As for the appropriate judicial attitude toward board-packing in such a setting, Kahan and Rock concluded:

> We believe that the Supreme Court [in *Liquid Audio*] was correct to apply *Blasius* even though the expansion of the board from five to seven did not make it hard for MM to obtain control. The Chancery Court analysis implicitly viewed the incumbent directors (and the MM representatives) as homogeneous groups: if each group member always votes with her group, then the only important factor is the difficulty each group faces in getting a board majority. The Supreme Court's holding, by contrast, is based on viewing each director as an individual. If some of the incumbent directors may vote, on some issues, with the MM representatives—because they may be convinced by their arguments—then it is significant whether the MM representatives occupy two or five or two of seven seats on the board. We think the Supreme Court's holding is more in tune with the modern aspiration for the board....

Should courts adopt different standards of review depending on whether a board defensive maneuver rests on a shareholder-approved structure or one created by the board? In *Blasius* the board arguably exercised (though not fully) its entrenching staggered-board authority. Should a reviewing court take this into account?

What would the result have been if the *Liquid Audio* board had expanded from five to seven directors not to thwart the MM bid, as revealed in an interrogatory answer in the case, but to satisfy the independent-director requirements of the Sarbanes–Oxley Act? Do board motives make a difference in reviewing measures that make takeovers more difficult, or only the effects of such board action?

Add at page 1172 (before "2. Other States' Approaches"):

Note: Joint Ventures and the Sale of Control

Joint ventures, through which companies pool resources and combine efforts for profit, are increasingly common, particularly in areas of fast-moving technology. However, joint ventures pose challenges in analyzing fiduciary duties. In particular, directors and officers owe duties, not only to their own companies, but also to their partners and to the joint venture, which typically is a separate legal entity. The following [heavily edited—I'd like to talk about editing styles] article excerpt addresses some of these complexities, and considers how courts might analyze the sale of control in the joint venture context.

Steven Fraidin & Radu Lelutiu, STRATEGIC ALLIANCES AND CORPORATE CONTROL

53 CASE W. RES. L. REV. 865 (2003).

A joint venture agreement can result in complex issues of fiduciary duties. In addition, the structure of a joint venture arrangement can have a more substantial impact on the fiduciary obligations of one or both of the joint venture partners if the joint venture agreements, taken as a whole, might be viewed as either: (1) a sale of control of one of the venturers; or (2) a defense against takeover by one of the venturers.

If a joint venture transaction would be viewed as a sale of fundamental control over one of the parties, the courts could apply a special fiduciary duty analysis upon the company's board of directors. The answer to the question of whether a given transaction would constitute a fundamental change of corporate control is a highly fact-specific inquiry.

In holding that the transfer of a majority of stock from public shareholders to a controlling shareholder triggered the duty to maximize shareholder value under the *Revlon* case, the *QVC* court found particularly significant the fact that a majority of Paramount's voting stock would transfer from "fluid aggregation of unaffiliated stockholders" to a single "controlling stockholder" who would have the power to (a) elect directors; (b) cause a breakup of the corporation; (c) merge it with another company; (d) cashout the public stockholders; (e) amend the certificate of incorporation; (f) sell all or substantially all of the corporate assets; or (g) otherwise alter materially the nature of the corporation and the public stockholders' interests.

The significance of the *Revlon* case and its progeny is simply that joint venture arrangements, with or without an ancillary equity investment agreement, have the potential to trigger the "duty to auction" if one or more of the factors outlined in the *QVC* case would result from the transaction. In order to prevent courts from second-guessing a company's decision to enter into a joint venture with a substantial equity investment, the board of directors of the investee company may wish to consider negotiating a standstill arrangement which would do one or more of the following:

- Place a cap on the investing party's ownership level and/or its ability to increase its voting power through other means;
- Place voting restrictions on the investing party's equity share;
- Limit the ability of the investing party to transfer its shares in large blocks to any single third party; or
- Limit the ability of the investing party to elect a majority of the board of directors.

Since there is no "magic bullet" answer to the question of "what constitutes a change in control," in order to get the benefit of the business judgment rule, the investee company must consider its fiduciary obligations thoroughly.

An effective standstill arrangement can eliminate many of the fiduciary risks associated with cross equity investments. However, there is still an open question as to how large an equity stake would be sufficient to effect a change in control even with a standstill agreement. What if the investor were to acquire a fifty-one percent interest in the investee? How long would the standstill have to last in this situation? What terms must the standstill contain?

The answer to these questions is uncertain, but the guiding principle would be that if, after the investment, the shareholders of the investee would be able to get a full takeover premium for their shares, a *Revlon* event probably has not have occurred.

If a joint venture agreement, or its equity investment component, is deemed to be a defensive maneuver of the type described in *Unocal* and its progeny, for the board to be protected by the business judgment rule, the board's actions must survive what the Delaware courts call "enhanced review." To satisfy the first prong of the *Unocal* review and show that a potential unsolicited takeover bid would be inimical to corporate effectiveness and policy, it is enough that the board establish that it acted in good faith and upon reasonable investigation. To satisfy the second prong of the *Unocal* review, the proportionality test, the board must establish that the challenged transaction is "not Draconian" in nature. The term "not Draconian" was later explained as referring to a measure that is "not either coercive or preclusive." If the measure is "not Draconian," then the *Unocal* proportionality test guides the enhanced judicial scrutiny towards the "the range of reasonableness."

Prominent commentators have noted that, as applied, the *Unocal* enhanced scrutiny is merely a "dressed up" business judgment review. Delaware law would suggest that joint venture agreements, where undertaken with an expectation of profit and as a means of leveling risks, would survive *Unocal* review. Furthermore, because ancillary equity investments are sometimes essential to the success of the venture, it is likely that they will survive *Unocal* review as well, especially where some safeguards described in this Article are considered or adopted.

Nonetheless, the board of directors of the investee company should take adequate steps, and ensure that it understands all the terms of the agreement, especially the implications the venture and investment will have on the potential takeover premium that may become available to shareholders of the company.

†